Virgil, Horace and Ovid are often cited
poets of classical Roman literature. An
is Ovid (43 BCE–17/18 CE) who has the most enduring legacy.
Carole Newlands introduces her subject as an ancient author with
a vital place in the modern cultural canon, and also as the inspira-
tion behind figures as diverse as Chaucer, Titian, Dryden and Ted
Hughes. She views Ovid as a Latin writer who is uniquely suit-
able for times of change: he appeals to post-modern sensibilities
because of his interest in psychology, his fascination with cultural
hybridity and his challenge to the conventional divide between
animal and human. This book explores the connection between
the historical poet and the works he produced: love elegies, the
Metamorphoses and the *Fasti*. It shows that unlike Virgil – who
wrote early in Augustus' reign, anticipating a Golden Age of
peace and prosperity – Ovid was a product of the late Augustan
age: one of hardening autocracy and the greater influence of
Tiberius behind the scenes. His elegies and erotic myths must
therefore be understood as the result of complex, shifting political
circumstances.

CAROLE E. NEWLANDS is Professor of Classics at the
University of Colorado, Boulder. Her previous publications
include *Playing with Time: Ovid and the Fasti* (1995), *Statius'
Silvae and the Poetics of Empire* (2002), *Statius, Poet Between Rome
and Naples* (2012) and *An Ovid Reader* (2013).

Lively and engrossing, Carole E. Newlands' *Ovid* offers a sure guide to the works of Rome's most entertaining and influential poet. Here the reader will find compact, readable and reliable discussions of all Ovid's writings, including the ever-popular love poetry and *Metamorphoses*, Ovid's epic of transformation. Especially to be recommended are the chapters on the *Heroides*, imaginary letters in verse written by heroines of myth; and the *Fasti*, a poem on the Roman calendar that incorporates tales of great variety. Newlands' book is unique among introductions to Ovid in that it draws on many later literary texts, from his time to ours, that are indebted to Ovid and offer genuine insight into his poetry. Ovidian reception appears not just in a concluding chapter, as in typical introductions to Ovid, but throughout the book. In introducing Ovid's early love elegies, for instance, Newlands calls upon his last elegies, written in wretched exile on the Black Sea, to show how he adapts old themes to new circumstances; and she cites the Northern Irish poet Derek Mahon for a modern re-imagining of Ovidian love elegy. Newlands' *Ovid* is an exemplary introduction not only to Ovid's writings but to their continuing importance from the first millennium to the third.

> – Garth Tissol, Professor of Classics, Emory University, author of *The Face of Nature: Wit, Narrative, and Cosmic Origins in Ovid's Metamorphoses*

UNDERSTANDING CLASSICS

EDITOR: RICHARD STONEMAN (UNIVERSITY OF EXETER)

When the great Roman poets of the Augustan Age – Ovid, Virgil and Horace – composed their odes, love poetry and lyrical verse, could they have imagined that their works would one day form a cornerstone of Western civilization, or serve as the basis of study for generations of schoolchildren learning Latin? Could Aeschylus or Euripides have envisaged the remarkable popularity of contemporary stagings of their tragedies? The legacy and continuing resonance of Homer's *Iliad* and *Odyssey* – Greek poetical epics written many millennia ago – again testify to the capacity of the classics to cross the divide of thousands of years and speak powerfully and relevantly to audiences quite different from those to which they were originally addressed.

Understanding Classics is a specially commissioned series which aims to introduce the outstanding authors and thinkers of antiquity to a wide audience of appreciative modern readers, whether undergraduate students of classics, literature, philosophy and ancient history or generalists interested in the classical world. Each volume – written by leading figures internationally – will examine the historical significance of the writer or writers in question; their social, political and cultural contexts; their use of language, literature and mythology; extracts from their major works; and their reception in later European literature, art, music and culture. *Understanding Classics* will build a library of readable, authoritative introductions offering fresh and elegant surveys of the greatest literatures, philosophies and poetries of the ancient world.

UNDERSTANDING CLASSICS

OVID

Carole E. Newlands

UNDERSTANDING CLASSICS SERIES EDITOR:
RICHARD STONEMAN

I.B. TAURIS
LONDON · NEW YORK

Published in 2015 by
I.B.Tauris & Co. Ltd
London • New York
www.ibtauris.com

ISBN: 978 1 84885 929 6 (HB)
          978 1 84885 930 2 (PB)
eISBN: 978 0 85773 984 1

A full CIP record for this book is available from the British Library
A full CIP record is available from the Library of Congress

Library of Congress Catalog Card Number: available

Text design, typesetting and eBook versions by Tetragon, London

Printed and bound in Great Britain by T.J. International, Padstow, Cornwall

CONTENTS

Acknowledgements

I WISH TO THANK Richard Stoneman for inviting me to write this book; Alex Wright for his patient shepherding of the process; Alex Middleton for his astute reading of the manuscript; and Nadia Ghosheh and Stephanie Krause for helping me get to the final post. Above all, thanks to Sheila Knapman for her constant support; this book is for her.

All translations are my own.

Key Dates in Ovid's Career

43 BCE	Birth of Ovid.
31 BCE	Augustus' victory over Mark Antony and Cleopatra at the Battle of Actium. Augustus begins a long reign as Rome's first emperor.
25 BCE	Ovid begins publishing individual *Amores*.
16 BCE	Approximate publication date for three-book edition of the *Amores*. Ovid possibly begins composition of the *Heroides*.
2 BCE	Publication of *Ars Amatoria* Books 1 and 2. Augustus assumes title 'pater patriae' (father of the country). Augustus' daughter is exiled on charges of adultery.
1/2 CE	Publication of *Ars Amatoria* Book 3 and probably *Remedia Amoris*.
8 CE	Publication of *Metamorphoses* and probably Books 1–6 of *Fasti*. Ovid is exiled to Tomis on the Roman frontier. Julia, Augustus' granddaughter, is exiled on charges of adultery (like her mother).
9–12 CE	Ovid writes *Tristia* (Books 1–5) from Tomis.
12–17 CE	Ovid writes *Epistulae ex Ponto* (Books 1–4) from Tomis.
14 CE	Death of Augustus; accession of his stepson Tiberius.
17/18 CE	Death of Ovid in exile.

Abbreviations

ABBREVIATIONS OF OVID'S WORKS FOLLOW the style of the *OLD* (*Oxford Latin Dictionary*), with one exception: the *Fasti* is not abbreviated.

Am. = *Amores*; *Ars* = *Ars Amatoria*; *Ep.* = *Heroides*; *Met.* = *Metamorphoses*; *Pont.* = *Epistulae ex Ponto*; *Rem.* = *Remedia Amoris*; *Tr.* = *Tristia*.

The following abbreviations refer to works cited frequently:

Blackwell Companion	Peter Knox (ed.), *A Companion to Ovid*, Blackwell Companions to the Ancient World (Oxford and Malden, MA, 2009)
Brill's Companion	Barbara Boyd (ed.), *Brill's Companion to Ovid* (Leiden, 2002)
Cambridge Companion	Philip Hardie (ed.), *The Cambridge Companion to Ovid* (Cambridge, 2002)
Handbook	John F. Miller and Carole E. Newlands (eds), *A Handbook to the Reception of Ovid*, Wiley Blackwell Handbooks to Classical Reception (Oxford, 2014)

Ovid in the Third Millennium and the First

THE ROMAN POET OVID (43 BCE–17/18 CE) continues to fascinate us today for the power of his visual imagination, his gift of narrative, his eloquence and his capacious, generous insight into human emotions. In a time of political oppression, his bold challenges to social and literary conventions give his poetry an exciting edge; he dared even confront the authority of the most powerful political leader in his day, the emperor Augustus. Poet of love and poet of change, Ovid speaks still to a generation for whom sudden, rapid change has become a dominant feature of modern life. When biotechnology can create hybrid forms beyond ancient imaginings, and the division between animal and human is being increasingly questioned, Ovid, who wrote a great poem on change as the fundamental principle of human existence, the *Metamorphoses*, is surely a poet for our times.[1]

In summer 2012, as part of Britain's cultural display during the Olympics, the National Gallery in London launched a stunning, multidisciplinary exhibition, *Metamorphosis: Titian 2012*. The show was organized around three paintings by the sixteenth-century Venetian artist Titian: *Diana and Callisto*, *Diana and Actaeon* and *The Death of Actaeon*. Titian drew on two myths from Ovid's epic poem, *Metamorphoses* (which the painter probably knew from an Italian translation). The first painting shows the moment when Diana, goddess of virginity, expels her devoted follower, Callisto, from her sacred precinct after the girl has been raped by Jupiter and has become pregnant; the second and third paintings show, respectively, the accidental trespass of the hunter Actaeon into Diana's grove when she is bathing, and the consequence of that trespass, his metamorphosis into a stag by the furious goddess and his savage killing by his own hounds. Titian referred to these paintings as 'poesie' (poetry), to suggest that he could rival Ovid's narrative art. They show mortals who, because they unwittingly transgressed on a divine domain, are at the mercy of an unpredictable, unjust and powerful deity; as often in Ovid's poem, scenes of cruelty and violence are depicted in a theatrical and aesthetically pleasing style. This artistic paradox makes demands on the spectator (or reader), who is seduced into moral engagement with the question of divine (in)justice on display.

New work by contemporary artists responded to these paintings and the Ovidian myths in a variety of ways. The Turner Prize-winning artist Chris Ofili downplayed the violence and intensified Titian's famous, vivid colours by transferring Ovid's myths to canvasses of glowing Caribbean colours and exuberant forms; a robotic sculpture by Conrad Shawcross entitled *Trophy* brilliantly epitomized the terror of surveillance and the psychology of revenge; Mark Wallinger played on the notion of voyeurism with his installation *Diana*, a black box with peepholes enclosing a nude woman bathing. Film clips were also displayed from three new ballets specially commissioned for the Royal Ballet (*Machina*, *Trespass* and *Diana and Actaeon*). Accompanying the exhibition was a publication of poems by leading modern poets, such as Seamus Heaney and Carol Ann Duffy, who explored the paintings and Ovid's myths from a variety of perspectives including the comic, the tragic and the feminist. The National Gallery thus showcased how a classic text, Ovid's *Metamorphoses*, inspired and continues to inspire new metamorphoses across different media.

This book will explore not only how to understand Ovid today, but also why we enjoy reading his poetry, not only his *Metamorphoses* but also his works written in elegiac metre: the *Amores*, the *Heroides*, the *Ars Amatoria*, the *Fasti*, the *Tristia* and the *Epistulae ex Ponto*. Ovid's work stands out among ancient poets for its sheer range and variety, its resistance to stereotype. It offers comedy and tragedy, celebration and lament, magic and miracle, beauty of style and deftness of wit; it explores the joys and sorrows of human existence, its highs and its lows. Ovid is a superb storyteller who brings ancient myths to life with his vivid visual imagination. Yet he began and ended his career by writing elegy, and the universal themes of love and sexual desire, among the most changeable of emotions, are central to all his poetry, examined from multiple perspectives and with psychological insight. The first six chapters of this book thus discuss all Ovid's major works. But while individual works receive special emphasis in each chapter, my focus is also thematic, as I examine how major preoccupations of Ovid's poetry reappear and are modified across genres and time. Throughout, in keeping with the series' aims of explaining the importance and continuing relevance of the author under discussion, I keep under consideration the creative vitality of Ovid's poetry, although the final chapter is devoted strictly to reception.

Ovid's reputation was not always as high as it is today. Charles Martindale argues that Ovid's works were a central point of reference for Western culture until the seventeenth century when, for political and cultural reasons, his critical reputation began to wane.[2] Although Ovid has always maintained at least a subterranean presence, until fairly recently he was regarded as a shallow, comic poet whose erotic verse was judged indecent in times of stricter sexual codes. But beginning in 1945 with Hermann Fränkel's study, *Ovid: A Poet between Two Worlds*, there has been a new scholarly appreciation of Ovid's poetry for its formal and humane qualities.[3] At the time Fränkel was criticized for viewing Ovid as essentially a tragic poet, wavering in metaphysical angst between the old world of pagan Antiquity and the new one of Christianity. This view of the poet, however, was recently reiterated by Ted Hughes in the introduction to his poetic renditions of 24 stories from the *Metamorphoses*, *Tales from Ovid*.[4] A striking aspect of the fresh scholarly appraisal of Ovid has been its transference to the public realm, where it has motivated new creative Ovidianisms in literature and art.

Ovid, born in Sulmo, a town north of Rome, in 43 BCE, the year after Julius Caesar's assassination, was the first of the Augustan poets to reach manhood in a time of peace. Although Ovid is often classified as an 'Augustan poet', he lived into the reign of Tiberius (14–37 CE). As Peter Knox has argued, Tiberius may well have had a decisive hand in Ovid's relegation to Tomis. In exile Ovid pleads to Augustus, and he pleads to Tiberius' nephew and heir Germanicus, but, perhaps tellingly, he does not plead to Tiberius.[5] And although Tiberius is occasionally mentioned in the exile poetry, he is never addressed by name, unlike Augustus and Germanicus.

The term 'Augustan', moreover, does not account for the significant changes that took place in the period between Augustus' assumption of sole power over the Roman world in 31 BCE and his death in 14 CE. Augustus' long rule eventually hardened into autocracy, and the political optimism of his early years, celebrated by the poets Horace and Virgil as a new Golden Age of peace, became blunted by the family tragedies and scandals that afflicted the Augustan household. Ovid's poetry, composed over a long time span, responds to political change and the dynastic strains within the imperial family. His poetry is also, however, the product of an empire that gave him the leisure to pursue a life of poetry, even if, in the end, he had too much leisure on his hands in Tomis.

Ovid also fascinates us because his life seems to mirror his art. In 8 CE, at the height of his career and for reasons never fully revealed, he was exiled by the emperor Augustus to Tomis on the Black Sea, a small town on the frontier of the Roman Empire, present-day Constanza in Romania.[6] He was never recalled to Rome and he died in exile, probably in 17 CE. Ovid's exile poetry is our only source for the circumstances of his banishment, and the reasons are left obscure. In *Tr.* 2.207 Ovid states that the causes were 'a poem and an error'.[7] The poem is generally understood to be the *Ars Amatoria*, and in his exile poetry Ovid represents himself as a tragic hero who has been victimized for his art.[8] The exact nature of the 'error', however, is never revealed, but it was probably political and perhaps tied up with the exile of Augustus' granddaughter Julia on the charge of adultery that same year. In recent decades, the continuing mystery of Ovid's exile has led to the creation of what Katharina Volk calls 'a mini-genre', the 'Ovid novel', which imagines alternative lives and outcomes for the banished poet.[9] Modern writers draw on our fascination with a life that provides a powerful case study of tragic downfall but also literary transcendence.

The dynamic principle of change underpins not only Ovid's life but also his poetry. Change is not restricted to bodily or emotional transformation but encompasses poetic form and genre; it is thus a constant preoccupation at the formal as well as thematic level of all Ovid's work. Moreover, few poets have probed so extensively into the instability of human identity or have drawn such attention to the passions as the driving force of human action; from the very beginning of his work, as we shall see shortly, Ovid fashions a crisis in his poetic identity involving the power of love.[10]

Ovid's works

Ovid's body of work is one of the most complete and extensive to survive from Antiquity, and its range is impressive; he was not a poet to stick to a well-worn groove. The exact chronology of his poetry is debatable – we have to rely mostly on internal dating – but it seems likely that Ovid began his career with elegiac love poems, the *Amores* ('Loves').[11] He may have begun writing and publishing them from 25 BCE (when he was only 17 or 18 years old), but what we possess today is a second, revised edition of the poems produced by Ovid and published some time after the deaths of Virgil and of the poet Tibullus in 19 BCE (*Am.* 3.9).

In the epigrammatic preface to the *Amores* we are told that an original set of five books has been reduced to three:

> We who had lately been five books of Naso
>> are three; the author preferred this work to that.
> Even though you still find no pleasure in reading us,
>> your pain will be lighter since two have been removed.

Already the principle of change is at work in this authorial decision to turn five books of poetry into three.[12] In these four short lines we also see characteristic Ovidian devices: personification – the book collection speaks, substituting for the poet's voice; direct address, thus engaging the reader in an intimate relationship with the text and its poet; humour, for the 'voice' of the poetry books is ironic and teasing; and lastly the prominence of the author's name (always 'Naso'), for throughout his career Ovid frequently signs off on his work with his own name or an equivalent form of self-reference, not just through pride but to set the seal of authenticity on his poems. Indeed, Ovid is unique in ancient literature for the sheer number of self-references in his elegiac poetry.[13] This paratext to Ovid's first work reveals a poet who tries to keep tight control over his work and its reception.

A persistent criticism of Ovid's poetry from Antiquity has been that he is a self-indulgent writer.[14] But Ovid shows himself as scrupulous in what he deemed fit to publish to the world. For instance, in exile he comments that 'I wrote prolifically, but what I thought defective I gave to the flames to take care of' (*Tr.* 4.10.61–2). Burning one's work is an extreme method of 'revision' and suggests the high standards Ovid set for his poetry.[15] His removal of a significant number of poems for his second edition of *Amores* gives the work an internal coherence not found in the more diverse elegiac collections of his predecessors, Tibullus and Propertius, which include love poems addressed to boys as well as to young women; in the *Amores* love is strictly heterosexual. The importance of authorial control, along with the notion of change, is thus inscribed into the very format of the *Amores* as we have them today, and so too is the key concept of pleasure. In the Latin text the word for 'pleasure' comes at the end of line 3, thus emphasizing that Ovid's poetry is meant to be enjoyed; the pleasures of lovemaking and of writing and reading elegiac verse are closely allied.

Probably towards the end of his work on the *Amores* Ovid began writing the single *Heroides* ('(Letters from) heroines'). They represent a new experiment with love elegy, for they take the form of letters written by famous legendary women to their absent lovers or family members; they accommodate epic and tragic themes to the elegiac genre, and use the first-person feminine voice to express and explore female psychology and experience. The double *Heroides*, exchanges of letters between famous mythological lovers such as Paris and Helen, are generally thought now to have occupied the later part of Ovid's career.[16] His interest in the female voice and passion possibly spurred his desire in the early period of his career to write a tragedy, *Medea*, which survives in only two fragments, quoted by other authors.[17]

In 2 BCE Ovid experimented again with elegy by turning to didactic poetry, traditionally written in epic metre; his most immediate model was Virgil's *Georgics*, a four-book poem on farming, and Lucretius' *de Rerum Natura* ('On the nature of things'), a poem on Epicurean philosophy. On the other hand, Ovid's wittily irreverent didactic poem, the *Ars Amatoria* ('The art of love') was written in elegiac couplets and set out to teach the art of seduction, rather than impart moral instruction or a practical, traditional Roman skill (such as Virgil's agriculture). The *Ars Amatoria* claims to teach men (in the first two books) and women (in the third book, published probably two or three years later) how to find a sexual partner, with the end point of bed.[18] In her recent *Latin Love Lessons: Put a Little Ovid in Your Life*, author Charlotte Higgins humorously distils some of Ovid's recommendations for contemporary youth; the advice on male grooming, for instance, she suggests, would probably not go amiss today.[19] However, the *Ars Amatoria* ran counter to the moral climate in Rome and to Augustan legislation, and it seems to have led to Ovid's eventual exile.[20] It was followed shortly thereafter, perhaps by the end of 1 CE, by the *Remedia Amoris* ('Remedies for love'), a one-book didactic poem in elegiac couplets which takes the opposite tack on love from the *Ars* by teaching how to get over heartbreak. Ovid also wrote a didactic poem on cosmetics, *Medicamina Faciei Feminae* ('Make-up for the female face'), but this exists now only as a fragment of uncertain date and may have been an early work.[21]

Between 2 and 8 CE Ovid composed the *Metamorphoses*, an innovative epic which explains the origins of the physical world through myths of metamorphosis; its time frame spans the creation of the world to his own times. His epic is paired with another ambitious work that he seems to have been writing at the same time, the *Fasti* (the title refers to the Roman calendar, known as (*dies*) *fasti*, that is, days on which it was permitted to conduct business). Though written in elegiacs, it complements the *Metamorphoses* in that it is also a poem about origins, in this case, using the Roman calendar as a framework, the origins of Roman customs, of religious rites, and of the stars and constellations that presided over the Roman year. Although its opening expresses the hope of letting 'the whole year unfold' (*Fasti* 1.26), the poem as we have it has only six books and stops at the end of June, broken off by exile, as Ovid claims in his one external reference to the poem (*Tr.* 2.552).[22] With the *Fasti* Ovid continued to emphasize the importance of elegy to his self-construction as a poet; together with the *Metamorphoses* it forms a 'monumental climax' to his career.[23]

In exile Ovid's poetic career essentially comes full circle with the composition in elegiacs of five books of the *Tristia* ('Sad poems'), published between 9 and 12 CE, and four books of *Epistulae ex Ponto* ('Letters from the Black Sea'), published between 12 and 17 CE, as well as an invective poem, *Ibis*.[24] In the *Tristia* and the *Epistulae ex Ponto*, he returns to the epistolary form that he explored with the *Heroides*, only now he himself assumes the place of his abandoned heroines, and the object of his desire is not a cruel mistress but cruel Rome. While his exile poetry alludes extensively to the *Metamorphoses*, it also is richly informed by his earlier elegiac poetry – for part of Ovid's strategy in exile is to remind his readers, including his 'super-reader' Augustus, that he is the greatest living Roman poet.[25]

First-person elegiac poetry occupied most of Ovid's career, from its beginning to its bitter end in exile. Part of the appeal of that poetry is its projection of a distinctive first-person voice, confiding and confessional, which always seems to include the reader, even when the primary addressee is a friend or a lover. As Philip Hardie argues, Ovid shows 'an obsessive drive to realize a maximum of immediate presence in his poetry, at the same time as he self-consciously unmasks the reality effects'; Ovid's poetry is predicated on the *illusion* of presence, and thus generates tension between vivid presence and absence.[26] In the *Metamorphoses*, which does not accommodate direct authorial self-expression, except in its proem and epilogue, we are nonetheless made conscious of the narrator, who frequently interjects his own opinions and emotions into events and cajoles the reader to respond. Ovid also of course adopts other first-person voices in his poetry. For instance, he frequently experiments with mimesis of female speech, most notably in his *Heroides*, and then in the *Metamorphoses*. Sometimes, too, fictional characters seem to act as voices for the poet or represent the act of authoring.

Thus although in Ovid's first-person elegiac poetry the poet's voice often seems direct, intimate and confiding, the author is ultimately elusive, for in each of his works his voice is modulated according to genre, to prior texts and, at the end of his life, by external events.[27] Thus the self-confident teacher of the *Ars Amatoria* and *Remedia Amoris* who relies entirely on his own experience in the matter of love becomes the researcher of the *Fasti*, who is deferential to experts who have knowledge of Rome's history and religious customs; in the exile poetry the poet's voice is modulated by the genre of lament. Even when Ovid talks to his readers about his life, he presents that life through a literary lens. He insists in his exile poetry that Augustus should make a distinction between the historical poet and the poetic speaker(s) when he writes, 'believe me, my character is different from my poetry; my life is chaste, my Muse playful' (*Tr.* 2.353–6). The various voices of Ovid's poetry are literary creations, including his own. Thus, when I write about Ovid, I mean, in short, his authorial self-representations, or the various, textually embedded forms he gives to the poetic 'I'.

Likewise, the personal tone of Ovid's poetry has encouraged readers to see historical women behind his female addressees in his *Amores*, women who by their liberated lifestyle flouted the orthodox constraints of marriage and motherhood. But when Ovid says to a prospective 'girlfriend' early on in the *Amores* (1.3.19), 'offer yourself as happy material for my poetry', he implies that the girl embodies the literary and political interests of the male elegiac poet. In the *Amores* and *Ars Amatoria* the social status of the 'girlfriend' is kept vague, sliding between the courtesan and the married woman. Such fluidity gives the poet flexibility in his own socially provocative roles of 'slave to love' and 'soldier of love'.[28]

One of the most controversial poems in terms of Ovid's authorial identity and his handling of gender relations is *Am.* 1.5, in which the main, but not exclusive, girlfriend in the *Amores*, Corinna, is first introduced by name. As Stephen Hinds argues, Corinna's unexpected arrival during Ovid's siesta takes the form of a quasi-epiphany.[29] She arrives not with a knock on the door but as if by magic, like a supernatural being: 'look, Corinna comes'

(*Am.* 1.5.9).[30] But the sense of an epiphany is dispelled when the poet peels off the girl's flimsy clothing, overcoming her half-hearted attempts at resistance (9–16). As Paul Allen Miller notes, this is 'Ovidian erotic theater'.[31]

In his poem 'Ovid in love', a version of *Am.* 1.5, the Northern Irish poet Derek Mahon beautifully captures the tensions in the poet's initial perception of his girl as both divine and mortal (9–12):[32]

> You entered in a muslin gown,
> bare-footed, your fine braids undone,
> a fabled goddess with an air
> as if in heat, yet debonair.

Ovid's description of Corinna's body, beginning with her shoulders and ending with her thighs (19–22), has been criticized as a display of male lechery and domination.[33] The denial of a voice or even a face, the site of individuality, objectifies the woman. Unlike Ovid, Mahon at least gives her an identity and suggests her face by addressing her as 'you'. But another fruitful way of reading Corinna's body is to recognize its metaphorical potential; the meeting between Ovid and Corinna is also an encounter between the poet and his new elegiac poetry. This is Corinna's first named appearance in the poem, and Ovid's first sexual encounter; the poet's observation that 'there was no blemish on her body' can be taken to refer also to the body of elegiac poetry, the *Amores*.[34] Thus, as Joan Booth has argued, if we take Corinna as a double for love elegy, then, for Ovid's poetry to be a success, he has to master her entirely.[35] This seems to me the right direction and allows us not to overlook either the powerful eroticism of the poem or the attractive literary qualities of the elegiac mistress that match Ovid's smooth but complex verse.[36] Moreover, in keeping with the refinement of his verse, Ovid is never coarse; the sex that follows the verbal striptease is left to the imagination: 'who does not know the rest?' (25). The very name of Ovid's Corinna captures the ambiguity in her status and person, including her ability to participate in various metaphorical discourses, for she is named after a renowned Greek female lyric poet of the sixth century, but her name also evokes the common Greek word for 'girl', *kore*.[37]

Poet of change

Ovid is a poet of change in his poetry and in his life, with his drastic exile from Rome to Tomis. Indeed, change is programmatically inscribed not only into the prefatory epigram to his first work, the *Amores*, as we have seen, but into the first poem, where Ovid undergoes a personal metamorphosis (*Am.* 1.1.1–4):

> Arma gravi numero violentaque bella parabam
> > edere, materia conveniente modis.
> par erat inferior versus; risisse Cupido
> > dicitur atque unum surripuisse pedem.

> I was beginning to write about arms and violent war in a serious metre,
> with subject matching the rhythm. The second verse was equal in length
> (to the first); Cupid is said to have laughed and to have snatched away
> one foot.

I have provided the Latin here because part of the joke of this opening poem depends on metrical and generic transformation. In these opening lines Ovid describes a swift coup on the part of Cupid, who interrupts Ovid as he starts to write an epic poem that, moreover, recalls Virgil's *Aeneid*: the first word *arma* ('arms') is also the first word of the *Aeneid* with its famous starting phrase, *arma virumque cano* ('I sing of arms and the man'). The joke also depends on the metrical difference between epic hexameter, that is, six-foot verse, and the elegiac couplet, with its alternating six-foot and five-foot (pentameter) verses. By snatching away a foot from the second line of Ovid's epic poem, Cupid changes what was meant to be a hexameter line into a pentameter, thus shortening the verse and ending the sentence. The two lines have become a self-contained elegiac couplet and, hey presto, Ovid is no longer writing epic but has become an elegiac poet of love! Here then is the first Ovidian metamorphosis, the poet's own, in the very first poem of his work. In a further joke, the opening line is very light and quick, lacking the weight and gravity of the 'serious metre of epic' and thus suggesting that our poet is predisposed to write elegy. Indeed, Ovid sexualizes the elegiac couplet by describing it as 'rising in six measures and falling in five' (27).[38] In a further witty turn on the conventions of erotic elegy, by the end of the poem the god has made the poet feel passion, despite his objections to this metamorphosis (*Am.* 1.1.26): 'I am on fire.'

In *Am.* 1.1 Ovid brings humour and originality to the *recusatio*, 'the formal refusal' of epic adopted by elegiac poets and by Virgil in his pastoral poetry. Their particular model was the Hellenistic poet Callimachus (*c.*310–240 B C E) and the programmatic opening to his elegiac *Aetia* where he refuses to write an epic about kings and heroes on the grounds that Apollo commanded him to write shorter, but also more innovative, poetry (15–38). In *Ecl.* 6 Virgil follows Callimachus by claiming that he is writing pastoral poetry because, 'when I was about to sing of kings and battles, Apollo plucked my ear and admonished me' (3–4). In *Am.* 1.1 Ovid uniquely substitutes for Apollo, the great god of poetry, the mischievous boy Cupid as his inspiring divinity, thus suggesting that he will become a great love poet. Moreover, Cupid's paradoxical nature – the naughty little boy who happens to be omnipotent – embodies the psychological effects of love as an emotion both delightful but also potentially devastating.

The genre of Latin love elegy was a particular phenomenon of the Augustan age, developing in resistance to dominant social and political Roman discourse. As a love poet Ovid followed in the prestigious footsteps of his distinguished predecessors Gallus, the founder of Roman erotic elegy, Propertius and Tibullus, as well as Catullus, but he also took the genre in new directions.[39] For instance, he reverses the gendered power relations of elegy that enslaved the man to a cruel mistress.[40] *Am.* 1.1 makes clear that Ovid will strike a different course with the elegiac genre. Propertius' first love elegy opens with the name of his girlfriend (1.1): 'Cynthia first captured wretched me with her eyes.' But although Ovid is on fire with love, outrageously he has not yet found someone to love; no girl is in sight until *Am.* 1.3. There, as we saw above, she appears not as a vividly realized individual but as the necessary material for Ovid's love poetry and as a primary generic signifier (19): 'give yourself to me as the happy material for my poetry'; she is, in other words, a conduit for elegiac tropes. Whereas Propertius characterized himself as loyal to a unique but faithless woman, Ovid represents himself as disloyal and a seductive game-player. Although a girl is finally named as Corinna in *Am*. 1.5 and dominates the *Amores*, other girls are written into the generic script. The 'slavery of love' is an elegiac trope and a strategic pose that Ovid plays with in the *Amores*, but never for long. He is a lifelong slave only to Cupid, who significantly appears in *Am*. 1.1 as god of elegiac poetry as well as god of love.

Ovid's *Amores* thus interact with and against his elegiac predecessors.[41] In *Am*. 1.1 Ovid's ironical approach to the genre is marked by the absence of a girl. The programmatic start to the *Amores* asserts the primary importance of text and genre and makes fun of elegy's obsession with serious, exclusive emotion; Ovid is on fire with love, to be sure – 'I burn, and Love reigns in an empty heart' (*Am*. 1.1.26) – but his passion is for writing love poetry, and he defines himself as a love poet, devoted first and foremost to elegiac poetry. As Joan Booth pithily comments, Ovid 'makes and fakes love'.[42]

Cupid in Ovid's poetry: a generic ally

In conclusion to this introductory chapter, let us look at the role of Cupid in Ovid's poetry, for above all, perhaps, love, however ironic the poet's perspective, is central to the continuing appeal of Ovid's poetry. Moreover, Cupid embodies the principles of change and continuity that underpin Ovid's work, for his appearance and actions are modified according to its varying genres. From Ovid's first publication, Cupid is a frequent presence in his poetry, not only as the god of love and love poetry but also the presider over generic disruption and change. As we have seen, he bursts into *Am*. 1.1 with the mischievous theft of a metrical foot; his practical joke has momentous consequences as it redirects Ovid's career from epic to elegiac poetry. This boyish but omnipotent god has the power of metamorphosis, for he makes Ovid an elegiac poet and lover.

In the *Amores* the poet represents himself as the prisoner of Cupid (*Am*. 1.2) and also as a soldier in Cupid's army (*Am*. 1.9). But at the start of the *Ars Amatoria* there is a surprising shift. Ovid has become the experienced teacher of love who claims mastery over Cupid (and thus love) through art (*Ars* 1.4); Cupid is represented as a young pupil and Ovid as his tutor (*Ars* 1.9–10):

> Of course he is wild, the sort to often rebel against me;
> but he is a boy, and a young age is fit for guidance.

In the *Ars* the poet attempts to teach love as a calculated system of seduction; love by the rules means success and pleasure, rather than pain. Readers of Ovid's *Amores* will suspect that Ovid may have taken on an impossible task in subjecting Love/love to a rational system of rules, especially since the poet acknowledges that even his mother Venus has found her boy ungovernable and hence has handed him over to Ovid to teach (*Ars* 1.3–24). As we will see in the next chapter, Ovid's rules are frequently countered in the *Ars* by evidence of the volatility of love, as embodied in the boy god Cupid. Indeed, Ovid's next didactic work, the *Remedia Amoris*, suggests the limitations of the *Ars Amatoria* in the realm of love; rules and techniques are still no guarantee against heartbreak.

The *Remedia Amoris* opens with Ovid confronting an indignant Cupid, who fears that Ovid has reverted to writing epic and is making war on his elegiac territory (*Rem.* 1.1–2):

> Cupid had read the title and name of this book:
> 'Wars, I see,' he said, 'wars are being prepared against me.'

Cupid acts here like the ungovernable boy of the *Ars*. He is not much of a student and blows up in anger after he has merely read the title of the *Remedia* (1–2). As we saw in *Am.* 1.1, this god prefers few words! In a long opening speech the poet placates Cupid, convincing him that love should be play, not pain, and that he is not destroying love, only restoring its pleasures (3–38). Ovid runs rings around Cupid, who is easily convinced by these half-truths, claiming that Ovid's new poem is no threat to his realm.[43] In a sign of favour, 'the golden boy moves his jewelled wings', and briefly tells the poet to complete his planned work (*Rem.* 39–40). The only other reference in literature, apparently, to Cupid's 'jewelled wings' occurs in *Am.* 1.2.41–2, where Cupid is also called 'golden' and rules over Ovid as a triumphing general over a slave.[44] In the *Remedia* the allusion underlines how much the poet has seized control of love's agenda from Cupid.

Cupid even actively supports the poet when, later in the poem, he appears in an epiphany to add some precepts of his own on cures for heartbreak (*Rem.* 549–78). He is here accommodated to the didactic thrust of the poem, for he assumes the unique role of *Lethaeus Amor*, 'the Cupid of Forgetting' (*Rem.* 551), probably Ovid's creation for his new didactic poem. E. J. Kenney argues that Cupid's theophany provides a welcome break to the potential monotony of the *Remedia*.[45] Yet the god's precepts are uninspiring and drily pragmatic, and again show Cupid's penchant for short speech (*Rem.* 557–74). For instance, Cupid advises the lover to focus on financial worries such as debts, agricultural ruin or the loss of merchandise in shipwreck.[46] Only the concluding mythological allusion to Paris, who could have turned against Helen if he had thought about the deaths of his many brothers, makes a more vivid point, yet it is of course an extreme example of little account for the average lover (573–4). With his dry speech, the 'Cupid of Forgetting' shows how the spark has gone out of love.

Cupid's role here is the reverse of Apollo's in the *Ars Amatoria*. Apollo supports the teachings of Ovid's *Ars* by announcing that the key tenet of his temple at Delphi, 'know yourself', allows Ovid's precepts to be applied intelligently and successfully to seduction (2.493–510). Apollo's basic message is to remember, whereas Cupid's is to forget; this may explain why, beyond the fact that Ovid's Cupid prefers action to rhetoric, the god's precepts are fairly unmemorable! And whereas in the *Ars* Apollo looks and acts divine, strumming a golden lyre and wreathed with laurel (*Ars* 2.493–6), the curious 'Cupid of Forgetting' is not described at all beyond his one gesture of extinguishing his torches with water, emblem of the fire of love (*Rem.* 552). Thus in the *Remedia Amoris* Cupid again acts as a generic marker of an erotic, elegiac work, accommodated however to a didactic message of forgetting love; he is a shadow of his former vital self.

Cupid functions as a flexible, generic marker also in Ovid's *Metamorphoses*. As in *Am.* 1.1, his introduction to the epic poem is programmatic and generically disruptive. He presides over the poem's first 'love' story, the myth of Apollo and Daphne, which occurs early in the poem, thus marking the poet's departure from martial epic norms (*Met*. 1.452–567). The epic Cupid looks back to the mischievous god of *Am*. 1.1 but is more powerful. His entry into the *Metamorphoses* recalls the *coup d'état* at the start of the *Amores*, only here he makes Apollo, the god of poetry himself, fall in love, rather than the poet. His metamorphic power is thus shown as more lethal, invincible and 'epic'.

At the start of Ovid's narrative, the god Apollo is filled with pride after killing the monstrous Python (*Met*. 1.438–51). So far the god's role conforms to epic expectations, although the narrative of his struggle against the monster is short and perfunctory, serving as a mere prelude to the longer tale of his 'first love'.[47] When Apollo spots Cupid sitting in a tree with bow and arrows, he carps at him (*Met*. 1.456–7):

> 'What, lascivious boy,' he said, 'are you doing with sturdy weapons?
> That equipment looks better on my shoulders.'

Apollo unwisely continues to boast about his own prowess with the bow. With a speech half as long as Apollo's, Cupid claims his superior power (*Met*. 1.463–5), and backs it up by removing from his quiver two arrows designed to have opposite effects: one with tip of gold to make Apollo on fire with love, and one with tip of lead to make the nymph Daphne spurn him (1.466–74). Cupid's adaptation to epic vastly increases the scope of his power. Not only does the great god Apollo fall in love, but his famous arts of poetry and healing cannot help him either secure the girl or rid him of his passion (*Met*. 1.523–4). The god who happened, furthermore, to be Augustus' patron deity, closely associated with his victory at the Battle of Actium, succumbs nonetheless to the greater power of love.[48]

This first erotic myth in the *Metamorphoses* shows Cupid in his most blatant contradictions: still a mischievous boy (who likes to climb trees), he has easy power over the greatest of the gods, and indeed power over life and death, for the game of love often proves deadly in the *Metamorphoses*. Daphne escapes Apollo only by losing her human identity through metamorphosis into the laurel tree (*Met.* 1.543–67). Cupid demonstrates in this first myth that love is the ruling force of the world. Moreover, by making Apollo, the god of poetry, fall in love, Cupid programmatically introduces erotic themes to the *Metamorphoses*, thus challenging the stability of Roman epic conventions that were traditionally historical and nationalistic. Cupid's appearance early on in the epic draws attention to the generically experimental nature of the *Metamorphoses* and its politically provocative edge. Thus Cupid plays a major role in both the *Metamorphoses* and the elegiac works as master of generic play and change, and as the wild card, so to speak, among the gods of Rome.

Cupid does not abandon Ovid in exile, and makes a final appearance in Ovid's poetry in *Pont.* 3.3. As E. J. Kenney points out, Cupid's epiphany recalls his previous appearance to the poet at *Rem.* 549–78. The two epiphanies, representing mid-career and end-career for Ovid, are poignantly interwoven. On both occasions the god appears to the poet who is in a dreamlike state.[49] 'I don't know if it was the real Cupid or a dream,' Ovid comments at *Rem.* 555–6, and, when Cupid finishes his short speech, the poet adds, 'there was more to come, but the boyish image left my peaceful dream – if it was in fact a dream' (*Rem.* 575–6). In exile Ovid recalls in similar concluding lines his earlier uncertainty over whether Cupid's appearance was merely a dream (*Pont.* 3.3.93–4): 'he spoke and then either slipped away into thin air, or my own senses began to waken.' The recall of the *Remedia Amoris* serves as a strategic reminder that Ovid wrote not only the controversial *Ars* but also a poem that aims to banish love; in exile he always had an eye on his pardon or at least an improvement in his harsh conditions. Indeed, one of the functions of Cupid's speech to Ovid in *Pont.* 3.3 is to exonerate the *Ars Amatoria*; he begins by swearing that 'there is no crime in your *Ars*' (70).

In describing Cupid's departure 'into thin air' (93), Ovid also echoes Virgil's lines on the departure of Mercury in *Aeneid* 4, after the god has given Aeneas Jupiter's orders that he must leave Dido's Carthage if he is to fulfil divine plans for Roman destiny (*Aen.* 4.276–8): 'thus Mercury spoke and left mortal vision mid-speech, vanishing far from sight into thin air.' Virgil's Mercury is an appropriate counterpart to Cupid, for both are winged gods notoriously clever at theft. The allusion to Virgil's epic puts Ovid cleverly in the position of Aeneas. As Aeneas in Carthage is in the wrong place at the wrong time, so too Ovid is out of place in Tomis, and like Aeneas, he needs to move from east to west, to the magnet of Rome. And as Mercury's speech is authoritative in changing the course of Aeneas' life, so too Cupid's speech predicting imperial clemency (*Pont.* 3.3.67–92) should mean that Ovid's hopes are not in vain.

Unlike in the first epiphany in the *Remedia Amoris*, Cupid's arrival and appearance are described in some detail (*Pont.* 3.3.5–20):

> It was night, and the moon was filtering through the twin-shuttered windows
>> with its usual mid-month brightness.
> Sleep, the common respite for care, possessed me,
>> and my languid limbs were sprawled all over the bed,
> when suddenly the air shivered, disturbed by wings,
>> and the window creaked slightly as it moved.
> Terrified, I propped myself up on my left elbow,
>> and sleep was driven from my terrified heart.
> There stood Cupid, not looking like his former self,
>> but sadly he held the maple post of the couch with his left hand.
> He did not have a torque on his neck or adornment on his hair,
>> nor was his hair well arranged, as before.
> His soft hair hung down over his horrid-looking face,
>> and his wings seemed horrid to me too,
> like those on the back of a winged dove,
>> which many hands have touched and handled.

Ovid plays here off epic dreams such as Aeneas' vision of the ghost of Hector on the night before the fall of Troy (*Aen.* 2.268–303). Like Cupid (13), Hector is greatly changed, no longer the glorious Homeric hero, for his beard is matted, his hair is clotted with blood and his body shows many wounds (*Aen.* 2.274–9). But although Ovid expects a ghost (9–12), instead he has an even greater vision of a god. Yet the Cupid who appears before him is not like the mischievous boy of *Am.* 1.1 who stole a foot from the poet's epic verse. Shabby and dejected, he symbolically represents the hard times that Ovid endures in exile and the nature of the exile poetry itself.

In his signature final poem to the *Amores*, Ovid twice calls Cupid 'elegant' (*Am.* 3.15.15): 'elegant boy and Amathusian parent [i.e. Venus] of the elegant boy' (*culte puer puerique parens Amathusia culti*). This line of verse too is made elegant through the framing of the line by the Latin word for 'elegant' (with a minor difference in ending, *culte / culti*), and the rare Greek title for Venus, 'Amathusian parent', borrowed from Catullus 68.51. *Cultus*, 'sophistication and polish', is the hallmark of Ovid's elegiac poetry. *Cultus* is what he tries to teach the lover in the *Ars Amatoria*. He famously says in *Ars Amatoria* 3 that he loves contemporary Rome because '*cultus* is here, and the rustic manners of our ancestors have not survived to our times' (*Ars* 3). The Cupid of the exile poetry is by contrast *incultus*, like Ovid's first book of *Tristia*, which is personified as *incultus*, that is, 'unkempt, as befits an exile' (*Tr.* 1.1.3), and 'looking shaggy with loose locks of hair' (*Tr.* 1.1.12).

Twice in *Pont.* 3.3 Ovid describes Cupid with the adjective 'horrid' (17, 18), a word that in Latin evokes strong feelings of horror and revulsion and is also used of 'rough, bristly hair'; Cupid is shocking to look at with his ungroomed, matted locks and wings. The concluding simile of the dove (19–20) is particularly appropriate, since the dove was the special bird of Cupid's mother Venus. But this dove is shop-soiled goods, handled and pawed over by many, the antithesis of Ovid's formerly elegant poetry. Described as 'sad' ('tristis', 14), Cupid bears the signature of Ovid's first collection of exile poetry, the *Tristia* ('Sad poems'). This is Cupid metamorphosed. The poet's suffering in exile as well as the altered character of his poetry are etched on the changed, bedraggled body of the god who, in Ovid's first elegiac poems, impudently introduced the poet to love poetry (*Am.* 1.1) and shone, triumphant and golden, with wings and hair glittering with jewels (*Am.* 1.2.41–2).

The appearance and demeanour of this Cupid show that he is in tune with his poet's elegiac sufferings, even though Ovid no longer writes erotic poetry. The theme of sympathy with Ovid's misfortune is conveyed by reference to Cupid's 'left hand' (14), which clutches the backrest of Ovid's couch and thus matches the 'left elbow' (11) on which Ovid props himself up, 'left' being the unlucky side; the bodily gestures show that Cupid shares in his poet's misfortune. Moreover, the detail that the backrest of Ovid's couch is made of maplewood (14) is probably not arbitrary, for the Latin word for 'maple', *acer*, recalls in sound the Latin adjective *acer* meaning 'painful'. The bed symbolizes Ovid's suffering as well as the changed material of his elegies. His limbs too take up the *whole* bed, which means that he is alone, no longer a lover, and his limbs are 'languid', thus lacking in virility (8). By contrast, in *Am.* 1.5, a poem that is evoked at the start of *Pont.* 3.3 by the similar dimly lit bedroom setting, the poet lies in the *middle* of the bed, meaning there is room to share, and his limbs are waiting for both arousal and relief (2).

Cupid, as the poet points out, has imperial connections through the genealogy of Augustus, which traced its origins to Venus.[50] He thus provocatively addresses Cupid as 'Aeneas' brother' and thus Augustus' relative (62). But Cupid's estrangement from the imperial house is suggested by his bedraggled appearance in *Pont.* 3.3, which represents too the estrangement of his poet from imperial Rome, from a circle of important friends and from a wife related to the imperial family, none of whom, however, could engineer his recall. Ovid's Cupid is an indictment of Augustus' shabby treatment of his kin – and of Rome's most illustrious living poet. Cupid alone of the Augustan family has shown loyalty to Ovid by travelling far to see him.

But this figure of a loyal Cupid also represents the continuity of Ovid's poetry even in exile. Like all Ovid's exile poetry, *Pont.* 3.3 is deeply informed by his earlier elegiac poetry as well as the *Metamorphoses*. *Am.* 3.9, Ovid's elegy for the death of the love poet Tibullus, grants us an anticipatory glimpse of this later, metamorphosed Cupid. In *Am.* 3.9 Cupid is in mourning and walks in the funeral procession of his beloved Tibullus with his quiver upturned, his bow broken, his torches without light, his wings drooping and his hair unbound; he beats his breast and shakes with sobs (*Am.* 3.9.7–12). The particular features of the drooping wings and unbound hair foreshadow the grieving Cupid of Ovid's exile, thus suggesting that Ovid too has experienced a kind of death in his banishment, a persistent trope of the exile poetry.[51] A related trope is that Ovid's poetry has suffered a decline, cut off from his important source of inspiration, Rome; Cupid is the physical manifestation of that trope, and with his shaggy hair (*Pont.* 3.3.17–18) recalls the personified, unkempt poetry book of *Tr.* 1.1.12 ('looking shaggy with loose locks of hair').[52] The recall of *Am.* 3.9, however, also draws attention to Ovid's importance as Tibullus' elegiac successor. In exile he represents himself as the last, but by no means the least, of the four canonical Augustan elegiac poets: Gallus, Propertius, Tibullus and now Ovid (*Tr.* 4.10.54). Recall of his own earlier elegiac poetry and his prominent place in literary history provides a poignant, self-defensive grammar for the description of the experience of exile, sharpening the nature of the poet's present plight and reminding Ovid's readers of his artistic greatness.

Pont. 3.3 is addressed to Paullus Fabius Maximus, a prominent member of the senatorial elite who was a close friend of Augustus and also a supporter of Ovid.[53] He had considerable literary as well as political heft, for as a young man he appeared in Horace's first poem in Book 4 of the *Odes* (9–27).[54] Horace begins *Carm.* 4.1 by begging Venus to leave him alone, for he is finished with love (1–8); she should instead transfer her attentions to the youthful Fabius, who will rightly worship her. The poem then describes a luxurious temple that Horace imagines Fabius will build in her honour (19–27). Ovid strategically follows Horace in honouring the now elderly Fabius with a poem featuring another imaginative centrepiece, the dream vision of Venus' son. He also castigates Cupid, as Horace castigates Venus; in Ovid's case he complains that Cupid ruined him – he is the only teacher who has been destroyed by his own pupil (*Pont.* 3.3.45–6).

The multifaceted Cupid of exile, however, is a figure of loyalty and an embodiment of Ovid's mature poetry. He now shows himself capable of eloquence and defends himself in a fairly lengthy speech that promises the lessening of Caesar's wrath (67–92). He has travelled far to give his poet hope, a sign of the unbroken bond between the god and his poet. Indeed, Cupid refers to having made a previous journey to Tomis in order to cause Medea to fall in love (*Pont.* 3.3.79–80), an allusion surely to the role of Medea in Ovid's poetry, both as the theme of his lost tragedy *Medea* and as an important, first-person female voice with a lengthy soliloquy in the seventh book of the *Metamorphoses* (11–71). Cupid thus signifies the continuity of Ovid's poetry over time and in a variety of genres. Linked to the imperial house through genealogy, he is also in *Pont.* 3.3 a surrogate for the return letter of official recall that Ovid longs for. Shabby, down at heel, but still faithful to his banished poet, Cupid is a generic sign of the complexity of Ovid's final poetry, written by a poet displaced, alienated, and yet richly and proudly engaged with his previous poetry and with his Augustan predecessors.

In his own time, Ovid's poetry had a broad popular basis. He frequently advertises the appeal of his poetry to the general populace, rather than simply to a literary elite; for instance, he begins the *Ars Amatoria* by addressing 'all those among this people [that is to say, of Rome] who do not know the art of love' (*Ars* 1.1). Indeed he refers to the performance of his poetry on stage before packed audiences, possibly danced by pantomime artists who did not sing but acted out mythical narratives through brilliantly executed bodily gestures conveying actions and emotions (*Tr.* 2.519–20).[55] Moreover, in Roman culture visual literacy was high. People navigated their cities by landmarks such as monuments; mythological figures and narratives were ubiquitous in public and private art. As Peter Knox, for instance, has shown, stories from the *Metamorphoses* were illustrated on the walls of houses in Pompeii, essentially what we would call a 'middle-class' town where art served both for private enjoyment and for public display to visitors and business associates; in the first century CE these paintings attest to the wide appeal and the cultural cachet of Ovid's poetry among not only the elite but also the general public.[56] The variety and humanity of Ovid's poetry and its vivid visual qualities, along with an active empire-wide book trade, helped it survive the vagaries of time and the condemnation of rulers. Although his friends could not recall Ovid from exile, they kept copies of his poetry in circulation – in the end, perhaps, a greater service to the poet (*Tr.* 1.7.23–4; *Tr.* 3.1.79–82).

The tensions in Ovid's poetry – eloquent, smooth-flowing verse applied to the depth and range of human emotions; violence frequently conjoined to beauty – create a dynamic role for the reader, whom the poet continues to draw into his world. 'To be at once the same and different: is that not somewhere near the heart of the virtue of Ovid's *Metamorphoses*?' asks Charles Martindale, but his remark applies to Ovid's poetry as a whole.[57]

II

WRITING FOR AN AGE OF GOLD: THE LOVE ELEGIST

Let Antiquity please others; as for me, I'm glad to have been born now: this age suits my temperament.

(ARS AMATORIA 3.121–2)

OVID WAS A GREAT COMIC poet in an era when comedy could be deemed politically incorrect. From the start of his literary career Ovid presents himself as a poet both very much of the Augustan age and on a nonconformist track in dialogue with, as Alison Sharrock puts it, 'the most powerful contemporary signifiers of the masculine order: Augustus, *arma* (war and epic), and political life'.[1] In Ovid's poetry we are frequently conscious of a parallel political discourse as the boundaries between the discourses of love and of politics become provocatively blurred. War, the driving force of Roman imperial power, becomes in Ovid's poetry not only a metaphor for love but also a similar practice for, as Ovid most blatantly put it in *Am.* 1.9.1, 'every lover is a soldier.' Love, moreover, in Rome was a political matter, subject to severe legislation.[2] Let us therefore take a look at the emperor who tired of Ovid's wit and in 8 CE banished him from the city that was the centre of his world.

Augustus

Augustus ruled between 31 BCE and 14 CE as Rome's first emperor. He rode to power on winds of change, for Rome was exhausted after two decades of civil war and was desperate for a leader who could bring political stability. Victorious over Mark Antony and Cleopatra at the Battle of Actium in 31 BCE, Augustus set about establishing a new form of governance for Rome and a lasting peace.[3] Although the idea of monarchy was anathema to the Romans, who had expelled their last king on the traditional date of 510 BCE when they established a republic, they now had to accept one-man rule. Augustus diplomatically styled himself not 'king' (Latin *rex*) but *princeps* ('first man of the state'), and the new form of government, which retained Republican institutions such as the Senate, was known as 'the principate'.

Over the course of a long reign of 45 years Augustus rebuilt Rome into a cosmopolitan, imperial city. The basis of his authority rested not only on the flourishing economy made possible by peace, but on his self-presentation, supported by laws, as a moral exemplar for his citizens. The recent past of civil wars was condemned as degenerate; Rome needed to turn to the virtues of the remote past for renewal.[4] Thus Augustus set in motion an impressive system of propaganda that looked both back to an idealized past of virtuous, hard-working ancestors and forward to a future of unparalleled prosperity, of global reach, of empire without end; the city of Rome itself was a microcosm of the idea of eternal empire.

Key also to Augustus' programme of renewal were art and architecture. He stamped Rome with his own image, altering the visual cityscape of Rome by building and restoring magnificent monuments and marble buildings, temples, porticoes, baths, theatres, many of them named after the imperial family, including, prominently, himself.[5] Temples and statues honouring

Augustus and his family were, moreover, erected all across the empire. Before his death Augustus wrote a lengthy record of his achievements, the *Res Gestae* ('Achievements'), which he ordered inscribed on bronze pillars in Rome as an example for posterity (*Res Gestae* 1). Copies also appeared on temples and monuments across the empire, including in Ancyra, Turkey, where a surviving text, in Latin with Greek translation, reflects the cosmopolitanism of Rome. Augustus made a monument out of his achievements, to be circulated throughout the empire.

Such public magnificence emblematized the peace Augustus had brought to the Roman world through imperial conquest. The Ara Pacis (Altar of Peace), dedicated by the Senate in 9 BCE in honour of Augustus' safe return from campaigns in France and Spain, provided, for instance, a striking visual image of Augustan ideals, an interweaving of political and religious iconography that depicted Rome's early founders Aeneas and Romulus, and the new founders, the imperial family, walking forward in sacrificial procession with their priests and children as the guarantors of a new peace, fertility and order. The interdependence of traditional civic and domestic virtues is shown as foundational to a successful, prosperous state. The public representation of families, however, was a striking artistic innovation that emphasized, moreover, the monument's dynastic aims.[6]

This new, cosmopolitan, imperial Rome was the centre of Ovid's world and of his elegiac poetry. In exile, when he writes that he was born in Sulmo, he identifies the town by reference to its distance of 90 miles from 'the city', that is, from Rome (*Tr.* 4.10.4), which continues to form the mental compass for his life.[7] He puns on the idea that Rome is the world, since *urbs*, the Latin word for 'the city' (i.e. Rome), resembles in sound that for the 'world', *orbs* (*Ars* 1.173–4; *Fasti* 2.683–4). The epigraph to this chapter highlights the provocative nature of Ovid's enthusiastic embrace of present-day Rome, with its implication that he is a sure guide to all that is contemporary and cool in Rome.[8] His dismissal of Antiquity, however, runs counter to the Augustan elevation of the past as the repository of the moral values that had made Rome great.[9] Augustus claimed he had brought back the Golden Age, meaning a time of prosperity and peace allied with traditional Roman virtues.[10] The poet of the *Ars* sees the present age as 'Golden' in a different sense: 'Rome is golden' (3.113) with glittering new buildings that are an invitation to pleasure and a sign of a sophisticated, forward-looking culture. Thus Ovid's Rome is not simply a celebration of the fabulous present but becomes, as Tony Boyle aptly puts it, 'the site of an ideological struggle' over what it meant to be Roman.[11]

Of particular impact on Roman erotic elegy was Augustus' moral legislation. Disturbed by what he perceived as neglect of the family among the governing classes, he introduced around 18 and 17 BCE the Julian laws on adultery and marriage.[12] Many details of the laws are unclear to us today. From what we can tell, severe financial penalties were imposed on unmarried men, who were legally required to marry and have children; to preserve Roman racial purity, senators could not marry freedwomen. And for the first time adultery was made a criminal offence rather than an offence that was handled within the family. The law fell more heavily on women than men: a woman could not bring a charge of adultery against her husband but a husband was required by law to divorce his adulterous wife and take her to court. Punishment for both male and female offenders generally meant relegation to an island and confiscation of some of their property.[13] These controversial laws, bitterly resented by the elite, intervened in an unprecedented fashion in the private lives of Roman citizens, and they confer a provocative edge on the sensual and promiscuous pleasures of Ovidian erotic elegy.

Also of crucial impact on Ovidian elegy is Roman militarism. As Alison Keith points out, the discourse of elegy was collusive with imperial expansion and military conquest, for they made possible the circulation of luxury goods and wealth in Rome. Ovid makes fun of Rome's military ethos with his development of the analogy between the lover and the soldier (e.g. *Am.* 1.9), and yet, like Propertius, he draws attention to the dependence of elegiac leisure, and pleasure, on the commercial spoils of imperialism.[14]

Amores *and* Ars Amatoria

In his early elegiac works, the *Amores* and *Ars Amatoria*, Ovid played the part of Rome's poet of sex and the city. The French scholar Paul Veyne, in an influential book published in English in 1988, claimed that Roman love poetry was pure fantasy, a 'game' without any relation to political and social issues.[15] Many scholars argue that, on the contrary, the language of Ovid's erotic elegy provocatively touches upon contemporary social issues, in particular Augustan moral legislation. The elegiac 'girl' may be an imaginary figure, shaped by the poet's literary and political agendas, but she also serves as a major provocation for the poet to devote his life to love and poetry rather than to the state. Despite the textualization of women in Latin love elegy, Ovid's love elegy also explores the social realities of men's and women's lives. The centrality of love in Ovid's poetry defies Augustus' infringement on Roman private life.

In the *Amores*, his first collection of elegiac love poetry, Ovid plays the game of love with few illusions and with often self-deprecatory humour that offsets his chauvinism. As Barbara Boyd argues, he revitalizes the genre.[16] He daringly brings social realism into the genre with poems about abortion (*Am.* 2.13 and 14), about the disastrous effects of hair dye on Corinna's beautiful tresses (*Am.* 1.14), about his unlimited sexual stamina (*Am.* 2.10), and even about his own impotence (*Am.* 3.7). In *Am.* 1.3 he plays with the ideal of fidelity by promising the girl he courts everlasting loyalty (13–16), but in *Am.* 2.4 he boasts of his promiscuity (*Am.* 2.4.10): 'there are a hundred reasons why I should always be in love.'[17]

Most provocatively, perhaps, the *Amores* flirt with adultery by assuming that love, to be exciting, should generally be forbidden. For example, *Am.* 1.4 is addressed to the poet's two-timing girlfriend who is to be at the same dinner party as he is, along with her man; the poem, 'an advance *Art of Love*', gives the girl instructions on how to enjoy erotic thrills in this charged situation, playing 'footsie' with the poet under the table, for instance (15–16), or passing her wine cup directly to him after her lips have touched the rim (31–2). The girl's social status is kept deliberately vague, however. For instance, in the poem's opening line, 'your man is going to the same dinner party as us', the Latin word for 'man', as in English, can mean either 'husband' or 'partner'. The poet's own marital status is not revealed until *Am.* 3.13, when we discover to our surprise that he has a wife. While critics assume that the introduction of his wife means that Ovid is winding up the project of writing the *Amores* and is turning to new themes and genres, it also invites us to reread the *Amores* as adulterous poetry.

As for the social status of the girls that the poet–lover pursues in his elegiac poetry, critics have oscillated between seeing them as high-class courtesans and adulterous married women. As we saw in Chapter 1, many critics now assume that the elegiac mistress such as Ovid's Corinna does not correspond to a real-life girlfriend but is shaped by the literary and political interests of the elegiac text; she participates metaphorically in various discourses.[18] As Sharon James has argued, moreover, the concept of the elegiac mistress is significantly shaped by the tradition of Greco-Roman New Comedy, where the independent, high-class courtesan, socially unavailable and often ruinously expensive, creates, like the elegiac mistress, obstacles to love; she was a particularly powerful model at a time when foreign courtesans were flooding into Rome, a product of Rome's new wealth and imperial power.[19] Thus the social status of the elegiac girl remains vague, allowing her to play flexible roles in the poetry. The frisson of seduction, moreover, depends on the beloved's unavailability. She has to be hard to get, and thus generally at least with another partner; in *Am.* 2.12.3–4 Corinna is described as being heavily guarded. The *Amores* present themselves in part as a male fantasy of love and sex where the attraction of the forbidden gives the poetry an erotic charge. At the same time, by interrogating prescriptive gender roles and social behaviour, they challenge the Augustan laws that attempted to regulate private sexual lives. The poet seems to exult in an unrepentant lifestyle (*Am.* 2.1.2): 'I am that Ovid, the poet of my mischievousness', but the elusiveness of the girl's social status also gives the poet a political safety net before the moralists.

In the exile poetry Ovid's wife replaces the girlfriend, although she plays a less central role. She is never named, and although there are hints that she is close to the imperial family, this is never made certain. Rather, she is constructed as the opposite of the destructive, wilful girlfriend(s) of the *Amores*, for Ovid's wife is to be the necessary loyal partner who will do her utmost to save her man. Whereas he commands his unnamed girlfriend in *Am.* 1.3.19 to 'offer yourself to me as happy material for my poetry', he commands his wife in *Tr.* 4.3.73 to 'fill my sad material with your virtues'. With this play on his poetry's title *Tristia* ('Sad poems'), Ovid's wife represents the generic diversification of elegy into lament. While the absence of *eros* marks the wife's wrongful, physical absence from her exiled husband, conjugal virtue replaces forbidden sex.

The *Ars Amatoria*, however, is generally agreed to be the poem that, along with the charge of 'an error', led to Ovid's exile in 8 CE (*Tr.* 2.207). Probably this mysterious 'error', which Ovid was not permitted to divulge, was the more serious charge, for why would Augustus wait ten years after the publication of the *Ars* (in 2 BCE) to banish Ovid?[20] The *Ars* was the equivalent of today's bestseller. It remained popular through the Middle Ages, both as an eloquent school text for teaching Latin grammar and style, and as a guide to ethical conduct towards lovers.[21] The first two books of this heteronormative poem teach men how to secure a love partner; the third book teaches women how to seduce a man.[22]

The *Ars Amatoria* breaks with didactic tradition in major ways. Ovid's Latin predecessors in didactic poetry, Lucretius and Virgil, open their *de Rerum Natura* and *Georgics* respectively with a request for divine inspiration. Ovid, however, claims that he does not need divine authority to inspire his teachings; rather, he relies purely on his personal expertise in love (*Ars* 1.25–30). Cupid, his master and inspiring deity in *Am.* 1.1, is now to be his pupil (*Ars* 1.3–24). Traditionally, moreover, from its origins with the archaic Greek poet Hesiod, didactic poetry was written in epic metre. By writing a didactic poem in elegiacs, Ovid emphasized both his break with the serious didactic tradition and also the continuity of his *Ars* with his *Amores*. The *Ars* shows a similar ironic approach to love, but the now highly experienced love poet specifically advocates for others love without pain. His claim that love is a technical skill which can be learned by following rules parodies traditional didactic methods. Such sexual pragmatism results in the objectification of the girl as a hunter's quarry, or as military plunder; little concession is made to her feelings. The instructions for the male lover in the *Ars* follow his amoral counterpart in the *Amores*: he may flatter and demean himself, but always with an eye to securing the girl. In the *Ars*, the poet teaches that love does not happen by accident; it must be sought, and every behaviour is rhetorical.

But the *Ars Amatoria* is not only about love; it is also about the new Augustan city, its monuments, its wealth and its opportunities for leisure. It offers a critical and playful enquiry into the Augustan order and its public representation. But the timing of the poem's publication in 2 BCE proved unfortunate. In that year, at the pinnacle of his rule, Augustus was granted by the Senate and the people of Rome the title of 'father of the nation'; he thus was able to validate his patriarchal model of government (avoiding the terminology of monarchy), and to assert the importance of family to a successful state. Augustus' particular pride in this title is reflected in his *Res Gestae*, where it forms the climax of his accomplishments (35). However, in the dual role of 'father of the nation' and 'father of his family', that same year he had to exercise his own punitive laws against his daughter Julia, sending her into exile on conviction of adultery.

In this moral climate there is much that could be seen as provocative about the playful *Ars Amatoria*.[23] Its opening premise that, by reading the poem and following Ovid's rules, anyone can enjoy love and sex with whomever he (or she, in Book 3) chooses, flies in the face of Augustus' legislation aimed at social control (*Ars* 1.1–2):

> If anyone among this population does not know the art of making love,
>> he should read this poem and, once it is read, be an experienced lover.

The poet does not restrict his readership to any particular social class in Rome. However, he makes an attempt to protect his *Ars Amatoria* from censure with the programmatic disclaimer that the poem is not for chaste young girls or respectable married women and, furthermore, that there is nothing criminal in his poem (1.31–34):

> Keep your distance, slender headbands, badge of modesty,
>> and you, long outer dress, who covers to the middle of the feet:
> I will sing of safe love and permitted cheatings;
>> there will be no crime in my poem.

Modest adornment and dress that covers the body are signs of female virtue that function here as synecdoches for chaste young girls and respectable Roman matrons. The disclaimer seems a disingenuous, questionable attempt to protect the poem from the new laws.[24] 'Safe love' (33) is love without consequences that exists solely for gratification; as Robert Edwards argues, such love belongs to an imaginary world where genuine passion and responsibility are absent.[25] And is there such a thing as 'permitted cheatings'? Finally, are we really to take at face value that an educated married woman would not read the latest poem by the most famous poet of the day?[26] As the poet argues later at *Tr.* 2.307–8, 'it is not a crime to peruse elegiac verse; chaste women may read of things they should not do.' Moreover, as in the *Amores*, so in the *Ars* the social status of the 'girls' that are to be pursued is kept generally ambiguous. As Roy Gibson points out, the text often makes it difficult to distinguish between the upper-class married woman and the courtesan.[27] The poet's opening disclaimer is thus an invitation to transgressive readings.

Indeed, from the perspective of the teacher of love, Augustus' new city has made a manual on seduction necessary, for it has attracted a flood of available girls (*Ars* 1.55–60):

> Rome will grant you so many and such beautiful girls
>> that you can say 'this city has everything in the world'.
> As many harvests and as much vintage as Gargara and Methymna provide,
>> as many fish and as many birds shelter in sea and trees,
> as many stars as are in the sky, just as many girls has your Rome:
>> Aeneas' mother has settled in her son's city.

Women, presumably foreign prostitutes, are represented here as part of the imperial trade pouring into Rome from fertile agricultural regions of western Asia and Greece (57); the city is represented as a physical body ruled by appetite. It is typical of the *Ars* that its views of women and of love are neither moral nor romantic but pragmatic; women are also frequently described as 'prey' to be hunted.[28] But the hunt does not take place in the wild woods characteristic of erotic pursuit in the *Metamorphoses* but rather within the Augustan city himself, which, as Carin Green suggests, resembles one big game preserve.[29] By calling Venus 'Aeneas' mother', the poet provocatively alludes to Augustus' claim of divine descent from Venus and her son Aeneas, physically realized in the temple of Venus Genetrix (Venus the

Mother), built by Julius Caesar in the heart of Rome. Ovid's poem wittily exploits the gap between Augustus' moral legislation and the social realities underpinning imperial prosperity. Venus has settled in Rome as the new capital of the empire of love.

Part of the political provocation of the *Ars* lies also in the poem's emphasis that many of the erotic 'hot spots' where men and women could cruise were buildings endowed by or named after the imperial family. In the *Amores* there are few topographical references to the city of Rome, but the *Ars Amatoria* situates itself squarely in the city among its splendid new monuments. Augustus had boasted that he had found 'a city of brick but left it a city of marble' (Suetonius, *Div. Aug.* 28.2), but in Ovid's *Ars* the majestic beauty of the imperial buildings matters only to the extent that, since many were open to the general public, they afforded perfect venues for erotic encounters (1.67–88). The colonnades of Augustus' sister Octavia, for instance, or of his wife Livia, served as attractive recreational spaces for the Roman public to promenade and look at splendid works of art; yet in this elegiac remapping of Rome these august imperial monuments are appropriated for sex (68–72). Moreover, they make seduction a public event conducted outdoors in the daylight rather than one conducted behind closed doors. Ironically, this shocking innovation in social and sexual conduct is made possible by the benefactions of imperial women, models for the state of traditional domestic values.[30]

Even the emperor's crowning glory on the Palatine, the temple of Apollo, was recommended to lovers, for it too had a colonnade with spectacular works of art, among them statues of the Danaids (1.73–4):

> [and go] where the Danaids dared to plot murder for their wretched cousins
> and their savage father stands with sword drawn.

For Propertius, who misses a date with his girlfriend to visit the temple of Apollo when it is first opened to the public, this is not a place for dalliance but for admiring stunning architecture and works of art (3.31). As Alison Keith points out, art, acquired by imperial conquest, played a major role in the promulgation of the Augustan peace; Propertius' poem augments the value both of imperial rule and of the art on display in the temple of Palatine Apollo.[31] By contrast, Ovid refers not to the beauty of the building or its works of art but to the scandalous myth associated with the statues of the Danaids. In his *Heroides* he tells, through the voice of Hypermnestra, how at the instigation of their father Danaus, his daughters killed their husband–cousins on their wedding night (*Ep.* 14).[32] The Danaids were punished by being condemned to carry water in leaky jars in Tartarus, an endlessly futile task.

As in the *Heroides*, the poet of the *Ars* invites a moral response to the statues, shifting the focus from the daughters to the father, whom he condemns as 'savage' (74). In *Tr.* 3.1 the poet alludes to this description of the Danaid statues, again condemning the father rather than the daughters (61–2):

> In between the columns of foreign marble are statues, the descendants
> of Belus [the Danaids] and their barbarous father with sword drawn.

The poet's focus on the father among the Palatine statues might perhaps recall the living Roman father on the Palatine who had banished his daughter Julia and, as 'father of the nation', had instituted draconian moral legislation. In the temple of Palatine Apollo, which was adjacent to the house of Augustus, the representation of the 'savage' or 'barbarous' father jars with Augustan/Apolline ideals of moderation, clemency and enlightened rule.[33]

The theatre too is a prime site for seduction, not only as an attractive public space but because of its origins. Provocatively, the poet locates the rape of the Sabine women – a desperate measure to boost the population of the new Roman settlement – in an early theatre on what had become in his day the Augustan Palatine (1.105–6). The story is told with a mixture of embarrassment and rationalization by Roman historians.[34] In the *Ars*, Ovid plays on Augustan reverence for Rome's early past to claim that sexual desire has been implicated in Roman expansion from its beginnings. Furthermore, lust was endorsed by Rome's first leader, Romulus (*Ars* 1.101–34), who set a 'solemn' precedent for seduction at the theatre to the present day (1.131–4). The poet suggests that the predatory didactic agenda of the *Ars* has ancient backing.

But myth in the *Ars* also often varies and expands the poem's emotional and didactic register. Countering the poet's irreverent pragmatism is the portrayal of the distress of the abducted women (1.115–24). This passage particularly emphasizes their fear, a word that is used four times in a short space (117, 119, 121 twice). The opening simile, moreover, represents the Roman predators in unflattering light (117–20):

> As doves, a most fearful group, fear eagles,
> > as the newborn lamb flees the wolves it has spotted,
> so they feared the men rushing lawlessly;
> > their faces were robbed of colour.

The men 'rushing lawlessly' are hardly good examples for a poem that teaches 'art' in love. Seen from the women's perspective, early Rome is not a hallowed time of simple dignity but of lawless violence, and the poet's concluding endorsement of Romulus' crude method for population expansion comes across as tongue-in-cheek. Moreover, eagles and wolves are the eminent symbols of Rome. Eagles crown Rome's military standards; indeed these very standards were on show in Augustus' signature forum, the Forum Augustum, dedicated in 2 BCE, the year of the publication of the *Ars*.[35] The wolf too, as the saviour of the divine twins, Romulus and Remus, is a major protective symbol of the Roman state. Yet these august emblems of Roman might and national identity are here metaphorically levelled against helpless women. The poetic narrative temporarily invites both sympathy for the young victims and criticism of the predators, the Roman 'eagles' who abuse their superior physical power to grab the defenceless women in a disreputable coup. The politics of love are here troublingly conflated with the politics of imperialism.

The *Ars Amatoria* thus offers not only guidelines in seduction. It provocatively applies the politics of imperialism to the sphere of love. Moreover, it is interleaved with mythological examples and narratives that not only illustrate the poet's teachings but also, ironically, hint at their limitations.[36] Myth enlarges the poem's emotional range and invites more complex, yet still politicized, perspectives on the nature of love.[37] For example, married love, which is not the didactic goal of the *Ars*, along with adultery, which was heavily penalized by Augustan legislation, emerge as the themes of the final mythological narrative in the poem (and also its longest), the story of Procris and Cephalus (3.685–746). In brief, Procris and Cephalus are a loving married couple, but suspicion of her husband's adultery leads to Procris' accidental death at his unknowing hand. Hiding in the woods to spy on Cephalus while he rests from the hunt, Procris discovers her fears are groundless and rushes into her husband's arms, only to be killed when he momentarily mistakes her for a wild beast; she dies in his embrace. (The myth is told in full at *Met.* 7.690–862.)

The poet's ostensible reason for introducing this myth is to illustrate the dangers of female jealousy. But his warning at the narrative's start that a woman should 'let infidelity stir her up moderately' (683) is a typical Ovidian paradox that hints at the real difficulty of limiting emotions once they are aroused; the rules for the poet–teacher's brand of 'love without pain' fail before deep human emotions and commitment. Moreover, as Victoria Rimell argues, this narrative thematizes mistrust between couples at the end of the *Ars*, an ironic by-product of the didactic pragmatism of the poem; 'readers [of the *Ars*] are never safe' under the Ovidian teacher's instruction.[38] But although the tragedy of Procris and Cephalus, wife and husband, shows the dangers and potentially tragic consequences of adultery – and thus undermines the dictate of Books 1 and 2 that deception is an integral pleasure of the game of love – it also suggests that love is too complex and powerful an emotion to be prescribed by textbook rules. This is surely a lesson for Augustus no less than for the teacher of love. Both Procris and Cephalus act rashly, she out of desire for her husband, he out of desire for the hunt, an erotic metaphor. As Robert Edwards puts it, 'desire remains beyond the technology of control.'[39]

The *Ars Amatoria* runs counter to the spirit of Augustan legislation in its set of amatory rules and in its insistence on the centrality of love and sexuality to human existence.[40] The poem's Rome, moreover, is not a city of imperial majesty but of imperial pleasures. But the poem's subtle admission that love and passion, despite the emperor's and the poet's rules, cannot be effectively codified, is perhaps its most serious provocation to Augustus' restrictive new legislation.

The triumph of art

Irreverent play with Augustan institutions is a feature of Ovid's erotic poetry that begins with the *Amores*. Latin erotic elegy was based on a generic opposition between love/elegy and war/epic; service to a woman replaced the service to the state expected of Roman males. Ovid challenges these strict polarities. Love is conceived of as a similar practice to war. As the poet states explicitly in *Am.* 1.9, 'every lover is a soldier' (1). The lover does not lie around sighing on a couch but engages, like a soldier in Caesar's army, in active service, such as bivouacking outside at night (hoping that his girl will admit him to her house), enduring harsh conditions to ward off the enemy (a rival lover), and keeping fit for nocturnal struggles in the bedroom. The lover and love poet, in short, is equal in mental and physical toughness to a Roman soldier and has the desired qualities of the elite male: discipline, perseverance, physical strength. War, the driving force of Roman imperial power, becomes in Ovid's poetry not only a metaphor for epic but also a metaphor for erotic elegy, as Ovid moves the genre away from its binary oppositions.[41]

The recurrent theme of the Roman triumph in Ovid's poetry is a development of the military metaphor that suggests the link between the lover's pleasures and the spoils of imperial conquest. The military triumph put Roman power and world conquest on display with a great procession through the centre of Rome to the temple of Capitoline Jupiter. The victorious general rode in a chariot drawn by four white horses and was followed by a procession of captives and floats decorated with representations of captured sites and towns. In the Republic such a stunning spectacle gave the triumphant general the chance to court popularity with the people and possibly to canvass political favour. Thus, in Ovid's day the triumph had become a particularly Augustan institution, restricted to the emperor and members of the imperial family. The theme attracted the elegiac poets, who used the spectacle of the triumph as a focal point for the opposition between private and public life.[42] As Mary Beard comments, Ovid in particular is a major source for our scant knowledge about the Roman triumph.[43] But, unlike his elegiac predecessors, in his first poem on the theme, Ovid uses the triumph to make love itself a public spectacle.

In *Am.* 1.2 Ovid literalizes a cliché, Cupid's triumph over his heart, by imagining himself as a captive led through the centre of Rome in the god's triumphal procession.[44] He here combines the elegiac trope of 'the slavery of love' with the military trope of love as a form of war. Typically, the 'slavery' of the male lover to the woman he desires is a striking gendered inversion.[45] But in *Am.* 1.2 Ovid imagines himself as a slave to a great god, not to a woman. Moreover, his enslavement does not occur in a domestic context but is on display in the greatest public spectacle in Rome, the triumph.

Am. 1.2 plays on the paradox that Cupid is enormously powerful but also regularly portrayed in ancient literature and art as a beautiful winged cherub. Ovid adds domestic, miniaturizing details to the scene of the triumph to keep in play the tension between Cupid's omnipotence and his playful demeanour and appearance. He thus demonstrates the tension between his grand military theme and unepic genre, and also the tension within elegy itself, 'a light genre', yet devoted to the overwhelming power of love.

There are no clashing weapons in this triumph, no proud horses; Cupid goes on display in a style that is true to the sophistication of the *Amores*. For instance, he decks himself out for the triumph by binding his hair with his mother's emblematic plant, the myrtle, not the laurel worn by Roman generals; his mother will lend doves (white birds, rather than white horses) to pull his chariot; his stepfather (whether this is Vulcan, Venus' husband and maker of weaponry, or her lover Mars, the war god, is left ambiguous) will provide the chariot itself; the people will shout in acclamation as Cupid drives the birds past (23–6). This is an amusing fantasy, a comic inversion of an institution that put on show 'the most tangible expression you could wish of world power.'[46] Ovid puts on show here love's power, acted with Ovidian style and sophistication.

But the next couplet brings a shock of realism into this fantasy, for it could describe a typical triumphal scene through Rome (27): 'captive young men and captive girls will be led in the procession.' As Mary Beard points out, the captives marching in the triumphal procession seem generally to have been chosen for their good looks;[47] Ovid's lovers therefore are assimilated to the captives of an actual triumph. And the reader is invited to imagine Ovid marching along with the beautiful young people (29–30). This was surely a magnificent occasion for him to put himself on display, to be in the limelight, and perhaps attract a partner or two.

As captive in a triumph, Ovid makes a sharp departure from Propertius, who celebrates his success in elegiac poetry with the image of himself as triumphal victor over other writers (3.1.9–12). He and his Muse ride in the triumphal chariot along with 'small Cupids', while a crowd of writers follows behind (11–12). But although Ovid marches instead as a captive, he is proud of his 'slavery' and openly displays his recent 'wound' (29). Displaying battle wounds was a gesture of honour for the Roman soldier, but Ovid proudly displays his wound of love and his enslavement to passion. In *Am.* 1.2 Ovid proposes a radically different view of love. Love is no longer a private, domestic matter. Instead, as Augustus did with his moral legislation, the poet brings love into the public sphere. But Ovid makes love imperial in its omnipotence.

In a further shift in *Am.* 1.2 between fantasy and historical realism, Cupid's captives and companions include personifications who suggest a definition of elegiac love that flies in the face of Augustus' moral legislation. Captives are 'Right-mindedness', 'Modesty' and 'Any Other Obstacles to Love'; companions are 'Flattery', 'Delusion' and 'Madness' (31–6). As if these were not controversial enough, the poet possibly alludes here to the famous passage in Virgil's first book of the *Aeneid* where, as a sign of the Augustan peace, 'Madness' (*Furor*, as in *Am.* 1.2.35) is now imprisoned in chains (*Aen.* 1.294–6); but in Cupid's triumph Madness is on the loose again and given, moreover, pride of place – a sign of love's destructive power.

The poem's final couplet is a provocative reminder, as we saw at *Ars* 1.60, that Cupid and Augustus Caesar are kin (51–2):

> Look at the well-omened weapons of your relative Caesar;
> he protects the conquered with his conquering hand.[48]

Although the poet makes a compliment to Caesar's clemency (or perhaps a plea for his indulgence), he also makes irreverent play with Augustus' divine genealogy. The famous Prima Porta statue of Augustus shows the emperor in full military dress with a tiny Cupid at his side, a discreet acknowledgement that the emperor traced his ancestry back to Venus, Cupid's mother. Ovid's poem is not so discreet. Since Augustus had forbidden anyone apart from a member of the imperial family from celebrating a triumph, Cupid as 'kin' has the right to a triumph! *Am.* 1.2 thus broadens the concept of the Augustan peace, which was dependent on military conquest, to include the imperial conquest of Cupid. By marching in Cupid's triumph, the poet demonstrates elegy's collusion with other fruits of empire, peace and the leisure necessary for love's pursuit.

In contrast to the imaginary triumph of *Am.* 1.2, in Book 1 of the *Ars Amatoria* Ovid, now a teacher of love, not its slave, describes a triumph that has a basis in a historical occasion (though it never took place): in 1 BCE Augustus' grandson and heir, Gaius Caesar, set off for a campaign in the East against the Parthians and Armenians. Ovid writes a 'send-off' for Gaius and predicts the triumph that will follow (1.177–228).[49] Gaius' anticipated triumph is accommodated to the erotic agenda of the *Ars* where public entertainments, such as chariot races and a mock sea battle staged by Augustus, are recommended as ideal occasions for picking up girls (163–76). Gaius' imagined triumph (213–28) likewise offers the young lover the chance to get a date. Military success will enable erotic success.

Ovid's model for Gaius' triumph is Propertius 3.4, where the poet imagines watching a triumphal procession with his girlfriend in his lap (11–18), but Ovid adapts that situation to the early stages of seduction. Thus he advises the young man to try to impress 'some girl' (219) standing beside him in the crowd by explaining the figures on the triumphal floats as they pass by, such as kings, captured sites, mountains and rivers; if he cannot identify the figures, he should improvise. For instance, when figures of river gods pass by on a float, the young man should guess, 'this is the Euphrates, its brow circled by reed, the one with blue hair hanging down will be the Tigris' (223–4); when a crowd of captives passes by, the poet advises (225), 'make these the Armenians'. The aim of the triumph is to impress a girl, not to be impressed by the spectacle of global power. The triumph is again co-opted for seduction, and its erotic purpose is further emphasized by a reminder of Ovid's part in Cupid's triumph in *Am.* 1.2. Line 217, 'joyful young men along with young women will be looking (at the spectacle)', which is a metrically and verbally similar echo of *Am.* 1.2.27, 'captured young men and captured young women will be led along.' The allusion marks the poet's shift from being part of the spectacle to part of the watching crowd, and it also wittily suggests his erotic credentials; given his hard-won experience in love, he can now use the triumph to promote his elegiac, amatory teachings and his new mastery of love.

Gaius' imagined triumph in the *Ars Amatoria* is provocative too in that, as Augustus' grandson, he was set on showing how well he could stand in his grandfather's footsteps. But the fight with the Parthians and the triumph never took place. As Adrian Hollis suggests, the whole affair was perhaps a mere propaganda exercise.[50] Ovid insists on Gaius' youth (181–96), three times calling him 'a boy' (182, 189, 191), although he had celebrated his twentieth birthday. This emphasis on youth could be seen as positive, indicating Gaius' vitality on the occasion of his departure for the East. A retrospective reading, however, after Gaius' death and the absence of a triumph, can see a suggestion of inexperience, a lack of the 'technical skills' that the *Ars Amatoria* insists are as important for success in love as in war.[51] Ovid was a careful editor of his own poetry, but curiously he never removed this passage from the poem, even after Gaius' death in Armenia in 4 CE. Gaius complements the mythological exemplum of Icarus at the start of Book 2 of *Ars Amatoria* (21–96), a boy who fails spectacularly at flying because he has not yet mastered the art.

Ovid returns to the theme of triumph in the exile poetry (*Tr.* 4.2; *Pont.* 2.1, 2.5, 3.4). He claims, however, that it is difficult to write of the triumph while absent from Rome. The triumph represents in acute form the poet's difficulty in appeasing the imperial family from afar. As he writes at *Pont* 3.4.39–40:

> I don't know the names of the chieftains, I don't know the names
> of the places; my hands did not have the material.[52]

Yet this apology reprises the situation in *Ars Amatoria* 1, where the lover, who can attend the triumphal procession, is advised to improvise when he cannot identify the figures on the floats. And improvisation of the triumph is what Ovid does in exile. There is thus a positive side to distance from Rome. With these imagined triumphs Ovid puts the power of his mind and creativity on display.[53]

Moreover, the triumph, with its models of captured rivers and towns, has a fictive quality that is ironically emphasized in the exile poetry.[54] Although Karl Galinsky, for instance, argues that in exile Ovid used the triumph theme to apologize for his earlier irreverent treatments, Mary Beard has argued that Ovid's poems also convey the sense that the Augustan triumph is all a bit of a show, more pageantry than substance that puts the imperial family on flattering display before the crowd 'to bolster bogus heroics'.[55]

In the final allusion to the imperial triumph in Ovid's poetry, the close of *Pont.* 3.4, this fictive quality is emphasized. Ovid addresses Livia, to whom he has predicted a triumph over Germany for her son Tiberius (101–12):

> Bring out the purple to throw over the victorious shoulders;
>   the wreath can recognize the customary head.
> Let shields and helmets shine with jewels and gold;
>   let the lopped trophies stand above the chained men;
> let towns of ivory be surrounded by turreted walls;
>   and let the illusion be done in such a way as to seem real.
> Let the Rhine, filthy, its hair hanging down under a broken reed,
>   carry along its waters stained with blood.
> Now the captured kings demand barbarian adornment,
>   and garments richer than their fate warrants,
> and add all the other things which the unconquered bravery of your sons, as often
>   in the past, makes you often have to prepare.

Here in his own domain of theatrical spectacle, the poet acts as stage manager, giving directions for this imagined triumph (103–8). Prospective orders shift suddenly into present tense as problems of stage-management occur (109–10); the captives, like actors wanting to look good for their parts, are demanding richer costumes than their fate warrants! Ovid's passage represents the triumph as a form of public theatre. As such, it implicitly raises the question of its integrity as a representation of actual military victory.

This triumph, moreover, has a formulaic quality, for Livia is preparing yet again standard features of an imperial triumph (111–12). Thus, when the poet orders that the 'illusion should be done in a way that seems real' (106), he suggests that a successful triumph demands art.[56] Indeed, it offers a prime opportunity for creative fictions. No longer a slave but a stage manager of the imperial triumph, Ovid hints that at least in his poetry he can create a true spectacle and elevate the imperial triumph through his transformative art.

In *Pont.* 3.4 one unconventional detail stands out, the river Rhine, here represented as a river god but covered in filth, his hair in disarray, his reed broken and his waters stained with blood (107–8).[57] By contrast, in Gaius Caesar's imagined triumph the rivers Euphrates and Tigris are conventionally described with reeds round the brow and blue hair, symbols of pacified territory (*Ars* 1.223–4). In *Pont.* 3.4 the bloodied Rhine is the one figure in the triumphal procession that does not glorify war but suggests the human price for Romans and barbarians alike. Indeed, Livia's repetition of triumphal preparations raises the question not only of the triumph's success as an artistic spectacle but also of when war against Germany will come to a successful end. Virgil ended *Aeneid* 8 with Augustus' triple triumph and the river Euphrates flowing more softly to mark the new era of Augustan peace (8.714–28), a far cry from Ovid's wounded Rhine. But life on the frontier some 40 years later provides a different picture. In 9 CE, for instance, the Roman army had suffered a stunning defeat in Germany with the loss of three legions. As the poet says of Tomis at *Pont.* 2.5.17–18, 'you will hardly find in the whole world a place which enjoys so little the Augustan peace.'

The late triumph imagined in *Pont.* 3.4 shows that elegy's collusion with imperialism persists, but on different terms. Seen through a critical, decentralized vision, imperialism now prompts new tropes of marginalization, disaffection, isolation and anger. Yet the poet, who lived for his craft, retains a fierce confidence in his art. At the end of *Am.* 1.15, his closural poem for Book 1 of the *Amores*, Ovid declares: 'let kings and triumphs over kings yield to poetry' (33). From the *Amores* to his final exile poetry the author emphasizes that the true triumph is the success of his art, a divine gift that 'triumphs' over death and the Caesars, and even, in the end, the condition of exile.

Ovid and the making of a poet

Like Augustus, who memorialized his accomplishments in his *Res Gestae* ('Achievements'), Ovid in *Tr.* 4.10 left behind a testament of his career. *Tr.* 4.10 is not an autobiography but a poem about the making of a brilliant poet. Here Ovid describes how from his youth he was dedicated to poetry, turning away from law and a political career (17–20), and how he was privileged to learn from many Augustan poets of the earlier generation (41–54). The poem thus also constructs a history of Augustan literature in which elegy has pride of place. Ovid makes the proud claim that he completes the canon of Augustan elegiac poets, and emphasizes that he was fourth in temporal succession to Gallus, Propertius and Tibullus, but certainly not fourth (or last) in the rank of fame (51–4).

What little of his 'life' Ovid presents in this poem is carefully fashioned to demonstrate both his virtuous character and his poetic genius. Next to *Tristia* 2, Ovid's letter to Augustus from exile, this poem must count as Ovid's most spirited, most well-crafted defence of his poetic achievements, written with a clear view to posterity. Since, as Alessandro Barchiesi and Philip Hardie put it, 'the same person in Rome is judge, emperor and supreme critic of Roman literature',[58] Ovid looks beyond Augustus to his loyal readers of the present and also the future; 'posterity' is the addressee of *Tr.* 4.10 (1–2). The poem has epitaphic overtones and can be seen as a poetic parallel to Augustus' *Res Gestae*, both final testaments.

In *Tr.* 4.10 the poet's voice is a compendium of strategies of self-promotion and self-defence drawn largely from moments of beginning and ending in his own earlier poetry, a reminder of his greatness from early on. Unlike *Tristia* 2, which begins by blaming poetry for his downfall, in particular his *Ars Amatoria* (1–8), *Tr.* 4.10 avoids explicit mention of that poem. Instead, Ovid introduces himself proudly as the poet of the *Amores*, and the opening couplet is suffused with its echoes (*Tr.* 4.10.1–2):

> Posterity, if you wish to know who the person you are reading was,
>> I, that person, was the playful poet of tender Loves/loves.

The title of his first work is inscribed in this first couplet, 'Loves' (*Amores*). Indeed, this is the only title of any of his works that Ovid mentions in this poem, and he thus suggests a close identification with his first love poetry. In addition, he echoes here the start of Book 2 of the *Amores*, where he describes himself as follows: 'I, that Naso, am poet of my mischievousness' (*Am.* 2.1.2). But the shift from the present tense of the verb to the past ('am' to 'was') emphasizes Ovid's change in fortunes and elegiac identity; erotic elegy has returned to its origins in lament and commemoration. The opening couplet of *Tr.* 4.10 has an epitaphic ring.

A further set of echoes of closural moments in his elegies emphasizes the retrospective, commemorative tone of *Tr.* 4.10 and provides a means of transition from poet to posterity. The phrase 'player of tender loves' alludes to Book 3 of the *Amores*, where the poet defines his erotic elegies as his 'tender loves' (*Am.* 3.1.69) and, in the final poem of the *Amores*, bids farewell to love elegy and Venus, 'mother of tender loves' (*Am.* 3.15.1); it also alludes to the epitaph that he writes for himself in exile: 'I who lie here was the player of tender loves' (*Tr.* 3.3.73). These echoes emphasize continuity in Ovid's poetry despite harsh change; the last poetry is suffused with echoes of the glorious first, while adroitly avoiding the problematic *Ars*.

The words of this opening self-description, 'player of tender loves', also have generic resonance. As we have seen, 'loves' (Latin *amores*) refers to Ovidian love elegy in general and to the *Amores* in particular; 'tender' is a frequent generic modifier. 'Tender', moreover, implies a contrast with the 'hardness' of martial epic, while 'play' often describes lighter, or non-epic genres; thus at *Fasti* 2.6 Ovid writes that 'my early youth played in its [i.e. love's] metre'. Ovid's self-presentation in this opening couplet as the poet of the *Amores* emphasizes his long poetic investment in elegy. It also emphasizes his political harmlessness, for what can be threatening about a poet of 'tender loves' who spurned a public career in law and politics (*Tr.* 4.10.17–26)? Ovid shows no remorse here for his erotic elegies but rather pride. In the *Ars Amatoria* he offered an elegiac view of the Augustan city of Rome. Here in *Tr.* 4.10 he shapes the literary history of the Augustan age by drawing attention to the centrality of elegy. The opening couplet of

Tr. 4.10 therefore lays out the two interrelated objectives of his exile elegies: vindication of his poetry, and a final concentrated authorial bid for its survival. Allusions in *Tr.* 4.10 to beginnings and endings in Ovid's *Amores* suggest that the poet's physical end nonetheless meant a new beginning for his poetry in reception.

III

WOMEN AS AUTHORS: LETTER WRITING AND THE HEROIDES

Sweet, sweet was the small song
That I sang,
Till I felt the squeeze of his fist.

(CAROL ANN DUFFY, 'THETIS')

OVID'S AUTHORIAL IDENTITY IS FLUID. He may be the playboy of Latin love elegy, but only in the *Amores* and *Ars Amatoria*; in the *Heroides*, his poetic letters from mythological heroines that were probably written concurrently with the *Amores*, women step into the author's position as the poet explores the possibilities of the female voice.[1] The breezy self-confidence of the 'teacher of love' is replaced by anguish, lament and anger. The *Heroides* represent a fictitious feminine reaction against male-centred elegiac norms. As writers, moreover, these heroines provide a fresh perspective on the myths and texts in which conventionally they play a subsidiary role. They thus provide a brilliant vehicle for critical scrutiny of the literary canon and its dominant narratives.

Today, for personal communication, people prefer alternative forms of social media to the written letter. However, the popularity of the website Letters of Note and of the letters' page in daily newspapers, for instance, suggests that letters still have a place in our culture for political argument, emotional expression and secrecy.[2] In the *Ars Amatoria*, letter writing is recommended as a key strategy of seduction. A letter can be craftily written, revised if necessary before sending, and sent undercover to avoid detection by a guardian. Ovid gives first men (*Ars* 1.437–86) and then women (*Ars* 3.467–98) advice on how to write a letter that will advance a love affair. However, men receive more explicit instruction on the style of letter writing than do women, who receive only four lines (3.479, 482): 'girls, write clean, regular prose using ordinary words [...] ah, how often barbarous mistakes have harmed a good-looking girl.' As Joseph Farrell points out, men are advised to use the letter as a skilful rhetorical weapon of seduction that conceals their true intentions.[3] The brief advice given to women, however, implies low expectations of their skills in letter writing and self-interestedly steers them away from deceit.

In the *Heroides* however, women are given a powerful voice through their letters. They talk back to the men who have deceived them. And because these men are absent, they cannot interrupt. On the one hand, the letter signals separation for the woman from her beloved; on the other hand, it gives her authority to write without the physical constraint of a male presence. The *Heroides* thus play with the dynamic between presence and absence that Philip Hardie, for instance, has identified as at the heart of Ovidian poetics.[4]

Through their position of narrative authority, Ovid's letter-writing heroines disrupt the elegiac norm of the *Amores* and the *Ars Amatoria* where the male lover controls the discourse. Indeed, in the Middle Ages the *Heroides* were recognized as foundational texts for exploring the possibilities of the female voice. As the medievalist Peter Dronke argues, 'Ovid's heroines [...] loom like exemplars' for subsequent literary traditions.[5] The critical dismissal of the *Heroides* for most of the twentieth century, on the grounds of monotony and repetitiveness, has thus been an aberration from their earlier, enthusiastic reception. Today, however, the *Heroides* have enjoyed a critical renascence.[6]

As Duncan Kennedy argues, recent critical interest in the epistolary form and in the distinctive aspects of letter writing 'as a discursive mode, as a model of communication and as a subject-position' has re-energized study of the *Heroides*, which are widely recognized as a foundational text in the epistolary tradition.[7]

The single *Heroides* consist of 15 poems. Questions of authenticity, in particular whether *Ep.* 15, Sappho's letter to Phaon, was written by Ovid, will not preoccupy us here, but rather the question of originality.[8] At *Ars* 3.345–6 Ovid recommends that women seeking to impress a lover should learn to read the *Heroides*, and he claims that they are his personal invention, 'he (i.e.) Ovid invented this work that is unknown to others' (346). Ovid is a notoriously slippery author, and this line has been much discussed, since the Latin word for 'invented' can also mean 'renewed'. How original were the *Heroides*? There were of course collections of letters in the Greek and Roman world, but they were written in prose.[9] Horace's *Epistles* provide a precedent for a collection of versified letters, but their philosophical content is quite different.

The one viable, possible precedent for the female-authored poetic letter in Latin poetry is Propertius 4.3, 'possible' because the uncertain dating of Propertius' poem and the *Heroides* means Propertius' priority is not certain.[10] Propertius 4.3 takes the form of a letter written by Arethusa to her husband, a Roman soldier away on campaign; from her elegiac perspective, war is a troubling obstacle to their married love. This poetic letter, however, is an isolated example in Propertius' work, and it does not involve mythological characters; the *Heroides*, on the other hand, engage closely through myth with prior literary texts. Thus we can probably safely say that Ovid was an innovator in his collection of verse epistles from mythological heroines. He created an important space for the female voice to talk back to tradition and provide a fresh perspective on well-known texts such as the *Odyssey*, *Iliad* and *Aeneid*. He also brought in silent, or virtually silent, women from the margins of texts, such as Briseis in *Ep.* 3, who barely speaks in the *Iliad* with the exception of *Il.* 19.282–300 (where she laments over Patroclus' body), and the Trojan nymph Oenone, Paris' first love (*Ep.* 5), whose story is not in Homer but first appears in Hellenistic literature. By providing commentary on events recorded in prior texts from their own unique perspective, the heroines' letters represent a creative engagement with both canonical and lesser-known literary works and figures. Through the women's letters Ovid challenges and rewrites literary tradition.

A common charge against the *Heroides* has been repetitiveness. But although the women of these letters have been abandoned by the men they love, the reasons are various; the women too vary in status from slave (e.g. Briseis of *Ep.* 3) to queen (e.g. Penelope of *Ep.* 1; Dido of *Ep.* 7); some are married (e.g. Hermione of *Ep.* 8; Laodamia of *Ep.* 13), some think they are married (e.g. Hypsipyle of *Ep.* 6 and Medea of *Ep.* 12, both Jason's women), and some are adulterous (e.g. Phaedra of Ep. 4) or incestuous (e.g. Canace of *Ep.* 11). Ovid thus greatly expands the range of elegiac voices from the certain, confident male voice of the *Amores* and the *Ars Amatoria.* As well as the writer's particular situation, her perception of her addressee and his hoped-for response shapes her discourse and her self-representation in the text;[11] so too does her awareness of her literary reputation and her recuperative involvement in literary canon formation.

The physical settings in which the women write are also varied and shape the female voice and its generic inflection. Penelope writes from her palace (*Ep.* 1), Oenone, a pastoral nymph who is Paris' first wife, from the rural slopes of Mount Ida above Troy (*Ep.* 5), and Hypermnestra from a prison within her palace (*Ep.* 14). Sometimes the women are far distant from their loved ones, like Laodamia in *Ep.* 13 whose husband Protesilaus has gone to Troy; sometimes they are physically near, like Dido, queen of Carthage in *Ep.* 7, whose addressee, Aeneas, is still in town. With the *Heroides* Ovid turns back to elegy's origins in lament, uniting grief with elegiac desire and thus enlarging the genre's perspective. Sappho defines this new composite genre at the start of her epistle (*Ep.* 15.7): 'my love is a cause for weeping; elegy is the poetry of tears.'

Ovid created women letter writers in a period when the writing woman was not a widespread phenomenon. For a woman to talk about her love and desire was also unusual, although, as Janet Altman points out of the later epistolary novel, 'the letter form seems tailored for the love plot, with its emphasis on separation and reunion.'[12] Critics however have objected that Ovid cannot lend authenticity to the female voice, for he is pulling the strings backstage.[13] But as Duncan Kennedy has argued, two voices are simultaneously inscribed in the text, that of the heroine and that of the author; through their interplay, the two 'authors' of the *Heroides* often generate the possibility for irony and invite a dynamic form of reading.[14]

Moreover, while Ovid plays with the fictional nature of his heroines' letter writing, the artificiality of the epistolary form need not preclude imaginative identification with female experience on the part of the author. A staple of the Roman school system was impersonation of different social roles and character types, including mythological heroines. The stability of the curriculum was such that a standard school exercise through the fourth century was that of Niobe lamenting her children, an episode from Book 6 of the *Metamorphoses* (157–312).[15] St Augustine (354–430 CE) writes in his *Confessions* that as a schoolboy he won a prize for his prose version of Juno's angry speech about the Trojans at the start of the *Aeneid* (*Confessions* 1.17); he also mentions his close emotional identification with Dido in a school exercise in which 'he wept for Dido because she died of love' (*Confessions* 1.13). Although the Roman school system was based on male acculturation and privilege, nonetheless, through the early practice of impersonation, value was conferred on the imaginative identification with female experience. As a young man Ovid became a skilled public declaimer of *suasoriae*, speeches in which a historical or mythological character debates how to handle a particular crisis;[16] his early pedagogical training would have been foundational for his exploration of female expression and emotion in the *Heroides*.

Formal renunciation of male narrative authority in the *Heroides* also allows for a greater plurality of voice and for diversity of gender. Efrossini Spentzou points out the importance of readers in the reception of the *Heroides*, for, just as there are two 'authors' of the *Heroides*, the legendary heroine and Ovid, so there are two readers, the intended addressee of the letter and the external reader; indeed, the poems often construct multiple addressees, for the intended recipient may not receive the letter or may reject it. Sometimes there are possible intermediary readers; Oenone, for instance, starts her letter by implying that Helen may be reading it over Paris' shoulder (5.1–4). Built into the collection is the possibility of diverse, even transgressive readings.[17]

Indeed, the *Heroides* repay the external reader multiple dividends, for the heroines, authors of single-standing letters, are 'decontextualized'; their letters are fragments of larger narratives that the external reader has to reconstruct from internal hints and personal knowledge of myth and literature. Moreover, letters are one half of a dialogue; as Janet Altman points out, their function is as 'a barrier and bridge', to emphasize absence from the beloved while attempting to eliminate it.[18] The external reader is thus dropping in on one part of an intimate conversation and has to work to understand the female author's unique version of her story, which diverges from traditional accounts. Although her perspective may also be shaped by a rhetorical need to persuade or injure her male addressee, 'resistant reading' by the elegiac woman, as Sharon James points out, destabilizes the conventional masculine script.[19] A modern successor to Ovid's *Heroides*, Ted Hughes' *Birthday Letters* (1998), addressed to his deceased wife Sylvia Plath, has been criticized precisely for what seems to be its male-centred desire to set the record straight about his marriage.[20] In this case, Hughes destabilizes the female literary prerogative of the elegiac letter.

The challenge to the reader to figure out the letter's context often begins with its opening. The first three letters have relatively straightforward beginnings in that they at least give the information of who is writing to whom. First in the collection is the letter by Penelope to Ulysses; it has pride of place since she is Antiquity's most celebrated loyal wife, and she and the intended recipient, Ulysses, are named in the opening line. The next two poems follow this model by naming the writer (although Briseis' addressee, Achilles, is assumed). The opening of *Ep.* 4, however, opens with a mythological teaser (1–2): 'the Cretan girl sends to the boy born of an Amazon wishes for well-being, which she will lack unless he reciprocates.' The writer is Phaedra and her addressee is her stepson Hippolytus; since she casts herself as a 'girl', she is not immediately identified with the mature married woman who is Theseus' wife. Other letters where the sender's name is delayed or obscured are *Ep.*

6, 7, 8 and 9. Dido's letter to Aeneas is not identified as such until almost the end, when she refers to her physical position as she writes (*Ep.* 7.183, 185), 'I wish you could see my face as I write [...] tears are gliding down my cheeks onto the drawn sword.' Until that point, her words read like another speech addressed to the Trojan hero, similar to those she hurled angrily at him in the *Aeneid* (4.305–30; 365–87). Some critics have speculated that each of the *Heroides* must have had titles that became lost in the course of transmission.[21] Enigmatic openings, however, immediately establish the need for critical, engaged readings, beginning with the decoding of the identity of the letter writer and the context. The delay in identifying Dido's words as a form of suicide note, not another speech haranguing Aeneas, gives the discovery dramatic impact. Aeneas is still nearby when Dido pens the fatal letter; but the psychological distance between them could not be greater.

The letters also invite their external readers to engage in further 'detective work' by working out the time and circumstances of composition and the motivation for the dramatic content. For instance, we learn towards the end of Ariadne's letter that Theseus is still under sail and not far off (10.151); Ariadne is therefore writing on the day that he abandoned her. In an important study of *Ep.* 1, Penelope's epistle to Ulysses, Duncan Kennedy showed that this first poem of the *Heroides* subtly reveals the precise time of its fictional composition, namely the day before Ulysses' slaughter of the suitors.[22] *Ep.* 1 is thus suffused with dramatic irony. In intending to hand over the letter to the beggar in the hopes that he will be able to deliver it to Ulysses, Penelope will be handing over the letter to Ulysses himself.

While Kennedy sees Ovid as following Homer's *Odyssey* to the letter, Penelope also speaks back to Homer's text where her character has a certain ambiguity: is she a loyal wife or not? Thus the first of the *Heroides* demonstrates the role that these poems play as a form of literary reception; in her attempt to control her reputation, Penelope displays her awareness of the dynamics of literary appropriation and selection. *Ep.* 1 allows her to set the record straight for her husband and subsequent readers. The final section of her letter emphasizes her chastity and loyalty (97–114). She writes that she has rebuffed proposals of marriage from all the suitors, despite urging from her father, for 'I am yours, I should be called yours' (83). The letter also seems to play on the ambiguity in Homer's poem over whether Penelope suspects that the beggar is her husband in disguise. At the end of the letter she outlines the limited manpower she has in the palace and explains that Telemachus is still young and in need of training from his father; she thus makes clear the need for Ulysses' quick return (97–114). Indeed, her letter begins by telling him not to write back but to come as quickly as he can instead (2). If she does suspect that the beggar is Ulysses, she has provided good evidence of her steadfast loyalty to her husband, while also imparting useful information on the precise state of the defences at home. Such disclosure strengthens the suspicion that she knows that Ulysses is nearby, for clever Penelope would not risk the letter falling into the wrong hands. Letters have a long tradition of secrecy and deception.[23] Heavily guarded by women servants, many of whom are disloyal, Penelope, through the covert means of a letter, gives her husband the necessary information to save his household and kingdom. In *Ep.* 1 Penelope controls her reputation by showing not only that she has been a chaste, faithful wife but also that she is a match for Ulysses in cunning.

Although all the women in the collection are in dire straits for a variety of reasons, the openings of their letters range widely in tone from the playful to the tragic. For instance, Briseis in *Ep.* 3 self-consciously writes to Achilles in Greek, apologizing for her mistakes (1–2), 'the letter which you are reading comes from stolen Briseis, and it is scarcely well written in Greek by my barbarian hand.' The joke of course lies in the fact that she is actually writing in Latin! Tears too have smudged her writing (3–4), a trope that Ovid will use effectively in exile to describe the stress on his own writings (*Tr.* 1.1.13–14). As Patricia Rosenmeyer points out, the modern reader, however, is confronted by the physical reality of a clean page that challenges the poetic illusion; we are reminded that we are reading fiction.[24] Yet Briseis' difficulties with writing highlight what can be seen now as a post-modern concern with the inadequacy of words as a form of communication.[25] Thus non-verbal signs can add to the rhetorical force of the letter as another form of persuasion, implying that 'in these blots you can see how much grief you have caused me'.[26] More grimly, Canace mentions that bloodstains are blotting her words and message, as she writes with a stylus in one hand, a sword in the other, shortly before committing suicide on her father's orders (*Ep.* 11.1–4).

Ovid also plays on the implausibility of letter writing in many instances. At the end of Hypermnestra's letter, we find out that she is shackled and her hands falter from the weight of chains (14.131–2), thus raising the question of how this woman, while imprisoned, could write a letter in the first place. More humorously, Ariadne's letter to Theseus (*Ep.* 10) is apparently written when he has abandoned her on a desert island without, presumably, postal service and she is clinging, furthermore, to a sea-lashed rock (136). The epistle begins by emphasizing that she is indeed writing him a letter (3): 'what you are reading, Theseus, I am sending from this shore.' Dealing with the weight of tradition derived from Catullus 64, his famous poem on the abandonment of Ariadne, the poet here gives a humorous turn to the landmark story in an extreme instance of an acknowledgement of the artificiality of letter writing in the *Heroides*. The various pressures on women as writers, such as dire physical circumstances and difficulties in writing, anticipate problems in communication across distance that Ovid will inscribe in his elegies from exile.

Women as critical readers: the case of Dido

The women of the *Heroides* play an important role as readers as well as writers of texts.[27] *Ep.* 7, Dido's suicide note to Aeneas, for instance, constitutes an early example of a critical reception of the *Aeneid*. Here Virgil's most famous episode, the love affair between Dido and Aeneas, is rewritten from a female point of view that responds directly to the controversial representation of Dido and Aeneas in *Aeneid* 4.[28] The letter seems to have been written after the last futile exchanges between Dido and Aeneas, when Aeneas has moved himself and his men to their ships in preparation for sailing.[29] Readers to this day have either condemned Dido as an obstacle to Aeneas' patriotic mission or have sympathized with her for her abandonment by Aeneas. *Ep.* 7 allows Dido the opportunity to set the record straight. She speaks as a lover, not as a political leader, and thus disrupts the imperial context of the *Aeneid*. Alternating between anger and special pleading, she does not ask for her lover's return, only for his delay (73–4; 169–80). From Dido's perspective, the Virgilian hero exploited her hospitality and betrayed her; she also accuses him of causing her death. Her letter is a form of elegiac commentary on *Aeneid* 1, 2 and 4 that offers a fresh critique of heroic values from outside the bounds of epic. Indeed, the persuasive rhetoric of *Ep.* 7 made it a key influence on a long tradition in the reception of Dido that was sympathetic to the queen. As Marilynn Desmond argues, so thoroughly does Ovid's Dido insinuate herself into the Virgilian text that often in medieval narratives the two Didos are conflated.[30]

Moreover, as Desmond argues, Ovid's Dido provides a model for the critical reader of texts, in particular here the politics of gender and empire in the *Aeneid*.[31] For instance, she questions the truth of Aeneas' version of events on fleeing Troy, the theme of *Aeneid* 2. Virgil's text indicates that Dido fell in love with Aeneas as much for the charm of his narrative as for his looks. Thus Dido cannot sleep after listening to Aeneas' adventures, because 'his face and words cling fixedly to her heart, and her obsession does not give soothing rest to her limbs' (*Aen.* 4.4–5). So powerful has been the effect of his narrative that the next evening she orders another banquet and another telling of Aeneas' story, 'and she hangs again on the lips of the narrator' (*Aen.* 4.77–9). In her Ovidian epistle, Dido now blames herself for being such a gullible listener. From outside Virgil's authoritative text Dido can question epic deeds and values and the hero's truth-telling.

For example, Ovid's Dido amplifies a moment of angry scepticism in *Aeneid* 4 when she finds Aeneas and his fleet have slipped away from Carthage in the night. Raging at her ex-lover, Virgil's Dido impugns the truthfulness of his heroic narrative of a divine mission (*Aen.* 4.598–9): 'people say that he is bringing his household gods with him, that he carried on his shoulders his father worn out with age.' In *Ep.* 7 Dido claims that she herself has not even seen these sacred relics (77–86). Thus the *Aeneid* itself anticipates here the alternative reading of Aeneas' narrative by Ovid's Dido.

Most scathingly, the Ovidian Dido targets a controversial part of the escape from Troy, Aeneas' loss of his wife Creusa (83–6):

> If anyone asks, where is Iulus' mother,
>> she died, abandoned by her hard-hearted husband.
> You told me this – it should have been warning enough for me.
>> Torture me, I deserve it; the punishment will be less than my fault.

In Book 2 of the *Aeneid* Aeneas loses his wife in admittedly murky circumstances. He carries his father on his shoulders and holds his son Iulus by hand; his wife, following behind, disappears in the chaos (*Aen.* 2.721–95). In his story to Dido and her court Aeneas presents the loss and death of Creusa as part of the divine plan. Ovid's Dido does not mention that Aeneas went back to look for Creusa and was confronted by her prophetic ghost, who urges him to set sail for Italy (*Aen.* 2.776–91). In her 'rereading' of Aeneas' words, Ovid's Dido sees Creusa only as a warning of her own abandonment by a heartless hero.

Dido's scepticism about Aeneas' tale of Troy draws attention to the fact that in Book 2 of the *Aeneid* the escape from Troy is focalized through Aeneas, who thus may be an untrustworthy narrator. His speech is conditioned by the circumstances in which he finds himself, specifically by the need to impress the foreign queen so that he and his men can have a secure refuge throughout the winter. Thus, while readers may not agree with the Ovidian Dido's blanket condemnation of Aeneas that (81–2) 'you lie about everything, and I am not the first your tongue has deceived, and I am not the first to be hurt', her accusations of Aeneas' narrative suggest the contingent nature of that narrative. Moreover, with the famous sack of Troy, Virgil was rewriting literary tradition. For instance, Aeneas' wife traditionally survived the chaos and accompanied her husband into exile.[32]

This letter is unusual in that it is not revealed until the end that Dido is writing a final letter, rather than simply uttering another speech of entreaty to Aeneas, as she did in *Aeneid* 4. Her stark words at the end, 'I write, and your Trojan sword sits in my lap' (184), thus come as a shock. She directly implicates Aeneas in her death in the self-written epitaph with which her letter ends (195–6):

> Aeneas provided the cause of death and the sword:
>> Dido fell by her own hand.

Dido's suicide with Aeneas' sword makes literal the erotic metaphor of the fatal wound with which *Aeneid* 4 begins, when she is described as a deer, wounded in its side by a careless shepherd's spear (*Aen.* 4.68–73). Her epitaph inculpates Aeneas directly in her suicide; it also seeks to interpret for future readers the events narrated in Virgil's text, namely that she has been betrayed by Aeneas. Even if Aeneas himself does not receive her letter, the inclusion of her epitaph suggests that Dido is rewriting Aeneas' pious reputation for posterity.

As Desmond points out, a long shadow of misogyny is cast over *Aeneid* 4 by Mercury's second speech to Aeneas (*Aen.* 4.560–70). Commanding the Trojan leader in a dream to leave Dido immediately and carry on with his patriotic mission, the god warns that 'woman is always an unstable and changeable thing' (*Aen.* 4.569–70). From the start of the *Aeneid*, much of the chaos and instability in society and the cosmos is attributed to the feminine; the poem's opening explains the causes of Juno's rage that drive her to persecute Aeneas (*Aen.* 1.1–33).[33] Ovid's Dido offers a different concept of the female, as a sceptical reader of language and meaning and a stable fulcrum for values such as peace, nurturance and family. For instance, Dido's wish in *Aeneid* 4.328–30 for a child, 'a little Aeneas', who would ease her feelings of abandonment, is realized in *Ep.* 7 where she writes that she is pregnant. She no longer sees the child as a consolation, however (133–8). Aeneas' abandonment of his innocent, unborn child doubles his guilt.[34] From the perspective of *Ep.* 7 it is not a woman but the male hero who is unstable and changeable, betraying wife and child for a possibly spurious, or at least uncertain mission.

In *Ep.* 7 Dido controls the moral narrative and shows Aeneas to be at fault. Writing not as a queen desiring dynastic support, but as a lover, she openly critiques the representation of epic deeds and patriarchal, Roman values in the *Aeneid*. Dido has no kin, no male defenders. Her letter shows the dangers of love for women. Of course this is a common theme of the *Heroides*, but the prominent status of the *Aeneid* in Roman culture casts a controversial light on the values on which this great epic poem's reputation rests. And to readers' doubts about the honour of Aeneas' conduct in *Aeneid* 4 she has a clear, if not definitive, answer.

Oenone on Helen, Paris and the Trojan War

In contrast to Dido, Oenone of *Ep.* 5 is one of the most obscure of heroines from the Trojan War. She comes from the margins of the literary canon to denigrate Paris and Helen and to expose the origins of the war as contemptible; from a woman's elegiac perspective, war means sorrow and betrayal, not glory. Oenone thus inverts the common metaphor of Ovid's erotic love elegy, the heroic *militia* of love. She does not appear in Homeric poetry but is first attested in Hellenistic literature. Parthenius (first century BCE), a major influence on the Roman elegiac poets, provides our most detailed extant prose summary of the story.[35] According to his account, Paris married the nymph Oenone while he lived as a shepherd on Mount Ida, swearing undying loyalty to her. Oenone, however, had the power of prophecy and would often foretell that he would bring war on his own people because of his infatuation with Helen. She also had the gift of healing, and knew that she alone would have the power to save him when he was injured. When later Paris was wounded in battle, he sent for Oenone, who at first delayed out of anger at Helen; when she finally reached Paris it was too late and she committed suicide in grief.

Ovid's Oenone writes her letter to Paris after he has returned to Troy with Helen; the dramatic date is just before the Trojan War begins. She is rather different from Parthenius' nymph. Oenone says nothing about her prophetic powers, and she has not anticipated Paris' return with Helen; Cassandra instead prophesies doom for Oenone's marriage (113–20). Moreover, Oenone refers to her healing arts only to complain how useless they are, for they cannot mend a broken heart (147–50). One of the most moving episodes in Oenone's letter is her traumatic memory of the moment when, unsuspecting of Paris' treachery, she sees from the clifftop his ship approach from its journey to Greece (61–76). In her excitement she wishes to skim over the waves (64), but delight at his return swiftly turns to fear when a flash of purple from the deck suggests that he is not alone. As the ship comes closer she realizes that Paris has betrayed their marriage by bringing another woman home: 'a disgraceful girlfriend clinging to your lap' (70).

In *Ep.* 5 elegy meets pastoral. Usually these two genres are opposed, for love elegy entails intense passion and suffering to which the pastoral world is immune. Thus Virgil's *Eclogue* 10, which celebrates the elegiac poet Gallus, ends with his expulsion from the pastoral world, for his enslavement to his mistress Lycoris means his life and poetry are not compatible with pastoral values. In *Ep.* 5 the conventional pastoral opposition between country and city is bound up with a moral choice about love, marriage and fidelity. Pastoral brings virtue and marriage to elegy. From the nymph's double perspective, Paris has rejected these values for adultery with Helen; war moreover is seen as a sorrowful, corrupting business. The pastoral setting is also implicated with ideas of feminine virtue. Oenone's country ways are associated with virtuous, married, faithful love that makes her, in her perspective, more than the equal of the adulterous Helen (5.77–88).

In *Ep.* 5 Oenone reminds Paris of their happy, loving marriage living on Mount Ida, herding sheep together, hunting together and sleeping together under the sheltering trees (13–30). In a detail full of pathos that symbolizes the end of this pastoral idyll, Oenone, on seeing Paris' ship come in, flees to mount Ida and drenches its rocks with tears (73–4). In happier days she lived with Paris among the mountain's woods, glades and streams (13–30); that landscape is now reduced to rocks, emblems of her harsh, pitiless, 'post-pastoral' plight.

Oenone assumes in her letter a complex position from which to judge Paris and the Trojan War. Her angry and sorrowful elegiac perspective on Paris and Helen's infidelity and its consequences is enlarged by a pastoral perspective that goes beyond personal injury to include ideals of peace for Troy and Greece as well as domestic happiness. By acknowledging his royal birth, Paris has entered the world of ambition, social rank and corruption. Had Paris stayed in the pastoral world there would have been no Trojan War. Oenone writes (89–90): 'remember, too, my love is safe; with my love no wars will come, no avenging ships will come over the sea.'

Oenone thus combines pastoral and elegiac strategies in the representation of loss and the denunciation of faithless princes. An interesting footnote to her letter is the paraphrase of *Ep.* 5 by the English author Aphra Behn (1640–89), writing during the Restoration of the monarchy after the failure of Cromwell's Commonwealth. Behn's epistle is particularly interesting because there is no need for Ovid's literary transvestism; here a female poet voices the sentiments of another woman. Yet rather than colluding with her female readers, Behn's Oenone seems to speak to a masculine world. Her Oenone extends the nymph's denunciation of Paris, his gender and his kingly class to a specific critique of the abuse of political power in her own day.[36] Ovid's Oenone invites such a reception, for the double perspective of her letter, both elegiac and pastoral, introduces moral and political ideas into the elegiac theme of personal abandonment. From that value-laden perspective, Paris' cause is shameful (98), for he did not consult his wise elders but short-sightedly preferred an adulterous woman to his country's welfare (93–8).

The power of the father

Not all the *Heroides* concern women's relationships with famous heroic lovers. Fathers also play a major role in the *Heroides*. In Roman society the father held absolute sway over the family; in 2 BCE Augustus was granted the title of 'father of the nation' and thus assumed the right of guardian over the state's family and moral life. But, seen from the women's perspective of the *Heroides*, fathers are weak, excessively cruel and devoid of moral authority. Although Canace in *Ep.* 11 is involved in an incestuous affair with her brother, her accusations are not against herself or her sibling but against her father. He does not know that Canace's newborn child is the result of an incestuous union, but all the same he orders the infant to be exposed on a hillside, there to be savaged by wild beasts. He also gives Canace a sword with the order to use it to commit suicide, for she has disgraced her family and noble position by giving birth out of wedlock. Canace's letter is addressed to her brother to explain that she must die and to request one final, grim act of love: that he gather the dismembered limbs of their son and place them in her tomb.

Like Dido, Canace writes with a sword in one hand, a stylus in the other; unlike Dido, she writes that any blots obscuring her message will be from blood already dripping onto the letter (*Ep.* 11.1–4). Her father Aeolus is the paradigmatic angry father, for he is god of the winds and by nature is unable to control his fearsome temper (11.7–16). Familial dysfunction, marked by a series of inversions, emanates from the father as well as from the incestuous siblings. Far from protecting his daughter, Canace's father orders her to commit suicide; he also cruelly rejects his newborn grandson rather than nurturing him. Canace is at the age for marriage, but wedding and funeral imagery become conflated when, in preparation for her death, she summons the torches of the Furies rather than the torches of Hymen, god of marriage (101–4).[37] The letter ends with a skewed statement of filial piety as Canace, about to kill herself, writes (128): 'I shall obey the commands of my father!' Patriarchal authority emerges here as disproportionately cruel; a daughter's piety to her father becomes, paradoxically, an act of self-destruction.

Even more confused is the relationship between Danaus and his daughter Hypermnestra in *Ep.* 14. As discussed in Chapter 2, Hypermnestra is the only one of the Danaid sisters who did not kill her husband on the wedding night, following her father's orders; the other 49 obeyed his command. She writes her letter to her husband Lynceus (who is also her cousin) from prison within her father's palace. She is in a situation of extreme duress, for she faces imminent death at the hands of her father. Even so, her letter is not a petition for release but a courageous, testamentary defence of her actions. Hypermnestra makes the case that as an elegiac heroine, constrained by genre and gender, she has no use for swords and thus could not obey her father's murderous orders (55–6; 65–6):

> I am a woman and a virgin, gentle by nature and in years;
>> my soft hands do not suit savage weapons [...]
> What have I to do with the sword? What have girls to do with weapons of war?
>> Weaving is more fitting for my fingers.

Hypermnestra embodies elegiac principles of softness and opposition to weapons and epic. But her father's order that his daughters kill their husbands because of a family feud with his twin brother creates a moral confusion that forces her beyond elegiac bounds. She dares to confront patriarchal authority by saving her husband, even though it means her death by the very sword her father gave her to kill her husband (11–14).

Hypermnestra's opposition to war arises not explicitly from love, as we might expect, but from piety, which is the surprising, central theme of *Ep.* 14.[38] Her letter thus takes a political turn with this particularly Roman virtue that meant a sacred sense of duty to the state and to the family. Virgil frequently refers to Aeneas as pious, although Ovid's Dido questions that. In *Ep.* 14 Hypermnestra repeatedly uses the word 'pious' of herself and her actions, despite her imprisonment by her father for 'impiety' in disobeying his orders. But from the start of her letter Hypermnestra redefines impiety as piety (4): 'the reason for my punishment is that I was pious.' For Hypermnestra, piety means not murdering someone who is doubly related to her as both husband and blood kin (7–8):

> It is better to be accused of crime than to have pleased my father thus;
> I am not ashamed to have hands free from blood.

Throughout her letter Hypermnestra privileges blood kinship by referring to Lynceus not as 'husband' but as 'brother' (meaning cousin). Roman culture highly valued fraternal loyalty: when Ovid in the *Fasti* summons family to a festival celebrating piety to ancestors, he first excludes from the invitation 'the impious brother' (*Fasti* 2.623–30). The first line of Hypermnestra's epistle establishes the importance of the 'fraternal' relationship with its inscription, 'Hypermnestra sends this to the one surviving from so many brothers.' The epitaph she has written for herself and that she asks Lynceus to engrave on her tomb again highlights piety, not married love, and the fraternal, not the spousal, relationship (129–30):

> Exiled Hypermnestra has herself paid the unjust price for her piety;
> she has suffered the death that she drove away from her brother.

Her double bonds with Lynceus trump the piety owed a father. She is willing to die in her husband's stead. Yet there is irony in her address to Lynceus, who, in a tradition she refers to, killed Hypermnestra's murderous sisters in revenge for his brothers (117). That he will receive her letter, written from prison, or that he will act upon it, are doubtful. Only at the end of her letter, by appealing to his piety, does she briefly request that he honour the inscription of her epitaph (123–30).

The central emphasis of Hypermnestra's letter is not her relationship with her husband, the ostensible addressee of her letter, but her relationship with her father. Danaus' cruelty is on display not only in his murderous orders but also in his subsequent, savage imprisonment of his brave daughter, her torture and his threat of execution (9–14). The inversion of proper family relations and rites is vividly illustrated by her allusion to her father's use of wedding torches as instruments of torture (9–10, 14):

> Although my father burn me with my wedding flame, which I did not violate,
> > and hold in my face the torches from the marriage ceremony [...]
> he will not make me say as I die 'I repent'.

The wedding imagery is a reminder of the happy married life that her father has inhumanly deprived her of. As we saw in the previous chapter, Hypermnestra was associated with Rome through the famous statue group of Danaus and his daughters in the portico of Augustus' temple of Palatine Apollo; moreover, her father's deadly feud with his twin brother evokes Rome's founding myth of Romulus and Remus, which cast a long shadow of moral pollution over Roman history. But most of all she is associated with Rome through her emphasis not on love, as we might expect, but on piety, a key concept of Roman society that Virgil applied to Aeneas and that Hypermnestra now applies to herself. Hypermnestra's letter implicitly challenges the patriarchal ideals on which Augustan power was based, for it shows that sometimes fathers are not avatars of moral rightness, and that sometimes they have to be resisted and disobeyed. She thus keeps her elegiac body intact and free from blood; it is the figure of the male, her father Danaus, who compromises elegiac, and also Roman, values. As Ellen O'Gorman points out, in *Ep.* 7 and 14, piety appears 'as the arena within which extreme violence and slaughter take place'.[39] Through the voice of a mythological woman, a key Roman virtue that was closely associated with patriarchal authority is subjected to harsh scrutiny.

In the *Metamorphoses*, which gives considerable space to the female voice, we also find women writing letters, but these letters are contextualized within a larger narrative and a set place and time in ways that the *Heroides* are not; the *Heroides* have greater autonomy as a reflection of a heroine's mind.[40] Letter writing occurs in the *Metamorphoses* with the myth of Byblis (9.450–665), where a letter actually receives a response.[41] Byblis, in love with her brother, like Canace in *Heroides* 11 (where, however, her love is returned), exhibits many of the traits of the elegiac letter writer of the *Heroides*: she struggles over what to say; she deletes and corrects with trembling hand (521–9); she moistens the wax seal of her letter with tears (566–7). The result is an ironic look at the efficacy of letter writing, for her brother does not even read the entire letter. He is so disgusted after reading only part that he casts the writing tablets furiously aside (9.574–5). Byblis attempts to follow the Ovidian teacher's advice to men in *Ars* 1.437–86, that letters can be an effective intermediary in the game of seduction. However, the fate of her letter suggests that, as well as the letter's content, her transgression into a male sphere of activity, the writing of a seductive letter, has militated against its success. Byblis ends up destitute and mute (655), her loss of speech a sign of both rhetorical failure and lack of authority as a female writer. The *Heroides*, however, grant authority to the female voice, not for its persuasive powers (for with the exception of Penelope, the letters fail to persuade), but for its fresh, interrogative examination of the literary tradition in which Ovid's mythological heroines are allowed to play an active, innovative part.

Weaving revenge: Philomela's 'letter' in the Metamorphoses

The most troubling exploration of female letter writing outside the *Heroides* occurs in the myth of Procne, Philomela and Tereus (*Met.* 6.424–674). Here, although the letter is granted the response that the writer wishes, it generates terrible violence; the letter invites a broader meditation on the ambiguous role of art in a dangerous, politically oppressive world.

According to Ovid, Philomela is foolishly allowed by her father, king of Athens, to sail with her brother-in-law Tereus to visit her sister in Thrace. When they land in his country among secluded woods he repeatedly rapes her and, to ensure her silence, brutally extracts her tongue. By the device of a secret 'letter' that takes the form of a woven tapestry, Philomela is rescued by Procne from her imprisonment in a woodland hut, and, in revenge, the two sisters kill Tereus' son and serve him up as a meal to the tyrant.[42] Escaping from Tereus' wrath, the two women are transformed into birds, the swallow and the nightingale. There is no end to the violence, however, for, although Philomela's voice is restored, Tereus becomes a hunting bird bent endlessly on the sisters' pursuit.

In this myth we have both a faithless spouse and a weak father who cannot protect his family so that, in the end, normative kinship relationships are shattered and the family destroyed. The myth is one of Ovid's most disturbing narratives in terms both of its graphic violence and of its dramatic shifts in moral authority among its violent agents.[43] Violence of course is characteristic of ancient epic, but Ovid's story involves domestic violence, not slaughter on the battlefield. Boundaries involving familial, sexual and culinary codes are violated, and hierarchical, kinship relations are overturned.

Authors and critics from Chaucer to contemporary feminist writers have been so troubled by the transformation of the women into murderers that they have omitted the myth's final, female act of revenge.[44] Andrew Feldherr has argued that 'the anguished redefinition of family roles' in the poem must have raised questions for Ovid's audience about what it meant to be Roman; the same was true, as we have seen, for several of the *Heroides*.[45] But in addition to its deeply problematic presentation of physical and psychological violence, a particularly striking feature of this myth is its exploration of the role of art as a double-edged weapon of resistance against physical and political repression. For at the heart of this myth, driving the plot, is Philomela's weaving and writing. Writing as a form of female communication is here effective, for it leads to Philomela's rescue.

But her letter also prompts a series of terrible events beyond the scope of the original communication.

Philomela weaves a letter to her sister because writing is the only power left to her in captivity. In his early tragedy, *Titus Andronicus*, Shakespeare ramped up the violence in Ovid's myth and deprived his heroine of even the power to write. His protagonists have read Ovid's *Metamorphoses*; when the heroine Lavinia is raped, her hands as well as her tongue are chopped off, so that she cannot speak or write. She communicates the facts of her violation by using a text of the *Metamorphoses* and pointing with a stick in her mouth to the story of Philomela; beyond that, Lavinia cannot act for herself, and the agents of her revenge are her male kin. In Ovid's myth the act of communication through Philomela's weaving of a letter is a pivotal episode in the narrative, an act of female agency that leads to her rescue but also galvanizes the sisters to take revenge on Tereus into their own hands.

Ovid draws here upon the long classical tradition of weaving as a metaphor for poetic composition.[46] In this myth, weaving is a form of cunning writing that transcends the extremity of Philomela's circumstances and allows her, despite her silencing, to escape the control of the tyrannical Tereus (6.576–8):

> Cunningly she hung threads upon a foreign loom
> and interwove purple marks with white threads,
> evidence of crime.

These 'marks' surely cannot be pictures of her rape, for that would give the game away to Philomela's custodians. Rather, I suggest, she weaves the story in her native language of Greek; the purple and white 'marks' are Greek letters which make an attractive design to the eyes of a Thracian barbarian, but represent a legible script to Greeks, in particular her Athenian sister, the intended recipient of this unconventional letter. Philomela thus writes with signs that only her sister, a reader who knows Greek, can understand.[47] From their Homeric origins, women letter writers were particularly associated with deceptive or dangerous writing.[48] Philomela's woven letter overcomes tyrannical oppression and the silencing of her voice through deceptive, visually attractive means.

Philomela's textile is represented as an unconventional form of letter. When Procne receives the tapestry, she unrolls it like a papyrus scroll and reads it like a letter (6.581–2):

> The wife of the savage tyrant unrolls the tapestry
> and reads the piteous poem of her misfortune.

The phrase 'piteous poem' is generally taken as an allusion to the nightingale's song at the end of Virgil's *Georgics* (4.514); it prefigures the women's transformation into birds and Philomela's return to song after their act of violent revenge.[49] The expression 'piteous poem' also links Philomela's letter with the poetic letters of the *Heroides*, which are defined in Sappho's epistle as 'poetry of tears' (*Ep.* 15.7). Read correctly by its destined primary reader, Philomela's sister Procne, this woven poetic letter provides material as well as emotional testimony of the violence done to Philomela; it thus triggers her escape. At the same time, the textile/text precipitates a terrible revenge against Tereus involving infanticide, matricide and cannibalism. The myth of Procne, Philomela and Tereus explores on the one hand traditional fears of the deceptive, violent nature of women and, on the other, the psychological impact of rape. The letter, with its power both to evoke sympathy for Philomela's plight and to instigate problematic retribution, invites broader reflection upon the ambiguous status of writing as a form of communication that, in an aesthetically pleasing form, can courageously challenge injustice but also provoke violence; that can persuade and seduce but also endanger the lives of both writer and recipient.

In their artfulness, the women's letters of the *Heroides* contradict the low expectations for their writing skills in *Ars* 3. Letter writing allows a woman to critique heroic values by showing the devastating personal impact of male treachery and deception; it also allows her to question or even defy her father's rights, when doing so face to face would be too dangerous. Letter writing is often undertaken *in extremis*; it is thus formulated as a new type of female heroism. In the decontextualized letters of the single *Heroides*, hope of a response is often not the point. Rather, these letters advertise their wider purposes of dynamic revision of social expectations and literary traditions. As figures of difference, women through letter writing can expose the inequality on which gender relations and patriarchal authority are based. Women's letters thus offer the poet the opportunity to challenge and recreate narrative traditions and to critique not only conventional male heroic values but social values central to Roman culture.

The *Heroides* anticipate the great dramatic monologues of the *Metamorphoses*, where women such as Medea, Scylla, Byblis and Myrrha explore the complexities of human experience in anguished debates over a conflict of loyalties. In both the *Metamorphoses* and *Heroides* Ovid pioneered the construction of 'a feminine subject with a substantially increased capacity for reflection and self-interrogation',[50] and also, I would add, with a capacity for interrogation of literary and cultural conventions. Despite its tragic outcome, the tale of Philomela is a particularly vivid example of what is true also for the *Heroides*, namely that letters, far more than oral speech, allow women's voices to be heard and remembered.

IV

WRITING FOR AN AGE OF IRON: THE METAMORPHOSES

You will not escape, yet you will be
separated from yourself while alive.

(MET. 10.566)

THE *METAMORPHOSES* BREAKS THE MOULD of Roman epic. It is not martial and nation-building in its focus. Rather, as a universal history, it investigates with epic sweep the origins of the known world from the beginning of time to Ovid's present – its plants, its animals, its rocks, even psychological conditions.[1] Although the gods play a major role, their justice is under intense scrutiny in the *Metamorphoses*; they come down to earth literally and metaphorically far more than in previous epics. The unifying theme of the poem, metamorphosis, generally implies downward change in physical form from human to animal or plant; in this magical, miraculous and unstable world, the gods are often the cruel or cruelly indifferent agents of transformation. Metamorphosis sometimes means escape from this world, but more often permanent punishment. Ovid's definition of metamorphosis, quoted at the head of this chapter, captures its paradoxical nature, for it suggests the horror of imprisonment or the glory of freedom – or possibly both. Despite the injustice and rapacity of the gods, Ovid's epic conveys a sense of wonder at the physical world, although from start to finish he emphasizes that the Golden Age, which Augustus claimed to have brought back, is firmly in the past (*Met.* 1.89–112; 15.96–110); the *Metamorphoses* is an epic of the age of Iron.[2]

The *Metamorphoses* draws upon a long tradition of transformation tales beginning with Homer and with Hesiod's *Catalogue of Women* and popularized in Hellenistic and Roman mythography in prose and verse, such as the source books written by Ovid's Augustan contemporaries, Conon and Hyginus.[3] The *Metamorphoses* is, however, far from a reference work. Rather, Ovid's epic explores the human predicament from shifting points of view and through an intermingling of comic, tragic, romantic and philosophic genres.[4] Central to the epic, moreover, is not war but love and the battles between the sexes and generations.

From the start of his literary career, Ovid played with the relationship between love and metamorphosis. In *Am.* 2.15 he imagined himself turned into a ring worn on his girl's finger, able therefore to enjoy physical intimacy with her and even capable of full sexual arousal! The *Metamorphoses* expands Ovid's earlier elegiac interests by exploring the physical and psychological changes wrought by many forms of love, including self-love, same-sex love, incest, and also the lust for power and revenge. With often urbane wit the *Metamorphoses* shows the ridiculous extremes to which lovers will go; it also does not flinch from articulating the tragic consequences of desire.

The *Metamorphoses* rewrites the epic code. It has no single hero, no unified plot; instead it has a multitude of internal narrators with diverse perspectives,[5] and an ambitious chronological scheme that attempts to impose order on the various narratives by linking them successively to one another. Stories vary in length and detail; sometimes they are enclosed within other stories; many are told by internal narrators and are sometimes grouped within storytelling sessions; the audience for a story can also affect its telling. Possibly the most ambitious example of the narrative style of the *Metamorphoses* is found in the episode of the rape of Persephone (*Met.* 5.332–661). The story is told to the goddess Minerva by an unnamed Muse; however, this Muse is repeating the song that her sister Muse, Calliope, sang in successful competition against their rivals, the Pierides. Also embedded in the reported story of Proserpina's rape is Arethusa's first-person narrative of attempted rape (5.572–641). Two first-person narratives, that of Calliope and that of Arethusa, are therefore repeated by an unnamed Muse to Minerva and are then narrated by the poet, the external narrator, to the reader in an ambitious form of narrative 'nesting'.

The *Metamorphoses*, moreover, has an ambitious temporal scheme. The *Iliad* took place during a few days of the last year of the siege of Troy; the *Aeneid* took place over a few years after the sack of Troy. Ovid's epic, however, spans the origins of the world to his own times and attempts to create a coherent, linear progression through time with myths of metamorphosis. In a four-line proem, impudently short for an ambitious, 15-book epic, the poet announces that he is 'spinning a continuous poem' (4). The phrase 'continuous poem' suggests linkage between individual stories; in a sense here it is a byword for a long, linear epic. But as Stephen Wheeler has argued, the reader of the *Metamorphoses* has to navigate two levels of continuity, 'that of the story-world and that of the discourse'.[6] The poem follows a general chronological pattern but with marked discontinuities. It divides into three temporal phases, corresponding to roughly five books each. First is the time when gods freely roamed the earth (Books 1–5); then a period focused on human beings (Books 6–10); and finally historical time (Books 11–15). However, this overarching time frame is not self-contained. Book 6 begins with a transitional myth, the confrontation between the mortal Arachne and the goddess Minerva; a marked line division between 6.420 and 421 announces a definitive change in the epic with the first myth focused entirely on human characters, Tereus, Philomela and Procne (6.424–674). The 'historical' time of the Trojan War and its heroes is not definitively marked until a further line division at 11.193 and 194 that brings the poem into historical time with the city of Troy and its heroes.[7] The significant time changes in the epic occur within books, not, where we might expect, at bookends, and stories sometimes run over into the following books, such as the story of Phaethon (1.747–2.400). The verb 'spinning' that describes the composition of 'the continuous poem' suggests the sophisticated narrative patterning within the linear chronology of this ambitious new epic.

Because the *Metamorphoses* is frequently read in segments in an anthology of selected stories, this patterning is often not appreciated. But as Erik Gray argues, at the narrative level the *Metamorphoses* exemplifies Peter Brook's Freudian account of the contradictory drives that govern our reading of narrative: the desire for an ending and the desire to delay an ending are kept in tension: 'Ovid's epic is composed of dozens of individual episodes; every few hundred lines, therefore, the narrative reaches a conclusion. Yet the sense of closure is never quite complete'; ambiguous transformations, including the merging of one episode into the starting-point of another, keep in play the dual impulse towards closure and continuity.[8] As Gray concludes, 'a large part of Ovid's achievement lies in his wondrous arrangement of discrete stories into one seamless, continuous discourse; his poem is continually concluding while also pressing tirelessly onward.'[9]

Individual stories are therefore ingeniously connected with one another, though often loosely by analogy and association rather than by strict temporal succession. Sometimes the connection between the tales seems particularly arbitrary, as when the story of Daphne and Apollo is connected to the following story of Io by reference to the absence of her father from a meeting of the river gods; they have gathered to support Daphne's father in the loss of his daughter, but Io's father cannot attend for he is searching for his own missing daughter (1.568–87). Often, however, the sequential relationships between stories are thematically pointed. For instance, Apollo's killing of the Python, which leads to the founding of the Pythian games (1.438–51), is not usually associated with the story of Daphne and Apollo (452–567), but Ovid connects them by commenting that Apollo cannot celebrate his victory with the traditional laurel wreath, for that plant did not yet exist (450–1) – not until Apollo fell in love with Daphne and she became a laurel tree.[10] By linking the two stories, the poet, in the first 'love story' of the epic, can demonstrate a major theme of his poem, the omnipotence of love; Apollo may kill a supernatural monster, but he cannot conquer love.

Another striking example of pointed narrative juxtaposition occurs with the story of Daedalus and Icarus, who attempted the first human flight; Ovid tells this story in both the *Ars Amatoria* and the *Metamorphoses* (*Ars* 2.21–96; *Met.* 8.183–235), both times with great sympathy for the father–son relationship. Pompeian wall paintings of this myth from the first century CE represent Icarus as an adolescent, whereas Ovid's Icarus in both his versions is a child who likes to play with the feathers and wax in his father's workshop and seems unaware of the magnitude of his father's invention of wings. Daedalus is an overly fond father, too trusting of his child's ability to follow instructions and keep a middle course in the sky. Daedalus fails to take account of the thrill of flying or of the youthful desire to test limits; as Robert Edwards comments, he does not reckon with 'the unforeseen arrival of desire'.[11] Icarus disobeys his father by flying too close to the sun; the heat melts the wax on his wings, and he plunges to his death. As told by Ovid, it is a story of great human pathos, of misguided fatherly love, and of a marvellous artistic invention foiled by both human fallibility and audacity. The *Metamorphoses* offers a new a new kind of epic hero, an artist who may fail but who courageously aims beyond human limits.

In the *Metamorphoses*, however, this story is followed by a tale that changes the reader's view of the inventor, that of Daedalus and Perdix (8.236–59). Perdix was Daedalus' nephew and ward; he was also a boy genius who invented the saw and the compass. Jealous of the boy's success, Daedalus pushed him over the walls of Athens; the goddess Minerva blocked his fall and turned Perdix into a partridge, a bird that dislikes heights and does not fly. The partridge now gloats at Icarus' death. The tale of Perdix provides the physical metamorphosis that the previous tale of flight lacks – although there is a quasi-metamorphosis as father and son soar in the sky like birds, or, more dangerously, like gods (8.211–20). It also enacts a metamorphosis on our reception of the Daedalus and Icarus myth. Chronologically, the Perdix myth should be placed before the story of the first flight. By placing it after, the poet alters our perspective on Daedalus; the loving father and brilliant inventor is shown here as the jealous murderer of his young nephew. The poet often leaves his stories open-ended and, by their pointed arrangement, invites dramatic change in the reader's moral and emotional response.

Although the *Metamorphoses* does not have a single hero like Odysseus or Aeneas guiding the plot, many traditional heroes appear in the poem; they do not, however, always act heroically and they often offer the opportunity for Ovidian play on ideas of conventional masculinity. In Book 8, for instance, the poem brings together many of the stars of the pre-Trojan heroic world to hunt a monstrous boar (267–546). Theseus heads an impressive group that includes Peleus, father of Achilles; Telamon, Peleus' brother and father of Ajax; Castor and Pollux, the divine twins; Jason, leader of the Argonauts; and the virgin huntress Atalanta (299–323). Although the boar is so huge that it should be hard to miss (281–97), the heroes bungle the hunt. The first shot sticks in the trunk of a tree (345–6); a younger, pre-Troy Nestor pole-vaults on a spear up a tree to escape the boar (365–8); Castor and Pollux, who always appear on horseback, cannot therefore pursue the boar through the thick of the woods (372–7); and Telamon trips on a tree root and falls flat on his face (378–9). The only female participant, Atalanta, is the first to wound the boar, shaming the male hunters (380–400). The hunt is a mock battle in which the poet playfully undermines ideas of epic masculinity. Moreover, the conventional notion of woman as a passive participant in epic is also challenged here; by coming temporarily out on top, Atlanta impinges on traditionally masculine spheres. But, as we saw with Philomela, a woman who assumes a male role usually ends badly; Atalanta loses her beloved Meleager as a result of a fight over the spoils of the hunt. The episode of the Trojan War in Book 12 is, like the hunt, distinguished by its battlefield stories that challenge epic masculine norms and privilege gender ambiguity.[12] But the longest narrative of 'heroic' fighting is Nestor's account, during a pause in Ovid's account of the Trojan War, of the fight between the Lapiths and Centaurs that took place not on the battlefield but at a wedding (*Met.* 12.168–535).[13]

Even the Roman hero Aeneas plays a minor role in the poem. His journey from Troy to Italy (*Met.* 13.623–14.582) offers a frame for stories about characters mostly incidental to Virgil's plot, with little focus on the pious Roman hero and his national quest. Ovid appropriates the *Aeneid* for his own poetic ends and vision of human history, countering Virgil's teleological, national goals.[14] An exception to the lack of central characters from the *Aeneid* is the Cyclops Polyphemus, an important figure in the *Odyssey* also and now in

Ovid's poem (13.740–899). But he is not the cannibalistic monster who terrified Odysseus and Aeneas; rather, this is the Cyclops temporarily metamorphosed. Traditionally solitary, self-sufficient and brutish, Ovid's Polyphemus has fallen in love with the sea nymph Galatea. This erotic story was popular in Hellenistic poetry, and Ovid draws particularly on Theocritus' *Idylls* 11 and 6. However, while the Hellenistic poet's Cyclops relies on his wealth in sheep and rural produce to lure his girl, Ovid's Cyclops seems to have taken a leaf out of the *Ars Amatoria* and attempts to spruce up his appearance. For instance, he tries to groom his hair but uses a rake instead of a comb, and he shaves with a sickle (765–6), details that remind us of his enormous size. Ovid plays on the comic disparity between the Cyclops' epic bulk and history and his new, lovesick heart. Epic here unites with elegy and pastoral as Polyphemus plays the shepherd lover and, using another amorous strategy, attempts to win over Galatea by a 'love song' (789–869). Mixing comedy and horror, flattery and threat, he praises her beauty, chastises her for spurning him, and offers her rustic gifts such as apples, a conventional token of love (812), and, as a climax, the far less conventional bear cubs (836–7) – which would be of no appeal to a sea nymph, and are destined to grow to epic proportions! He also recommends to her his physical 'assets', including his single eye, which he boasts is as large as a great shield (851–4) – an unfortunate comparison, for in *Aeneid* 3 the Cyclops' eye is compared to a shield at the moment when Ulysses and his men pierce it and blind him (*Aen.* 3.635–7).

The transformative power of love upon people and literary genres has been an Ovidian theme from the very start of his career. At *Am.* 1.1.7–12 Ovid reflects on the chaos Cupid can cause when gods – and poets – abandon their traditional roles and dress for the opposite (7–12) – 'just imagine Venus grabbing Minerva's armour,' the poet exclaims (7). With Polyphemus Ovid gives a comic spin to this theme while also accommodating it to an epic register – the Cyclops' gigantic size is emphasized, and the story of his passion for Galatea is incorporated into Ovid's version of Aeneas' journey to Italy. Moreover, we see in this story a recurrent pattern of the *Metamorphoses*: change occurring swiftly at the level of narrative. The mutual love of Galatea and Acis is interrupted by sudden death; the Cyclops reveals his true, monstrous nature by crushing Acis in a jealous rage with an enormous boulder torn from the mountainside (870–97). Comedy turns in a heartbeat to tragedy, and the artifice of the pastoral idyll is revealed with the return to epic mode. The concluding metamorphosis of Acis into a river god (885–97) provides another shift in register, an elegiac coda to a generically complex narrative.

The power of love

A significant feature of the *Metamorphoses* is its sustained exploration of love and sexual desire. Fatherly love as well as erotic love comes under scrutiny, as do tragic desires that deviate from the social heterosexual norm, for example, the self-love of Narcissus (*Met.* 3.339–510). Through the tropes of love elegy the narrative ironically articulates the youth's tragicomic obsession with his reflected image, among them the topos of the 'locked-out lover', humorously treated in *Am.* 1.6; here a thin barrier of water, not a locked door or a surly doorkeeper, keeps Narcissus from the object of his passion. In the tale of Pyramus and Thisbe, young lovers whose courtship is forbidden by their parents (4.55–166), the party wall between their houses acts alternately as a barrier and as a surrogate lover that each can kiss (65–80); like Narcissus' film of water, the wall drolly symbolizes the lovers' frustration at being separated from one another.[15] In the myth of Narcissus, the longing of lovers to be physically united is pushed to a paradoxical, tragic extreme.

The plot hangs on the assumption that mirrors were relatively rare commodities in the ancient world; thus Narcissus does not at first recognize himself in the pool. Enamoured of what he believes is a beautiful boy looking at him, Narcissus faces a unique rhetorical dilemma (456): 'should I be propositioned? Or should I proposition?' The water, the flimsiest of barriers, becomes a Lacanian mirror, an interface between self and other, reality and illusion.[16] In an important innovation in the myth, Narcissus does not however remain in ignorance but eventually realizes that the captivating boy in the water is in fact himself (463): 'I am that boy! I know it, and the image does not deceive me.'[17] The tale of Narcissus shifts between comic and tragic registers. Narcissus is from Thebes, the tragic city par excellence of the ancient world; like King Oedipus, whose famous story Ovid eschews for that of Narcissus, the boy finds that 'knowing oneself' is fatal.[18] But despite his recognition, he is unable to leave the pool, although he knows it will kill him; the narrative explores the paradox that he cannot walk away from the one he loves. Thus, for instance, Narcissus longs for impossible physical separation from himself so that he can pursue his self-love (467): 'oh, how I wish I could be split from this body!' Ultimately he has to reconcile himself to union through death, not in one urn, as was the fate of Pyramus and Thisbe (4.166), but in the same life spirit (3.473).

Ovid is unique in linking this tale with the story of the nymph Echo and her unrequited love for Narcissus (356–401).[19] When Echo helps Jupiter in his philandering with some sister nymphs, Juno suppresses her voice (359–69), a typical punishment for women in the *Metamorphoses*, as we have seen. Echo is cursed with being able to repeat only the last words of another, and thus she cannot communicate her love to Narcissus. The echo is the auditory equivalent of the mirror, reflecting back imperfect sound as the antique mirror reflected back an imperfect image. Like Narcissus, Echo suffers from unrequited love, and like him she wastes away from love. But her selfless, empathetic love contrasts with Narcissus' obsessive self-love. Echo stays with Narcissus until he dies, and her truncated voice finds a melancholy harmony with Narcissus in echoing his final words, 'alas' and 'farewell' (492–507). Echo's interwoven story highlights the damaging nature of narcissism to others as well as to Narcissus. In their similar fates Ovid literalizes the metaphor of 'dying for love'.

Another significant feature of this myth, especially characteristic of the early books of the *Metamorphoses*, is its beautiful clear, shaded pool; such *loci amoeni* (pleasant places) are inevitably in this epic the unexpected sites of shocking violence.[20] For example, Diana's pool where Actaeon surprises the goddess bathing, described shortly before the myth of Narcissus (3.155–62), is a lovely place, yet its water turns out to possess the deadly power of metamorphosis (189–98). Likewise, Narcissus' pool is both the instrument and the site of Narcissus' painful death (407–12). Its description hovers between the boundary of art and reality. It emphasizes the pool's uncanny, deceptive calm: no leaves, no branches, no cattle have sullied its waters; the pool is untouched, cool and unheated by the sun, like the virginal boy who has, until now, rejected all lovers and the heat of passion. This perfectly clear, still and lustrous pool symbolically mirrors Narcissus' self; it also acts as an actual mirror in which Narcissus, like the viewer of a work of art, looks in astonishment at a beautiful image. Indeed, comparisons of Narcissus in the narrative to a marble or ivory statue, and to the mingling of the colours red and white (418–25), as well as his fixation on the reflected image, probably influenced his more positive metamorphosis in the Renaissance into a cultural hero; in his *de Pictura* (1435), Leon Battista Alberti acclaimed Narcissus as the world's first painter and a figure of the subjectivity of the self-reflective artist.[21]

With the stories of Byblis and Myrrha (9.450–665; 10.298–502), the *Metamorphoses* also explores the taboo of incest.[22] A sister's love of her brother or a daughter's dutiful love of her father here exceeds the bounds of piety and becomes a crime. While Byblis' brother passionately rejects his unnatural sister, Myrrha's father is easily duped into having sex (in the dark of night) with his daughter (10.437–41). This story, one of a series of tales told by the legendary poet Orpheus, is flagged as particularly shocking and comes with an X-rated warning to parents and daughters either to skip this tale, or, if they are charmed by the poetry, to believe Myrrha's punishment was deserved (300–3).

But despite this moralizing introduction, Myrrha's unnatural obsession is sympathetically rendered. Unlike Narcissus, who is cursed by an unhappy lover and by the goddess Nemesis with an unnatural love (3.402–6), no external power seems to have inflicted Myrrha with this unholy passion; she has done nothing to deserve her fate (10.311–14). In a long dramatic soliloquy, a favourite device for women in the *Metamorphoses* facing a forbidden love, Myrrha debates and fights her terrible passion, drawing the reader into her mental and emotional world (315–55).[23] She eventually tries to escape what she condemns as 'a love that is a worse crime than hatred of a father' (315) by hanging herself, only for her nurse to intervene (368–88). In the end, metamorphosis into a tree brings her welcome escape from an incestuous passion and a father who, when the crime is exposed, tries to kill her (471–5). The tears that she endlessly weeps become myrrh. Orpheus, the narrator, who began the story by condemning Myrrha's crime (300–3), ends it by claiming that Myrrha will be honoured for ever through the perfume to which she gave her name (501–2). The 'moral' of the story, and the narrator's perspective, have changed. Metamorphosis here creates beauty from exceptional grief and exceptional crime; the child of Myrrha's union with her father is Adonis, whose ideal beauty makes him Venus' lover, though he is fated for a short life (503–739). The story of Myrrha ultimately invites a compassionate reading, for the story of Venus' doomed passion for Myrrha's son emphasizes that love is so powerful a force that it can come in any form and can strike even the goddess of love herself.

Orpheus seems the appropriate choice for the narrator of this story. He too is exceptional both in his poetic gifts and in his great love for his wife Eurydice who died on their wedding day; he too makes a fatal error because of love, for, after daring to descend to the Underworld and persuading its gods to return his Eurydice to him, he loses her a second time with a fatal backward glance just as he is about to emerge (10.1–85). Ovid's Orpheus also rejects all women after Eurydice, either because he has been deeply wounded by his loss, or because he had pledged fidelity to her; after three years he turns instead to the transient love of young men (78–85). Only a narrator who has known deep love, terrible loss and hell itself, perhaps, could do sympathetic justice to the complex, transgressive story of Myrrha's sufferings.

Incest also colours the story of Pygmalion, one of the most popular stories of the *Metamorphoses* (10.243–97). In earlier sources Pygmalion was a disreputable king who attempted sex with a beautiful statue. Ovid, through the voice of the legendary poet Orpheus, significantly changes the story by making Pygmalion an artist who sculpts a statue of his ideal woman and then falls in love with it; thanks to Venus' favour, his dream that his perfect work of art come to life is realized. This myth obviously reflects Orpheus' interest in perfection in the arts; moreover, the poet who has lost his wife chooses to tell a compelling story about an artist who creates and thus can keep his perfect woman.

The story of Pygmalion and his miraculous statue has often been read as a celebration of the perfect artist, yet George Bernard Shaw's play *Pygmalion* and its successful spin-off, the musical *My Fair Lady*, about a professor of linguistics who attempts to make a Cockney girl speak and act like a duchess, revealed the misogyny underlying the creation of a 'designer girl', a theme also brought out by the 2012 film *Ruby Sparks*, for instance.[24] But Ovid's tales should not be read in isolation. The following tale is that of the incestuous Myrrha, who is the great-granddaughter of Pygmalion and his perfect new wife. When we reread the Pygmalion myth, we see that Venus' gift is double-edged. For the sculptor who creates and brings to life the perfect woman acts in the role of father. When he marries her, he sows the seed of incest for future generations. Yet again, the artist who attempts to surpass human limits ultimately pays a penalty.

The story of Myrrha is an extreme example of the failure of the father–child relationship that is a significant theme in the *Metamorphoses* as well as in the *Heroides*. The question of the proper authority of a father over his children had topical relevance in a Rome guided by the strict moral rule of the 'father of the nation', Augustus, whose personal role as a father, however, was a public disaster. In Ovid's epic, fatherly love is often traduced by weakness and folly, as we saw with Daedalus and Myrrha's father, for instance. The theme emerges early in the poem when the cataclysmic event of the fire that threatens to engulf the world is tied to an exploration of failed fatherly love (*Met.* 1.750–2.400). Instead of a Platonic allegory of the failure of reason to control the chariot of the soul, Ovid provides psychological drama. Phaethon, who as a teenager discovers that his father is the Sun god, visits his father's shining palace at the edge of the world and, by playing on his absentee father's guilt, persuades the Sun foolishly to agree to grant the boy anything he wishes. Phaethon asks to drive his father's car, the horse-drawn chariot that the Sun drives daily across the sky. Having given the boy his promise, the Sun cannot refuse, and the result is a disaster. Phaethon cannot control the horses, the chariot bucks around the sky setting earth and heavens alight, and Jupiter finally hurls a thunderbolt at the boy that burns him to a crisp but saves the planet. Like Icarus, Phaethon is a young man who wants physically and metaphorically to fly but does not have the art. Moreover, the Sun, despite his cosmic power to light and warm the earth, not only loses his son but almost destroys the earth because of his misguided fatherly love. Like Augustus, perhaps, the Sun can guide the world, but not his own family.

There are very few instances of happy, married love in the *Metamorphoses*. Brooks Otis claimed that the tale of King Ceyx and his wife Alcyone provides a heroic, triumphant validation of conjugal love in the *Metamorphoses* (*Met.* 11.379–748).[25] And yet, in this long tale of epic complexity Ceyx, despite his loving wife's desperate pleas and misgivings, chooses to leave her for an ill-defined mission by sea where he drowns, thus placing her in the elegiac role of the abandoned woman. In *The Book of the Duchess* Chaucer perceptively tells this Ovidian story as a tragic tale, without Ovid's partially consoling metamorphosis of the couple into birds who enjoy seven days of peace together each day on the high seas ('the halcyon days').

The tale of Baucis and Philemon, an elderly devoted couple who host the gods in their humble cottage, is often anthologized as a myth showcasing piety to the gods and also contented married love (8.611–724). Their story has a particular connection with the virtues promoted by Augustus in his moral and religious reforms of Rome: marriage, simple living, obedience to the gods. When Jupiter and Mercury, who have come to earth disguised as mortals, find that Baucis and Philemon alone offer them hospitality, despite the poverty of their home and table, they reward the couple with the transformation of their humble cottage into a golden temple. And eventually the gods honour their request to die at the same time by turning them simultaneously into sacred trees growing side by side (707–24). However, one wonders who will worship at the beautiful golden temple, since the gods have destroyed by flood all the couple's inhospitable neighbours (696–7). The gods' reward of the couple's piety is decidedly self-interested; would a more comfortable cottage not have been in order?[26]

The story is also generically complex.[27] Placed in the centre of the *Metamorphoses*, it draws upon non-epic sources, in particular Callimachus' poetic versions of the hospitality theme in his *Aetia* and *Hecale*, in which a guest of much higher status is entertained at the humble table of a poor and virtuous host. Theseus is the hero of the *Hecale*, and he plays a role here in *Metamorphoses* 8 as an auditor at a storytelling session with fellow heroes in the cave of the river god Achelous. Theseus particularly enjoys the story of Baucis and Philemon since it replays his stay with a poor old woman in the *Hecale* (725–6).[28] Moreover, the emphasis of the narrator Lelex on the couple's mutual devotion and piety is conditioned by the tense circumstances in which he speaks, for the river Achelous is in spate, blocking the onward journey of Theseus and his men, one of whom unwisely questions the gods' power of metamorphosis (611–16); Lelex jumps quickly into the dangerous breech with his story of human beings' piety. He overemphasizes that the story of the couple's metamorphosis into sacred trees is true, for he himself has seen them being worshipped still (719–24).

The role of the internal narrator and his audience gives the story of Baucis and Philemon a certain contingency. Moreover, narrative juxtaposition further unsettles the concluding metamorphosis of the couple into trees. The story immediately following, told by Achelous to enforce human respect for the gods, concerns an oak tree sacred to Ceres that is ruthlessly cut down by the king Erysichthon (8.738–878). Metamorphosis often means stasis, fixation in a new form. But in the flux of the Ovidian universe, the fate of Ceres' special oak tells us that even the most sacred of trees is not immune to divine or human violence and destruction – and mutual, conjugal love is not for ever. Jonathan Swift's eighteenth-century 'Baucis and Philemon', a satiric imitation of Ovid's tale, ironically emphasizes the theme of mutability in the couple's ultimate fate:

> Old Goodman Dobson of the green
> Remembers he the trees has seen;
> He'll talk of them from noon till night,
> And goes with folks to show the sight;
> On Sundays, after evening prayer,
> He gathers all the parish there,
> Points out the place of either Yew:
> Here Baucis, there Philemon grew,
> Till once a parson of our town,
> To mend his barn, cut Baucis down;
> At which, 'tis hard to be believed
> How much the other tree was grieved,
> Grew scrubby, died a-top, was stunted:
> So the next parson stubbed and burnt it.

One of the most troubling features of the *Metamorphoses* for modern readers is its high number of rape narratives; love and sexual desire are often linked with violence.[29] Not all female characters in the *Metamorphoses* are the victims of male sexual desire; for example the sexually aggressive nymph Salmacis lusts after the youth Hermaphroditus (*Met.* 4.274–388), but she is an exception to the rule.[30] The first five books initiate a pattern of sexual violence with their numerous tales of nymphs raped by gods. As Erik Gray points out, scenes of running, involving the chase or a race, are a crucial feature of the *Metamorphoses* that derives from the chase scenes of earlier epic, for instance Achilles' famous pursuit of Hector round the walls of Troy (*Il.* 22.131–247). Moreover, the shifting or exchange of identities that we find in martial epic, for instance when Hector wears Achilles' armour in the chase, occurs not symbolically but in actuality in Ovid's poem.[31] Yet whereas the Homeric chase involves virtual peers, in the *Metamorphoses* the chase is emphatically unequal, with god against nymph. Nonetheless, this first triad of the poem is framed by stories of failed rape. The nymphs may not be as strong or powerful as the male gods who pursue them, but a life of hunting and dedication to virginity has made them fast. Though the nymphs evoke pity, they also have some of the patina of heroism derived from their epic male predecessors in the chase.

Book 5 ends with the story of Arethusa, a huntress and follower of Diana (*Met.* 5.577–641), who seeks respite at the noon hour in a river so translucent that every pebble can be counted. After the treacherously clear and calm pools of the Narcissus and Actaeon myths, the reader knows to expect sudden violence in such unnaturally beautiful water. True enough, when Arethusa strips off for a swim in the clear stream, she is salaciously exposed to the river god. A terrifying chase across the countryside ensues that recalls the first sexual hunt of the poem, Apollo's pursuit of Daphne (*Met.* 1.452–567). In particular, comparable animal similes emphasize the brutal power discrepancy between hunter and hunted (*Met.* 1.533–9, hound and hare; *Met.* 5.605–6, hawk and dove; 626–9, wolf and lamb, hound and hare); each narrative also provides the perspective of the girl, including her terrified feeling of the god's breath on her neck (*Met.* 1.541–2; *Met.* 5.616–17), emotions brilliantly conveyed by Bernini's sculpture of Apollo and Daphne.[32] Indeed, as Arethusa is the narrator of her own story, the narrative perspective is particularly hers, and we see the god only through her experience in the chase, for instance as a terrifyingly long shadow cast before her as she flees (*Met.* 5.614–15).

Arethusa is rescued by Diana, who first hides her in a mist and then sends her plunging underground. She is not trapped there, like Proserpina, but re-emerges in Sicily as a sacred fountain (5.621–41). The island that was the site of Proserpina's abduction by Pluto to Hell (5.346–424) also, by contrast, produces from underground a sacred, chaste fountain.[33] Arethusa is a survivor of rape who, in a poem where women often lose the power of speech when subjected to violence, lives on to tell her story.[34] By contrast the nymph Cyane, who observes the rape of Proserpina and tries to block Pluto's chariot, is violated and, in grief, loses her physical form and is rendered mute; her visual display of Proserpina's girdle on the surface of her waters is her only form of communication (5.411–37; 465–70).

Daphne too is a follower of Diana and is dedicated, moreover, to the hunt and virginity (*Met.* 1.474–87). But although she escapes rape by her metamorphosis into a laurel tree, she does not keep her voice. Arethusa's story concludes in the form of ring composition the pattern of divine rape in the first five books of the *Metamorphoses*; but instead of tragedy there is, for once, escape. Daphne's fate is left more ambiguous. At the myth's conclusion (1.557–67), Apollo announces that even if Daphne cannot be his wife, she will be his special tree; the poet's crown will be of laurel. Furthermore, her leaves will have special Roman significance, forming the crowns of generals who have earned the honour of a triumph. The failed lover thus saves face. Apollo, moreover, was Augustus' patron deity; two laurel trees flanked the door of Augustus' house on the Palatine. In addition to her association with poetry, Daphne becomes a political symbol of the Augustan regime. From the poem's start, political, sexual and autocratic power are correlated. And daringly, the poet inserts metamorphosis as a founding principle into Roman and Augustan institutions.

Arethusa, however, with the help of Diana, defies one of the most powerful Olympian deities, Venus, who was also, as founder of the Julian family, a major Augustan goddess, honoured as Venus Genetrix (Venus the

Founding Mother). In the *Metamorphoses*, Venus is an imperialist rather than patron of lovers. Pluto's rape of Ceres' daughter, Prosperina (5.346–571), is motivated by Venus' request to her son Cupid that he make Pluto, a determined bachelor, a lover; thus she will bring the third part of the cosmos, the Underworld, under her control and gain universal *imperium* (5.363–79). She also singles out Diana, Minerva and, potentially, Proserpina, as troubling renegades (5.375–7). As Patricia Johnson comments, Venus is a political and sexual empire builder, very much on a Roman model.[35] In the first tale of erotic seduction in the *Metamorphoses* Apollo, Diana's twin brother, proves no match for the power of the boy Cupid. But in keeping with Ovid's poetics of flux and resistance to closure, Diana's intervention at the end of *Metamorphoses* 5 leaves Venus' empire building incomplete.

In the first metamorphosis of the poem, that of King Lycaon into a wolf, there is continuity between his human looks and character and his animal form (1.235–9):

> He still now rejoices in blood.
> His clothes change to shaggy hair, his arms to legs:
> he becomes a wolf, yet keeps traces of his former shape;
> his grey hair is the same, the savagery in his face is the same,
> he has the same glinting eyes, the same look of bestiality.

Even when human, Lycaon looks and acts like a wolf. By contrast, the metamorphosis of the nymph Daphne, who can outrun Apollo, roots her to the spot. Her transformation into a tree is as much imprisonment as an escape, for the god can do as he wills with the tree. Plucking her leaves for a poet's or a general's crown is also a symbolic act of defloration. And as Charles Martindale notes, the nymph who resisted love now stands as a tree outside Augustus' door, like a locked-out lover, an elegiac trope.[36]

The poem, moreover, leaves ambiguous Daphne's degree of human consciousness. In a later myth Dryope, a nymph punished for an innocent transgression, is turned into a tree in slow, agonizing detail; metamorphosis takes the form of gradual suffocation and complete loss of human identity as the bark creeps upwards and robs Dryope of her child and her speech

(9.336–93). But Daphne metamorphosed can still perhaps react to the god's announcement of the honours she will have as his tree (1.566–7):

> The laurel, with its newly made branches, nodded,
> and seemed to toss its top like a head.

The word 'seemed' and the simile 'like a head' leaves in doubt, however, the meaning of the tree's movement – assent, dissent or the arbitrary tossing of the treetop in perhaps a gust of wind? With the ambiguity of the word 'seemed', the poet keeps us suspended among these possibilities.[37] Unlike Lycaon, who keeps his essential cruelty yet runs free, Daphne changes her identity when she becomes Apollo's tree. There remains just a hint of the former Daphne in the sheen of her leaves (552), the shrinking of her bark from Apollo's kisses (556), and the ambiguous tossing of the treetop that could mean acceptance of or resistance to her artistic and political appropriation by Apollo and his imperial ambitions as Augustus' patron deity.

The story of Daphne and Apollo is introduced as the 'first love' of Apollo (452); it is also the first love story of the poem, and it programmatically suggests that love and desire will play a major role in this new epic, reshaping the genre's rules that traditionally put war, history and Rome at its centre. As in *Am.* 1.1, Cupid is made responsible for the generic shift in the *Metamorphoses*, but his opponent is now the god of poetry himself, not our poet. Apollo taunts Cupid when he sees him with a bow and arrows, claiming that these are weapons only for grown-up gods (461–2): 'be content to stir up any loves with your torch and don't claim our honours.' The Latin word for 'loves' is *amores*, which evokes Ovid's first love poetry; repeating Cupid's advice to Ovid in *Am.* 1.1, Apollo now warns Cupid himself to stick to love and elegiac poetry. The Cupid of Ovid's epic, however, now has global reach; all creation is under his sway (464–5). Apollo is made to look foolish in his challenge to Cupid, and comically his arts of eloquence and of healing fail him in the pursuit of Daphne. The elegiac impulse is fully incorporated into imperial ambition. And the transformation of the god of poetry into a lover at the start of an epic poem suggests the generic malleability and inventiveness of the *Metamorphoses*. Change encompasses physical form, psychological states, narrative registers and also literary genres.

Often in these stories of rape in the *Metamorphoses* the poet explores the aftermath, not the act of rape itself. One of the most complex stories in this regard is that of Callisto, the victim not only of Jupiter's lust and Juno's jealousy but also of Diana's inflexible rules of virginity (2.401–530); Titian paired his painting of *Callisto and Diana* with his paintings of *Actaeon and Diana* and *The Death of Actaeon* to emphasize the common theme of cruel divinities and unjust punishment. As in Titian's source text, the *Metamorphoses*, the paintings disturb the viewer with their striking conjunction of sensuous beauty and scenes of cruelty.[38]

In the *Metamorphoses*, Jupiter shows himself a master of change who uses his powers to slip in and out of other physical forms as a strategy for seduction. He rapes Callisto by disguising himself as Diana; he catches the nymph unawares while she is resting at the noon hour (417–37). She tries to fight him off, 'but what girl could get the better of Jove?' (436–7). After the rape, the story is over for Jupiter but Callisto's story is just beginning. In the aftermath of the rape she is distraught and hates the grove and woods that she once loved (438–40). But a series of further punishments awaits her. She can expect no sympathy from her sister nymphs, who disclose her full-term pregnancy at Diana's pool, thus opposing fecundity with virginity. As a result the goddess peremptorily expels Callisto from her pure waters (453–65). Then, after Callisto's child Arcas is born, Juno in anger turns Callisto into a bear with a huge, ungainly, hairy body, the very opposite of a lovely nymph (466–95). Human speech is 'snatched' (483) from her, and she can only growl; she cannot effectively accuse or appeal. Like Actaeon (3.193–8), however, Callisto retains human consciousness (485), so that her suffering is acute, and, though she has animal form, she lives in fear of wild beasts (489–95). But unlike Actaeon, who is soon torn apart by his own hounds, Callisto survives for 15 years in the wild, abandoned by the gods.

The story comes to a resolution when Jupiter places Callisto and Arcas in the sky as the constellations Great Bear and Little Bear (496–530). He does so, however, not out of pity or a sense of guilt but to avoid an impious act; Arcas was out hunting and was about to shoot his 'mother' when

Jupiter intervenes to prevent the sacrilege. But Juno's vengeance still follows Callisto, and she forbids the new constellations ever to set in the sea.[39] She has the final word.

The *Metamorphoses* presents Jupiter in contradictory lights, as the omnipotent, thunderbolt-wielding ruler of the heavens, and as the philandering adulterer with a suspicious, vindictive wife. The poet comments on the disorienting contrast between the god who orders the cosmos and the god who sexually exploits humans with the pointed remark that 'majesty and love do not go well together' (2.846–7).[40] Yet common to these two aspects of Jupiter is his excessive, unleashed power. We see in this first triad of the poem that, whereas metamorphosis is often a punishment for mortals, for Jupiter it is a ruse that allows him to satisfy his lust by deceptive means. In the *Metamorphoses* the god's shape-shifting arts are a metaphor for the seemingly arbitrary nature of autocratic power.

Mary Lefkowitz has argued that Greek myths in which gods seduce mortal women should not be called 'rape' but rather 'seduction', for the experience enhances the status of the woman and her family.[41] In contrast, the stories of rape in the *Metamorphoses* emphasize the psychological and physical suffering of the victim. Callisto's 'ungrateful Jupiter' is deaf to her groans when she is metamorphosed (487–8); her 'family' of nymphs reject her; and although she was Diana's favourite (415–16), the goddess has no pity for a nymph who has transgressed, even if against her will. It is true that in the end Callisto becomes a constellation; very rarely does a rape result in an upward metamorphosis.[42] But thanks to Juno's continuing vengeance, she is still treated, as she was by Diana, as polluted and adulterous (471), and thus forbidden to dip into the sea's 'pure waters' (530). As is true for the majority of stories of rape in the *Metamorphoses*, Ovid's narrative emphasizes not the glory of divine seduction but the suffering.

The love of power

The myth of Callisto ends with a special kind of metamorphosis, what the ancients called 'catasterism', that is, a form of deification that involved transformation into a star or constellation. Thus Juno complains that 'the woman she forbade to be human has been made a goddess' (2.520). The idea of catasterism was topical in Ovid's Rome, since 'proof' of Julius Caesar's divinity was the appearance at his funeral games of a comet that shone for seven days and was popularly acclaimed as the metamorphosis of his deified soul; a star was thereafter added to Caesar's forehead on his statues. Augustus later interpreted the comet as predicting his own rise to power as well as his eventual deification.[43] Deification was crucial to the legitimation of the new regime. But the myth of Callisto shows from early in the poem how apotheosis could be politically manipulated.

In Ovid's epic, metamorphosis reaches its terminus in the monumental deification of its Roman heroes. First of all the apotheosis of Hercules (9.229–72), and then, in the final two books of the *Metamorphoses*, the deification of Aeneas (14.581–608) and the catasterisms of Romulus and his wife Hersilia (14.805–51) establish a precedent for the deification of Julius Caesar (15.843–51). Ovid omits any mention of the deliberations of the Senate who eventually decreed Julius Caesar's deification; rather, in Ovid's poem deification is presented as a gift of the empire-building Venus, founder of the Julian clan, who secures this boon from Jupiter (760–851).[44] Thus, according to Ovid's epic it was not merit, the conventional qualification for divinity, that made Julius Caesar a god; rather, 'he had to be made a god' so that Augustus could be deified on his death (15.760–1). Augustus thus appears as an agent of metamorphosis who hopes too to be its beneficiary.

Ovid's approach to deification perhaps reflects the debate that this essentially foreign, Hellenistic practice aroused.[45] His description of the process of catasterism alternates between serious reverence and comic zest and literalism.[46] Romulus' soul, released from his body, ricochets through the air like a lead bullet (14.825–6); Venus nurses the soul of Julius Caesar in her breast as they ascend heavenward but finds it too hot to handle and, lest she be burned, releases it to the sky as a comet (15.843–51). In the corresponding scene in the *Fasti*, it is the Roman goddess Vesta who takes Caesar's soul heavenward since Caesar, as 'pontifex maximus', was her special priest (*Fasti* 3.697–710). And yet the manner in which she 'snatched his body [from the scene of assassination] and left behind a nude statue of him' (701) humorously raises questions of propriety for the goddess of chastity.[47]

Augustus is compared explicitly to Jupiter at two points in the *Metamorphoses*, in its first book and its last. In Book 1, when Jupiter summons the other gods to a council, they travel along the Milky Way, which the poet boldly compares to the 'Sacred Way' that led from the Roman forum to the Palatine hill where Augustus had his house (*Met.* 1.166–76); indeed, Ovid explicitly refers to Jupiter's citadel as 'the Palatine of the sky' (176). Then, when the gods murmur in shock at the news that King Lycaon has attempted sacrilege against Jupiter, their reaction is compared to the horror of the Roman people when they learned of an attempt to extinguish the Caesarean line (199–205). The sudden move from myth to contemporary politics is striking. Here, moreover, for the only time in the poem until the final book, the poet directly addresses Augustus (204–5): 'your people's piety was no less pleasing to you, Augustus, than was the gods' piety to Jupiter.' The emperor is thus established from the start as a reader of the poem who perhaps, moreover, takes, or should take, particular interest in this section of the poem with its satirical representation of an autocratic ruler and his ineffective council.

The first emotion that Jupiter displays on entry to Ovid's *Metamorphoses* at the council of the gods is not the calm reason of an enlightened ruler but enormous anger (1.166): 'he gathers great wrath in his heart, worthy of Jove.' He informs the other gods that he has decided to destroy the entire human race for impiety, even though he can demonstrate only one heinous example, King Lycaon, who served Jupiter human flesh (1.221–31); Lycaon's people had, however, dutifully worshipped the god (1.218–21). Tantalus, who served up his own son at a banquet of the gods, was punished with an eternity of thirst and hunger in the Underworld, but Jupiter, for a similar crime, targets the whole human race for extinction. There is no debate at Jupiter's council. His gods are cowed and do not dare to oppose his decision to eliminate the human race (1.244–9), even though Lycaon has already been punished by metamorphosis into a wolf (1.232–9). The gods care only about who will provide them with their customary gifts of incense.

Jupiter's first appearance in the *Metamorphoses* is in the political role of tyrant, a figure of excess and brutal injustice. His suppression of open speech possibly had topical relevance in Ovid's Rome with its increasingly fearful and sycophantic Senate. The imperial poet Statius (*c.*45–96 CE) certainly thought so. In the council of the gods in his epic poem the *Thebaid*, a scene that plays off Ovid's council, Jupiter's sweeping pronouncement that the gods are not to interfere in his plans for war leaves the gods astounded and cowed; the poet then ironically alludes to present government under autocracy (*Theb.* 3.253–4): 'you would have thought that their nature was human, so curbed they all were in speech and thought.' Be that as it may, with Jupiter's introduction into Ovid's epic, brutally unequal power relations are established as fundamental to the way the divine universe works from the beginning of time.

The comparison between Jupiter and Augustus is thus troubling and hard to take as simply honorific. As Denis Feeney points out, comparisons of humans with the gods are always slippery and hard to limit.[48] At the end of the *Metamorphoses* the poet makes a final, bold comparison between Jupiter and Augustus (15.858–60):

> Jupiter rules the citadels of the heaven
> and the kingdom of the tripartite world, while the earth
> is under the rule of Augustus; each is father and ruler.

The immediate context is encomiastic, with Augustus granted global reach and equivalent power and status to Jupiter on earth. Yet this division of power can also be read as oppressive in the overall context of the *Metamorphoses*, with its often angry and lustful Jupiter, and its abusive and foolish fathers; Jupiter has not proved an enlightened model for governance.

There are very few deities in the *Metamorphoses* who act benevolently towards humans. Venus grants Pygmalion his wish for his statue to become alive, but the eventual outcome for his family is not a happy one. The one deity who stands apart from the petty vindictiveness and abusive power of the Olympian gods is the Egyptian goddess Isis. Formerly Io, she was forced to wander across the earth in the form of a cow after her rape by Jupiter

(*Met*. 1.583–747). In being restored to her human shape and becoming a goddess, she is a rare example of reverse and upward metamorphosis in the poem, and she is not persecuted thereafter, like Callisto, by Juno's eternal jealousy.

In the *Metamorphoses*, Isis intervenes in a tale of same-sex love between two girls, Iphis and Ianthe (9.666–797). The story takes place on Crete, an island widely associated with deviant sexuality, for instance with Queen Pasiphae, who conceived a mad passion for a bull and gave birth to the Minotaur (*Met*. 8.155–8). The protagonist, Iphis, is the child of humble parents who, at birth, survives her father's order that a girl child should be killed. There are generally two types of fathers in the *Metamorphoses*, the weak and the harsh, though both are foolish; Iphis' father is of the latter type. But his wife dares to disguise the baby as a boy, thanks to the appearance of Isis, who urges her to disobey her husband's cruel command (684–701). But when Iphis reaches puberty, she is engaged to marry the girl Ianthe, whom she loves desperately. Iphis now laments the deception, not so much because she fears her father, but because she regards same-sex love between two women as against the laws of nature. In a dramatic soliloquy where she wrestles with her forbidden emotions (726–63), she accepts, unlike Byblis or Myrrha, her mortal limits. Alluding, for instance, to Daedalus' invention of wings, she is sceptical that the famous inventor could change her sex through his arts (742–4). Despite her passion for Ianthe, she is not tempted to transgress social conventions and norms and appeals instead to the gods for help.

The story of Iphis and Ianthe depicts a highly conservative society in which the father's law rules supreme, although his command that the daughter be killed is marked as impious (711). And even though the mother dares to defy her husband, it is out of the question that same-sex love between women is socially viable, let alone acceptable to her high-handed husband. (By contrast, in the modern rendition of this myth by Ali Smith, *Girl Meets Boy*, the final message is 'that things can always change, because things will always change, and things will always be different, because things can always be different.'[49] In the ancient myth, the goddess Isis intervenes to change the sex of Iphis to that of male just before the wedding day (766–84). The metamorphosis is delicately marked first by Iphis' longer strides as he leaves the temple, accompanied by a shift in grammatical gender; then by the deepening of his once fair complexion, the shortening of his hair, and a more manly expression and demeanour (786–90). However, although in the end the wedding goes off smoothly and patriarchal order is restored (766–97), Iphis records in writing on the temple the miracle of his sex change with an inscription: 'a boy pays the gifts which as a girl Iphis had vowed.' He thus publicly validates his experience as female and, in a sacred context, challenges his father's misguided, impious authority over his gender.

Perhaps because of Isis' experience as a victim of Jupiter, when she suffered for a long time in an alien body, the goddess acts with compassion and without self-interest to help Iphis, who feels trapped in the wrong body. In another version of this story by the Hellenistic poet Nicander, the helping deity is Leto, a major Olympian deity who is the mother of Apollo and Diana.[50] In the *Metamorphoses*, however, the deity who performs the transformation is the non-Olympian Isis, who is untarnished by the lust for power and disregard for human needs and emotions that characterize Ovid's Olympian gods.

The Romans regarded their deified rulers as special guardians of the people of Rome. Ovid's poem shows the Olympian gods for the most part as selfish autocrats in love with power; his narratives of apotheosis implicitly raise doubt about whether deified rulers will act differently. Predicting Augustus' deification, Ovid prays at the end of the *Metamorphoses* (870), 'may he [Augustus] favour our prayers, though absent.' The Caesars too are subject to metamorphosis, but 'absent' is a strange last word to use of the deified Augustus. Indeed the emperor does not claim the last words of the poem, for he disappears from the text. That final honour goes to the poet, whose epilogue (871–9) defiantly declares that he has completed a work that 'the wrath of Jupiter will never be able to destroy' (871–2).

The art of change

When, towards the end of Book 6, Philomela weaves her tapestry/letter, she creates an aesthetically pleasing object that belies its terrible message

95

and prompts both her escape from captivity and a terrible revenge (*Met.* 6.571–86).[51] Her woven writing combines aesthetics with politics, and white and purple threads that give pleasure to the eye also incite violent action. The *Metamorphoses* explores the double-edged nature of art, its civilizing and also its destructive propensities. It also examines the precarious role of the artist in confrontation with higher, and often unjust, authority.[52] Tapestry-weaving is the focus of the first story of Book 6 (1–145), the contest between Minerva and Arachne where a girl of poor background but who is a brilliant weaver challenges the goddess of arts and crafts; the art of weaving thus frames Book 6.

In this contest Minerva weaves a tapestry that represents the Olympian gods as she wishes them to be seen: grave, dignified arbiters of justice, in contradiction to their general role so far in the *Metamorphoses* (70–102). The central scene is her victory over Neptune in the competition for the patronage of Athens; the other Olympian gods, with Jupiter in the centre, face the two protagonists in their role as judges. The style is a kind of high classicism, ordered, uncluttered and symmetrical; the four corners of her tapestry depict arrogant humans punished by the gods with metamorphosis for their hubris. Minerva constructs her tapestry as a warning to humans, Arachne above all, of the dangers of challenging the gods.

Arachne's tapestry, by contrast, depicts the gods as we often see them in the *Metamorphoses*, as seducers who resort to metamorphosis to con their victims (103–28). The first, most prominent example is Jupiter's rape of Europa when disguised as a bull (103–7), a story that concludes Book 2 of the *Metamorphoses* (836–75). Thereafter the stories come thick and fast, with Jupiter disguised as an eagle, a swan, a satyr, a shower of gold, flame, a shepherd, a spotted snake (108–14), and the other male Olympians follow suit. Arachne's tapestry shows the gods ridiculed by their lusts in animal and other non-anthropomorphic forms. In style too her tapestry is similar to that of the *Metamorphoses* with its asymmetrical variation in length of scene and detail.[53] The tapestry is so perfectly woven that not even Minerva could find fault with it, but shockingly, she abandons her Olympian dignity and rips apart the beautiful work of art; she then beats Arachne with a shuttle so that in despair the girl hangs herself (129–35). Out of pity, we are told

(135), Minerva changes Arachne into a spider and thus allows her to keep weaving, but without the colours and vivid narratives that once characterized her work (135–45). Minerva's 'pity' condemns Arachne to an eternity of subsistence work.

Despite some key similarities in theme and style between Arachne's tapestry and Ovid's epic, Arachne cannot be fully identified with the poet; but her tapestry represents key features of his metamorphic, edgy, yet aesthetically pleasing art. Typically, the fate of Arachne remains morally ambiguous. For she is punished not only for her art but for her presumption in challenging the goddess. Before the contest she boasted that she could surpass Minerva in weaving, and she dismissed with insulting, arrogant words a warning from the goddess, disguised as an old woman (25–44). The poet thus depicts a world in which free speech is dangerous in the face of power; but he also shows Arachne as foolishly arrogant. Like Daedalus, the first aviator (*Met.* 8.183–235), Arachne, a girl of humble background (10–13), aspires to the realm of the gods. Thus the poet shows too the tragic irony of the human lot; divine aspirations, the upward reach of humans for greatness, almost inevitably end in downfall not only because of jealous gods but because of human fallibility.

The local people react to Arachne's fate as a punishment that is also a lesson in politics, not in divine justice; one must always cede authority to the gods and 'use lesser words', that is avoid bold, confrontational speech (150–1). But not only is Arachne changed at the end of the story, so too is Minerva, who on her tapestry represented the divine justice and dignity of the gods. Now she appears as a poor loser and philistine, a divine patroness of art who wilfully destroys a perfect work. Minerva's jealous destruction of Arachne's tapestry demonstrates the precarious heroism of nonconformist art, though brilliant and perfectly executed, in a world dominated by self-interested, autocratic rulers who generally wield power in an arbitrary fashion.

The world of the *Metamorphoses* is subject to constant change and flux. Since the poem extends to the Augustan age, such a view challenges the Virgilian hopes of divinely granted, stable empire without end (*Aen.* 1.278–9). In the Ovidian universe, the gods are often harsh and cruel, but no power lasts for ever. Thus in the final book of the poem, Book 15, the philosopher Pythagoras argues that all creation is subject to the law of change, even great cities and empires (15.418–52). Athens once was great, now Rome is rising to be a major power – but the implication is that Rome too, like cities before it, will not maintain its supremacy for ever.[54]

Admittedly apotheosis, a Roman form of metamorphosis, counters historical flux by the new fixed position of the deified Roman heroes Hercules, Aeneas, Romulus (with his wife Hersilia) and Julius Caesar, in the heavens. Ovid's poem leaves in doubt the power that these new gods of Rome may possess. But, as Leonard Barkan suggests, true power resides with the poet who speaks at the poem's end with a voice that runs assertively counter to the construction of empire, one that postulates 'an order of continuing change beyond human control'.[55] Yet in the poem's epilogue (15.871–9), an exception appears to the laws of change in the form of our poet, the artist-as-hero. As Ovid announces, although his body will die (875–6), 'nevertheless, in my better part, I will be borne above the lofty stars, eternal, and my name will never be extinguished.' The Caesars may become stars after death, but Ovid, embodied in the fame of his poetry, will go even higher in the heavens. In this poem without a unifying mythological hero, the poet emerges as the true hero with wide-ranging ambitions and his own glorious apotheosis.

Ingo Gildenhard and Andrew Zissos' edited collection of essays, *Transformative Change in Western Thought: Metamorphosis from Homer to Hollywood* (London, 2013), claims that Ovid's epic, along with the Bible, is a touchstone in the history of ideas of metamorphosis. In their introduction the authors show how stories of metamorphosis, which existed on the margins of early Greek literature, became immensely popular in the Hellenistic period, underpinned by a tension between fact and fiction; Ovid's *Metamorphoses* is at once the ambitious culmination of these Hellenistic trends and the gateway to countless realms of transformative possibilities. In our era, this is perhaps particularly true in the novel and film. But we will explore this topic more fully in the final chapters.

V

THE FASTI: POEM
OF ROMAN TIME

Let the good times roll.

THE *FASTI*, A DIDACTIC POEM based on the Roman calendar, is probably the most radical of Ovid's experiments with the elegiac genre. It was composed at the same time as the *Metamorphoses*, around 2–8 CE, and seems to have been partly revised in Tomis, although the poet claims that only the first six books were completed because of exile (*Tr.* 2.549–52).¹ The poem explores the origins of significant dates in the Roman calendar such as state festivals, temple foundations and dedications, and occasions such as birthdays, triumphs and religious benefactions connected with the imperial house. The state calendar was not an inert document but rather was always subject to change, deletion and accretion; it thus reflected changing ideas of what it meant to be Roman.² Using the calendar as a framework, with each month corresponding to a book, Ovid's *Fasti* provides an elegiac commentary not only on Roman history and religion but also on ideas of what it meant to be 'Roman' in the late Augustan age. In the *Ars Amatoria*, his earlier elegiac didactic poem, the poet confronted the Augustan regime over the control of love and sexuality; in the *Fasti* the confrontation is over control of time.[3]

Augustus understood the value of time as an instrument of propaganda.[4] In addition to his building and restoration of temples, Augustus reordered time through the state calendar, which had been revised by Julius Caesar to bring civic time in line with natural time;[5] Augustus altered the calendar further to include new imperial festivals.[6] The Augustan state calendar was monumental in form, often inscribed on marble in prominent civic locations.[7] A surviving Augustan calendar from Praeneste (modern Palestrina, just outside Rome) formed part of the imposing temple of Fortune. It shows the new imperial dates and includes commentary by Verrius Flaccus, a scholar and tutor to the imperial children.[8] The most striking monument to time, however, was erected in the Campus Martius, in a complex that included Augustus' Altar of Peace and Mausoleum. A massive Egyptian obelisk, topped with a globe and dedicated to the Sun (as was the custom of Hellenistic monarchs), acted as a sundial and zodiac.[9] Time was thus monumentalized as a soaring emblem of imperial dominion.

In Rome the calendar measured time; but it was probably even more important as a religious and political instrument for creating cultural memory.[10] In the United States today, for instance, the addition to the calendar of Martin Luther King Day as an official national holiday memorializes the civil-rights leader and associates American identity with the principles of diversity and tolerance. Ovid's *Fasti*, therefore, had an ambitious literary and political agenda for elegy, to provide a distinctly Ovidian, elegiac perspective on Roman history and time.

Beginnings and influences

In the poem's opening couplet the poet outlines his new elegiac programme and acknowledges its multiple literary influences (1.1–2):

> Times distributed throughout the Roman year with their origins,
>   and the stars gliding below and above the earth, of these I will sing.

With the initial word 'times' Ovid places the *Fasti* in the tradition of Hesiod (eighth/seventh century BCE), the father of didactic poetry and author of a poem concerning time, *Works and Days*. This initial word of the *Fasti* is also the last word of the short proem to the *Metamorphoses* (1.1–4), which announces its linear, temporal scheme 'from the start of the world [...] to my times' (*Met.* 1.4).[11] Ovid thus advertises the connections between the two poems. Although the *Fasti* is composed in elegiac couplets and its concept of time is cyclical, not linear, it complements and in a sense continues Ovid's epic, which enters Roman time only in its final two books.[12]

The word 'origins' in the first line of the *Fasti* marks Ovid's debt to the Hellenistic poet Callimachus (*c.*310–240 BCE), whose *Aetia* ('Origins'), a four-book elegiac poem on the origins of Greek cults and festivals, was an important precedent for Roman elegiac poets. In Roman literature, Propertius' fourth book of *Elegies*, which was inspired by Callimachus' *Aetia*, provided a significant model for the *Fasti*;[13] Ovid's opening line echoes Propertius' programmatic statement at 4.1.69: 'I shall sing of sacred rites and days and the ancient origins of places.' The reference in the second line of the *Fasti* to the movements of the stars acknowledges the *Phaenomena* by Callimachus' contemporary Aratus, a didactic poem on the constellations and weather signs.[14] Despite this rich didactic background, however, the *Fasti* is unique in its use of the calendar as a unifying principle for time and place. Here natural time (the constellations) is meshed with civic time, for stars too fell under the political dispensation of the principate through apotheosis.

In the proem to the second book, Ovid refers back to his earlier elegies when he asks: 'who would have thought that the way led from this to that?' (*Fasti* 2.8). But the *Fasti* shares common preoccupations with the didactic *Ars*. In the *Ars* Ovid imposes a personal view of time by challenging the Augustan elevation of a virtuous past; the present is the best time in which to live (*Ars* 3.121–8), because of its cultural chic and amatory opportunities. The *Ars* also has its own internal calendar of special days for the lover (1.399–436), who needs to observe the appropriate times for seduction or for keeping one's distance (such as the girl's birthday, when expensive presents are expected). Mocking the serious didacticism of Hesiod's *Works and Days*, the 'teacher' advises lovers (1.399–400): 'times [seasons] are not just the concern of farmers or sailors; lovers need to watch the times too.'[15]

Like the *Ars Amatoria*, moreover, the *Fasti* is a poem of cosmopolitan, urban Rome; it makes only occasional forays to rural festivals in the countryside.[16] But it departs from the *Ars* in its novel modification of the conventional elegiac opposition between love and war (1.13–14):

> Let others sing of Caesar's wars. I will sing of Caesar's altars
> and the days he added to our sacred rites.

Altars (or religion and history) now substitute for love as the theme of the elegiac poem. And Augustan Rome is viewed from a fresh perspective as a living archive rather than an erotic playground. Sex is not in fact absent from the *Fasti*, but it is generally bracketed off in the poem and connected with licensed occasions for festive fun.[17] Significant in this regard is Ovid's address to Venus (*Fasti* 4.1–18), who is upset to learn that the poet is intent on 'greater' themes (1–4). Teasingly Ovid reassures the goddess (7), 'whether wounded or whole, have I ever abandoned your standards?' But Venus too has changed. Ovid addresses her as 'nurturing mother', an allusion both to her position as the founding figure of the family of the Caesars (19–132), and to her role as 'nurturing Venus' in the opening of Lucretius' great didactic poem *de Rerum Natura* ('On the nature of things'), where she presides over serious didactic poetry.

This then is elegy on a higher register (*Fasti* 2.3–4):

> Now for the first time, elegy, you advance with greater sails:
> lately, I recall, you were a tiny work.

The erotic metaphor of love as a form of military service, which Ovid developed most explicitly in *Am*. 1.9, assumes new semantic value as antiquarian research, a far cry from the earlier poetry of dinner parties and bedroom wrestling (2.9–10):

> This is my military service; I carry the weapons I can,
> and my right hand is not available for every duty.

But, as in the proem to Book 1 of the *Fasti*, where the poet declares his theme of 'Caesar's altars, not Caesar's arms' (13), the metaphor of 'military service' continues a self-conscious generic opposition to epic, marked prominently by the elegiac metre and by its peaceful themes. But Ovid no longer claims parity with the soldier, as he did in his erotic elegies. His fighting arm (his right) will not take on every task, for his exploration of Roman origins demands not the aggression of the lover but the peaceful deference of the enquirer after knowledge.

In the *Fasti* Ovid represents himself as a researcher of ancient cults rather than the 'know-all' of the *Ars*. The late Republican and Augustan age showed considerable interest in the origins of Roman religious practices and deities. The antiquarian prose writer Varro, for instance, wrote a major, multi-volume work on Roman antiquities and dedicated its 16 books on the gods to Julius Caesar in 47 BCE;[18] he also wrote a work on the Latin language whose sixth book discusses the origins of Roman festivals and names. But although Ovid refers at the start of the *Fasti* to digging out 'ancient annals' (1.7), his main strategy is fieldwork, not the library.[19] He injects physical energy into research as he moves through place as well as time, enjoying lively, first-person engagement with a variety of informants, both human and divine. The first informant of the *Fasti*, for instance, is the god Janus, ancient Italian deity of openings and closings, and therefore represented as facing in two directions (1.89–288); as the poet points out, he conveniently speaks to Ovid from his front mouth (100). Through the plurality of narrative voices and characters, the *Fasti* displays a rich diversity of Roman festivals and celebratory occasions, many of Republican origins. Ovid is not always the deferential researcher, moreover. Sometimes he takes on an active performative role, as when at the festival of Ceres he directs the farmers how to perform the sacrifice to the goddess (1.633–96).

The *Fasti* is more ambitious in scope and theme than the *Ars Amatoria*. Indeed, the poet shows his audacity when he shows that the distich of love poetry can take possession of epic and historical material through its emphasis on peace. As Alessandro Barchiesi argues, 'the *Fasti* is the Augustan poem that both dissociates itself most completely from *arma* ['weapons'] and accounts for this dissociation and dislike most exhaustively.'[20] Although

Janus, the poet's first informant, was traditionally associated closely with both war and peace, the god states in the *Fasti*, 'I have nothing to do with war; I watch over peace as well as doors' (1.253).[21]

The *Fasti* is thus introduced in Book 1 as poetry of peace that expands the generic range of Roman elegy. Yet as poetry of Rome the *Fasti* sometimes confronts a generic dilemma when it has to acknowledge the state's military foundations and its 'arms'. For instance, Mars, the god of war, creates a generic crisis in the poem when the poet has no choice but to invoke him at the start of the month to which he gave his name, March (3.1–2):

> Warrior god, put down your spear and shield for a little;
>> come, Mars, and loosen your shining hair from your helmet.

As Stephen Hinds has shown, the god is accommodated to the elegiac *Fasti* by his genial, temporary disarming; the generic crisis is thus defused (3.1–8).[22] Mars' book and month too begin with the reminder that he is associated with 'love' through his rape of Ilia, mother of Romulus and Remus (3.9–11).[23]

Yet later, Mars' arms encroach more uneasily on the elegiac poem as the god enters the city of Rome to inspect his new temple in the Forum of Augustus (5.545–98). Although the god's mission is peaceful, he comes fully armed, and the poet expresses his alarm at the disruptive sound of weapons in an elegiac poem (5.549–50):

> Am I wrong, or do I hear the sound of arms? Yes, that was the sound of arms.
>> Mars is coming, and at his coming he gives warlike sounds.

The poet attempts to contain generic disruption by comic repetition and by the placement of Mars' arrival in the pentameter, the short line that identifies the elegiac couplet. Yet elegy cannot quite contain the disruptive force of Mars as the Avenger (Mars Ultor). The temple of Mars Ultor had two origins. It was vowed by Octavian (the future emperor Augustus) at the civil war Battle of Philippi in 42 BCE in order to avenge the assassination of Julius Caesar; it was vowed again when, as emperor, he recovered Rome's captured military standards from the Parthians (5.569–80).[24] The *Fasti* foregrounds Philippi. The future emperor is imagined invoking Mars' presence in front of his troops before the battle (5.571–7). Echoing the poet's invocation of *Fasti* 3.2 ('Mars, come'), his address, however, is stark (575): 'Mars, come and glut your sword with criminal blood.' The 'criminal blood' were fellow Romans fighting on the opposite side, whose bodies in the aftermath of the battle were left unburied (*Fasti* 3.707–8). The future emperor's words, however, overwrite civil war as a pious duty to avenge a father, the murdered Julius Caesar. Yet his phrase 'criminal blood' alludes to the troubling, morally difficult end of Virgil's *Aeneid*, when Aeneas, in his last words of the poem, claims revenge from his opponent Turnus' 'criminal blood' (*Aen.* 12.949) before he kills him in terrible anger. Elegy, the genre of peace, turns to Virgil's epic to question the ideology of revenge. The temple of Mars Ultor in Augustus' new forum was a masterpiece of wonderful architecture, but the elegiac poet here reminds us of its problematic origins.[25] The double weight of Mars and Augustus cannot keep the sounds and memory of war out of the *Fasti*, but the elegiac poet can nonetheless indicate the huge personal cost of the Augustan peace that his poem now celebrates, with the reminder that elegy was associated in its generic origins with lament.

Fasti, *or 'permitted speech'*

The poem's title is not simply shorthand for the state calendar but also means 'permitted speech', for the calendar documented the times when it was allowed to speak in court; on major religious occasions judicial proceedings could not be held. The idea of 'permitted speech' takes on broader political ramifications in Ovid's poem, which, more so even than the *Metamorphoses*, is permeated with references to curbs on speech and silencing imposed by powerful gods and human leaders.[26]

The political matter of speech and time confronts the reader from the start of the poem in its rededication to Germanicus (*c.*15 BCE–19 CE), the emperor Tiberius' nephew and heir (1.1–26).[27] The new dedication draws attention to the poet's changed times as well as changed verse. Unlike the

Ars Amatoria, which specifically refuses the traditional didactic dedication to a distinguished individual (*Ars* 1.25–30), Ovid makes a politic choice of dedicatee, for Germanicus was connected by blood to both Augustus and Tiberius and seems to have enjoyed the patronage of both emperors.[28] He was also a skilled orator and poet. Like Cicero before him, he translated and updated Aratus' astronomical poem the *Phaenomena*. Ovid looks to Germanicus as fellow poet and Muse (15–26) and also as potential imperial patron with whom, however, he has to observe careful linguistic protocol. He concludes his address to Germanicus by acknowledging the constraints imposed by his imperial addressee (25–6):

> If it is allowed and it is right, as a poet guide the reins of a poet,
>> so that the whole year may proceed favourably under your auspices.

Ovid here acknowledges the new political dispensation under which he writes, where speech offensive to the imperial house could and did have dire consequences for the publication and success of his verse, and indeed his own livelihood. The reference to 'the whole year' is particularly pointed for a passage written in exile. Denis Feeney for instance has argued that in the *Fasti* Ovid retaliates against his exile by voluntary suppression of speech.[29] Thus he published only six books of *Fasti*, although he hints that the other six had been completed in draft (*Tr.* 2.549).[30] The extant poem is possibly a mute reproach to the principate, which never received its special months of July and August.

Although the *Fasti* thematizes silence and constraint of speech, it also takes considerable narrative liberties; the calendrical structure is not a chronological straitjacket. True, the sequence of months and festivals provides a clearer and nominally more restrictive temporal framework for the poem than for the *Metamorphoses*, but nonetheless Ovid shows considerable freedom in his manipulation of days and events. Specific dates often prompt stories or narrative digressions that have tenuous links with the original day commemorated, and as in the *Metamorphoses*, narratives are often linked by thematic association.[31] Ovid also sometimes draws attention to his narrative liberties with the calendar.[32] For instance, when introducing the expulsion of the Tarquin royal family from Rome, Ovid comments (*Fasti* 2.685): 'now is the time when I must speak of the king's flight [the 'Regifugium'].' But he does not, as an antiquarian might, discuss the obscure origins of the Regifugium, which possibly referred not to the Tarquins but to rites involving a sacred priest.[33] Rather, he associates the day with the end of monarchy but almost as an afterthought to a substantial narrative concerning the rape and suicide of Lucretia (2.687–852).[34] Ovid's narrative of Lucretia is a good example of the freedom and flexibility of elegy in taking on historical and epic material. Moreover, Lucretia, modelled as an elegiac woman, demonstrates the close connection between elegy and constraints on speech in the *Fasti*.

Three important literary models lie behind Ovid's Lucretia: Propertius' Arethusa, the loving wife who writes a letter to her absent soldier husband in 4.3; Philomela, the mythological heroine who was raped and silenced by the Thracian king Tereus (*Met.* 6.424–674);[35] and Livy's Lucretia. In Ovid's day the story of Lucretia would have been familiar to contemporary readers through the Augustan historian Livy, who concludes his first book of Rome's history with the sudden end of monarchy in Rome, thanks to the heroism of Brutus and of Lucretia (1.57–60). Whereas Livy focuses on Lucretia's rape by the king's son as the catalyst for political change, Ovid focuses on Lucretia as an elegiac woman; political change is incidental to his version.[36] Livy's Lucretia advocates for revenge and provides the motive for the establishment of the Roman Republic. Brutus is present at her death to use her body as a symbol of the wounded state that dramatized the need for political revolution. Livy's Lucretia also has primary social significance as a model for future generations of Roman women; her suicide is an example of the central importance of chastity (1.58). Ovid transforms Livy's stern matron into a largely elegiac figure and emphasizes the emotional impact of the rape on Lucretia and her close family, rather than its political and social implications. He thus invites the reader to consider the human cost of political revolution and the violence, here sexual, at the heart of Roman history.

Lucretia is first represented in Ovid's poem spinning with her hand-maidens late at night (2.741–60), a conventional sign of Roman matronly virtue, but Ovid makes Lucretia's work and her voice elegiac. Her wool is pleasingly 'soft' (742), and her voice is 'delicate' (744). She mentions to her handmaidens that she is weaving a warm cloak for her husband (2.745–6). She thus recalls Propertius' Arethusa, who has advanced to making a fourth cloak for her absent soldier husband (4.3.18). Like Arethusa, Lucretia sees war from an elegiac perspective as an activity that takes men away from their loved ones, rather than one that brings battle glory (2.749–50); like Arethusa again (4.3.63–72), she fears for the safety of her husband, who is a rash warrior (2.751–4). Her speech ends with the physical accompaniment of elegy, her tears (2.755–8), which make her stop spinning.

Lucretia is seen here through the eyes of her husband and of the king's son Sextus Tarquinius in particular, who, along with other noblemen, have briefly returned from war to check on their wives; all were found carousing, except for Lucretia (2.723–60). The reader is put in the position of voyeur along with the young men, who see and overhear Lucretia as 'she hangs a sweet burden on his [her husband's] neck' (760). Lucretia's husband gains proof of his wife's virtue and her love. But Lucretia's words and voice also stir the illicit, fatal passion of Sextus Tarquinius. Lucretia's innocent embrace of her husband enflames him (2.761–6); so too was Tereus enflamed by Philomela's frequent embrace of her father (*Met.* 6.475–82). As with Tereus' lust for Philomela, this is blind, obsessive love that shatters kinship and family ties (*Met.* 6.472–3; *Fasti* 2.762).

Lucretia is not mutilated, like Philomela, but rape almost entirely deprives her of speech. The scene of her suicide shows Ovid's focus, typical of the *Metamorphoses*, on the emotional and psychological consequences of rape. Livy's political narrative, on the other hand, uses Lucretia as an exemplary female figure. For example, Livy introduces Lucretia 'sitting sadly in her bedroom' (1.58.7), whereas Ovid's Lucretia sits with loose flowing locks (2.813); so too Philomela's locks after her rape were unbound, a sign of deep emotional distress (*Met.* 6.531). In a striking simile, Ovid's Lucretia is compared to a 'mother about to attend the funeral pyre of her son' (2.814). At first sight this comparison seems inept, for Lucretia was a young bride, not yet a mother. But the simile not only evokes her suffering over the violent loss of her chastity but also suggests that, as with Philomela, the psychological trauma of rape has changed her to a mature woman. There is a hint too at another possible consequence of the rape, unwanted pregnancy, which adds to Lucretia's moral dilemma. Lucretia dies not for political liberty, as in Livy, but through fear of '*liberi*', children.

After the rape, Livy's Lucretia invites to her bedroom her father and her husband, as in Ovid, but also Brutus and another friend (1.58.5). Her testimony about the rape becomes almost a public forum, and she speaks at length about the outrage done to her (1.58.7–10). But Ovid's Lucretia is silent for a long time and weeps copiously (2.819–20) until finally summoning the courage for a few disjointed words (2.823–8):

> Three times she tries to speak, three times she halted,
>   and though daring a fourth time she did not however raise her eyes.
> 'Will I owe this too to Tarquin? Shall I speak,' she said,
>   'shall I, unhappy woman, speak of my disgrace?'
> She tells what she can; the rest remained unspoken;
>   she wept and her matronly cheeks blushed.

Silence is a unique feature of Ovid's Lucretia. But she represents a recurrent figure in Ovid's *Metamorphoses* and *Fasti*, the woman silenced by trauma. As in the myth of Philomela, so in this Roman legend speech and silence are gender-coded. Here too in her matronly blush is a reason for her suicide that is not the political one chosen by Livy. Blushing identifies the chaste woman and virgin, but 'matronly' suggests both married respectability and the threat of motherhood. Rape has confused Lucretia's identity. She is no longer chaste but she cannot take on the role of mother. This is the dilemma that traps her and forces her to suicide, although her father and husband do not blame her (2.829–30). When she suddenly stabs herself to death, she does so in a chaste manner (2.833–4): 'dying she even then took care to fall with modesty.'[37]

Some critics have argued that Ovid plays down the political aspects of this myth out of sensitivity to the man who ended the Roman Republic, Augustus.[38] Even so, the literary context emphasizes the overlap between myth and history in the theme of the woman whose speech has been violently silenced by a prince. The elegiac distich offers new perspectives on Roman history from the traditional margins of female suffering, now made central. The end of Lucretia's narrative is immediately followed by a seasonal reference to the swallow's arrival at the start of spring that includes a specific allusion to the Procne, Tereus and Philomela myth (2.852–6). In his narrative poem *The Rape of Lucrece*, which is deeply indebted to Ovid's telling, Shakespeare blurs the boundary between Lucretia's lament and that of Philomela, the nightingale (1079–80). The themes of female speech, violence and silence that are embedded in Ovid's version of the Lucretia narrative are reinforced in the reference to both natural and mythological time in which the cycle of violence is endlessly and troublingly repeated.

In the *Fasti*, Lucretia does not stand alone in Roman history. Her tragic narrative is linked to the unique story of Lara, mother of the Lares, Roman guardians of homes and neighbourhoods (2.583–616). According to Ovid, Lara was a nymph punished by Jupiter for warning Juno of his adulterous intentions. Jupiter wrenched out Lara's tongue for her offensive speech. But the horror did not end there. After Jupiter commanded Mercury to take Lara to the Underworld, Mercury raped her on the way; she subsequently gave birth to the Lares, twin deities who guarded the crossroads in Rome.

The cult of the Lares was revived by Augustus when in 7 BCE he reorganized the city of Rome into new districts and appropriated the Lares as the 'Lares of Augustus'. Augustan ideology thus permeated the daily life of Rome's artisanal and merchant class; the bases of the altars to the Lares were often sculpted with figures demonstrating the sanctity of Augustus and the ruling family.[39] Yet according to Ovid's unique myth, the Lares are the product of mutilation, silencing and rape. The poem here casts on an ironic eye on Augustus' revival of an ancient cult, uncovering its violent origins. The Lares are a sign of Jupiter's power to control and suppress speech that would upset the social and political order. Augustus is thus connected with a cult that in its origins, according to Ovid's *Fasti*, was closely connected with a leader's suppression of speech that seemed threatening to his supremacy.[40] The notion that the threat to free speech is a concomitant of autocratic power is reinforced by a reference to Philomela that directly follows the episode of Lara (2.629). The interweaving of Roman cult with Greek mythological exemplars suggests that the suppression of speech is not just a feature of Greek myth but is an integral, disturbing feature of Roman cult and history with continuing pertinence to Ovid's day.

Where the poet of the *Fasti* can claim particular licence is in so-called 'comic rape narratives'. Unlike the *Metamorphoses*, the *Fasti* is distinguished by bawdy tales of foiled rape.[41] These stories, however, come with a sort of 'X-rated warning' that the poet is indulging for a limited time only in free speech.[42] Three of these stories involve Roman fertility deities exposed in absurd situations: Priapus, Roman god of the male libido, is caught out twice with trousers down by the braying of a donkey when he is attempting to rape the nymph Lotis and the goddess Vesta (1.391–440; 6.319–48); the equally sex-driven Roman god Faunus is foiled by cross-dressed lovers Hercules and Omphale when, bent on rape of the latter, he is shocked to discover the hairy legs of the Greek hero under a dress (2.303–58).[43] Peter Wiseman argues that these stories derive from the Republican comic stage.[44] The tales involving Lotis and Hercules and Omphale end with the laughter of the internal audience at the god's disgrace (1.437–8; 2.355–6), thus emphasizing the comic tone of the narratives and suggesting their possible farcical origins in Roman theatre.

The first of these stories, Lotis and Priapus, is depicted in Giovanni Bellini's early sixteenth-century painting *The Feast of the Gods*. On the right of the canvas Priapus, with an obvious bulge beneath his tunic, leans over the sleeping nymph. The gods themselves are not sleeping but sit calmly watching the incipient assault as if in a theatre watching a play unfold. Only the donkey seems alert, with ears fully extended, although its body is turned away from Priapus. Bellini here has brilliantly combined a narrative from the *Fasti* with a critique of the gods such as we find in the *Metamorphoses*, where the gods regard sex with nymphs as their prerogative. He also brings out the theatrical nature of the story in the *Fasti*, even if he did not know its possibly theatrical origins.

The calendar provides only a tenuous excuse for these comic narratives. Each is bracketed off, as it were, from the mainstream of the poem by the poet's warning to the reader of the risqué nature of the coming tale: 'the reason is shameful, but still fitting for the god' (1.392); 'but to explain

why Faunus especially shuns clothes, a funny tale is told from days of old'
(2.303–4); 'should I skip over your disgrace, ruddy Priapus? It's just a little
story but very funny' (6.319–20). In fact this 'little story' interrupts a lengthy
account of Vesta's sacred rites (6.249–460) and shows the poet at his most
audacious, for Priapus, in a virtually identical narrative to that involving
Lotis, attempts to rape Vesta, Roman goddess of chastity, who was particu-
larly dear to Augustus.[45] The parallelism between these two tales draws Vesta
down to the level of a nymph, the traditional target of Priapus' and Faunus'
lust. With this pornographic scenario the poet exploits the transgressiveness
of comedy to sail close to the political wind. However, unlike at the end
of the tale of Lotis, laughter is absent from the ending of the tale of Vesta,
perhaps in acknowledgement of how far the story has transgressed political
decorum. Instead, the narrative makes a concluding acknowledgement of
outrage as an alternative, appropriate response to laughter, for the goddess
is terrified, and a hostile crowd vainly tries to capture Priapus. With the
end of laughter, proper reverence for the gods is restored (6.343–4). Yet
since Priapus is not caught, as he is in the Lotis myth, he thus embodies the
arbitrary licence that can threaten the most impregnable of characters and
institutions, even Augustus' goddess of chastity. The Priapus of the *Fasti* is
the spirit of old Rome, a reminder of a robust sexuality and comic licence
that were at the heart of Roman identity before speech, except on special
occasions, had to be politically correct.

Women on the loose

On the Ides of March, the notorious date of Julius Caesar's assassination,
the poet highlights instead the bawdy, drunken festival of Anna Perenna
and the origins of this goddess (3.523–696). Here his caveat about correct
speech is reserved for politics, not for the licentious feast. He claims that
he was about to pass over Caesar's assassination and apotheosis entirely
when the Roman goddess Vesta admonished him to write a commemora-
tion (3.697–710). Ovid keeps it short; Anna is given 174 lines to 14 for
Caesar. Certainly, as we have seen, murder and bloodshed were generically

inappropriate to the *Fasti*. Moreover, the memory of Caesar's death was sensitive for Augustus and his family, although his apotheosis was important as a precedent for Augustus' deification. In this highly compressed passage the poet adopts an official, encomiastic voice, emphasizing that Julius Caesar, as 'chief priest' ('pontifex maximus') was under Vesta's special care and thus she was responsible for his rescue from the assassins and for his apotheosis (3.697–704).[46] Even so, an ambiguous note is struck by a brief reference to Philippi, the battle where, as we saw above, Octavian avenged himself on the assassins of Julius Caesar, Brutus and Cassius, and their troops (706–8):

> Those who polluted the priestly head
> lie in deserved death; bear witness, Philippi,
> and you whose bones are whitening, scattered on the ground.

Commissioned by Vesta, the poet condemns the assassins, and yet, at the same time, provides a reminder of the barbarity of the victors' decision to leave the bodies unburied on the battlefield.

Be that as it may, the imbalance in length between the imperial commemoration and the Republican festival is matched by the imbalance in the character of these two events on the Ides of March. The festival of Anna Perenna is described as an outdoor festival for the commoners. The rustic shelters made by the celebrants in a parody of elite architecture, with reeds instead of columns and togas serving as roof coverings (527–30), play on Augustan nostalgia for a simpler, more virtuous past. Yet this is a festival where couples let their hair down with sex, drinking, dancing and raunchy songs (3.523–42); the poet's eyewitness image of 'a drunken old man dragging along a drunken old woman' in the crowd of celebrants (542) is far from the elite concept of respectable seniority, especially for women.[47] On the Ides of March, a carnivalesque vision of streetwise Rome with its free, loose speech is juxtaposed with the elevated politics of elite deification and with commissioned panegyric.[48] Who then is this goddess Anna Perenna, and why might the poet wish to commemorate her at such length on this highly charged date? This is one of the poem's most ambitious episodes, for the discussion of the goddess's origins ranges from Virgil's *Aeneid* to comic burlesque, and yet in all these versions the goddess is also subtly associated with the Julian family.[49]

Given the obscurity of the origins of many of Rome's deities and cults, Roman antiquarians often offered several explanations in their research.[50] Ovid provides three main explanations for the identity of Anna Perenna: literary, historical and comic.[51] He does not follow the most popular explanations of Antiquity, namely that she was associated with the year (Latin *annus*) and new beginnings in spring and thus with fertility.[52] The first explanation (3.545–654) is written as a sequel both to the *Aeneid* and to the seventh *Heroides*, Dido's suicide letter. Anna Perenna is identified as Dido's sister Anna; her story begins where *Heroides* 7 ends. Dido has burned on the pyre, and the epitaph that she wrote for herself (*Ep.* 7.195–6) has now been etched with exactly the same words on her marble tomb (*Fasti* 3.549–50): 'Aeneas provided the cause of death and the sword: Dido fell by her own hand.' The narrative in the *Fasti* inherits from the *Heroides* the negative interpretation of Aeneas' actions towards Dido and stamps Ovidian authority yet again on the Virgilian characters.

According to this unique narrative in the *Fasti*, Anna has to flee from Carthage after Dido's suicide and eventually, after wanderings at sea that imitate those of Virgil's Aeneas, she is shipwrecked on the Laurentine shore of Aeneas' new kingdom in Italy (551–600). The story now enters 'post-*Aeneid* 12' territory. Aeneas has prospered (601–2):

> Now pious Aeneas had benefited from a kingdom
> and Latinus' daughter, and he had united two peoples.

Aeneas is introduced with his stereotypical Virgilian epithet 'pious', but, as in *Ep.* 7, he does not come out well in this elegiac narrative. Although he welcomes Anna into his palace, richly attired in Carthaginian dress – despite her recent shipwreck in which she lost everything (3.600)! – her presence as an exotic foreigner arouses the jealousy of the less cosmopolitan Lavinia. In a striking rewriting of Virgil's epic, his silent virgin, while she still does not speak, at last has definite thoughts and feelings, but they are vengeful ones (633–8). Mistrust of Aeneas' actions is inherited from Dido's letter (*Ep.* 7), and although Lavinia promises to treat Anna like a sister, she secretly begrudges the gifts that Aeneas gives his foreign guest (633–4):

> She promises everything, and conceals her deceitful wound
>   with silent thoughts, and disguises her fear.

The marriage for which much blood was spilled on Italian soil in *Aeneid* 7–12 is seriously compromised by Lavinia's desire to kill Anna and then die avenged (637–8).

Ovid's engagement with Virgil's canonical text and his elegiac rewriting of its characters touch on an alternative tradition according to which Anna, not Dido, was in love with Aeneas in Carthage.[53] As Frederick Ahl points out, moreover, Virgil in *Aeneid* 4 represents Anna, the devoted sister and messenger between Dido and Aeneas, as virtually a doublet of her sister, preparing the way for Ovid's 'further adventures of Anna.'[54] Lavinia's suspicions, therefore, have some textual basis. Tragedy is averted when Dido's bloodied ghost appears to Anna in the night to warn her. By jumping out of her bedroom window, Anna escapes to the embraces of the river Numicius and is deified (639–56). Even so, it is understandable that when a century later the Flavian poet Silius Italicus in his *Punica* reclaims Anna Perenna for epic (8.25–201), her loyalties go with the Carthaginians.

Like Lucretia, Anna is sacrificed to Rome's political development, yet the tonal register of her story is far different.[55] Rome's glorious foundation story continues here in the *Fasti* as a domestic melodrama with elements of hatred, fear, moral weakness and sheer farce. In his dealings with women, Aeneas, ancestor of the Julian race, has yet again emerged in an Ovidian text as inept and weak, unable to read or control the mind of his own wife, just as he was unable to comprehend or acknowledge the feelings of Dido. Ironically, Anna is said to become a goddess in the very river, the Numicius, that will later be the site of Aeneas' deification (*Met.* 14.581–608). In this elegiac sequel to *Aeneid* 4, Dido's double does finally make it to Italy and is joined after death with Aeneas through 'bedding down' in the same river.[56]

The second main explanation for Anna's identity has a populist basis true to the character of the festival and draws on a historical occasion (661–74). In 493 BCE the plebeian class of citizens, or commoners, wanting their own representatives, revolted against the nobility by leaving Rome and occupying the 'Sacred Mountain' a few miles distant; they stayed there until the elite eventually agreed to let them be represented by two 'tribunes of the people' (Livy 2.32–3). According to Ovid's *Fasti*, an old woman named Anna from the nearby town of Bovillae distributed her home-baked cakes to the commoners when they were starving during their secession from Rome. When peace was made, a statue was erected in her honour and she was made a goddess (3.679). This story of the old woman seems to be Ovid's invention. On the Ides of March, a major day in the imperial calendar that commemorates the assassination and deification of Caesar, the route to female deification is provocatively associated with populist, political, Republican sympathies.

Scholars have wondered why Ovid made this elderly Anna come from Bovillae, a small town south of Rome near the Alban lake. I suggest that this is because Bovillae had a major connection with Julius Caesar and his family. Bovillae was closely associated with Trojan foundation legends; it was near Alban Longa, which was founded supposedly by Aeneas' son Iulus. The Julian family had their family shrines there and also special games and festivals, and after Augustus' death there was a major public shrine to the deified emperor.[57]

A third story explains why girls sing obscene songs at Anna's festival (675–96). The songs themselves are not repeated, but since young girls were traditionally associated with modest silence, reference to their singing emphasizes that the festival is a licensed occasion for free speech and social inversion. Since earlier the poet referred to the singing of songs learned in the theatre (535), not surprisingly the origin of the custom is told as a bawdy tale that is possibly derived from comic mime.[58] The story involves an erotic triangle of Mars, Minerva and Anna Perenna, here imagined as the old woman from Bovillae, lately deified. As at the start of Book 3, Mars is again in an elegiac situation, for he is in love with Minerva, and he asks Anna to arrange an assignation; she owes him a favour as she recently became a goddess in his month (677–88). Anna, however, dupes Mars by disguising herself, veiled, as Minerva. In a version of the foiled rape motif, her deceit is discovered when he is about to bed her (689–92), and the story ends with characteristic ridicule of the god and laughter on the part of Anna; Venus too is pleased that her cheating lover has been caught (693–4). This comic farce mocks the solemn status of the two ancestral deities of Rome and the Julian family, Mars and Venus.[59] The story's punchline, 'it is satisfying that she [Anna] outwitted the great god' (696), emphasizes the people's pleasure in the besting of the powerful Roman god of war and the Roman state by a minor female deity; in a carnivalesque, generic inversion, elegy metaphorically trumps war through comedy. Just as Mars had to disarm at the start of Book 3 (1–8) to enter the elegiac poem, so here he appears as a god who can at times wear the jester's bells. Ovid's account of the festival of Anna Perenna emphasizes its populist roots and reminds us of the importance of ancient traditions of feasting, song, love and liberty of speech that had traditionally formed a key part of Roman identity and the city's celebration of time.

Although this comic licence seems to create a dissonance with the date's political importance to the principate (675–710), connections to the Caesars run like a subtle, contrapuntal thread throughout the festive fun. With his idiosyncratic explanations for Anna Perenna's identity and cult, Ovid subtly underwrites a reminder of the importance of the Ides of March to the Julian family. But he does so in a provocative way, by emphasizing populist traditions and resistance to elite control that are at odds with the autocratic tendencies of Julius Caesar and his successor Augustus.

That the populist festival was regarded as incompatible with Augustan values seems to be corroborated by a recent archaeological discovery in Rome. At the start of this century an altar dedicated to Anna Perenna and a fountain containing votive offerings and coins dating from the first to the fourth century were found in piazza Euclide in Rome, providing evidence that the cult lasted well beyond the Augustan age.[60] But the piazza Euclide is distant from the central location that Ovid's *Fasti* provides for celebration of the festival 'not far from the banks of the Tiber' (3.524), a site confirmed by the first-century calendar *Fasti Vaticani* which records the festival taking place at the first milestone on the Via Flaminia (*ILS* XIII.2.23). The piazza

Euclide, on the other hand, is beyond the third milestone. Stephen Heyworth has argued that the site for the festival was moved in the first century for political reasons. At the first milestone it was too close to Augustan sacred space, in particular the emperor's Mausoleum.[61] Moreover, a calendar of the fourth century CE, the *Fasti Filocaliani*, records the date of Anna Perenna's festival as not the Ides of March, but 18 June. Thus the tensions that can be traced in Ovid's text between a populist, female fertility cult and an elite male ruler cult seem to have been officially recognized by the removal of Anna Perenna further from the imperial centre of Rome, and by the removal of her festival from the Ides of March. Archaeology and epigraphy thus give us a clearer sense of the audacity of the poet's highlighting of Anna Perenna on the Ides of March.

Ovid's muse of good times

With Anna Perenna, the poet shows time and freedom of speech under pressure from the new imperial ruler cult. A similar tension occurs on 28 April, a day which celebrated two goddesses with opposing spheres of influence: Flora, an ancient fertility goddess with patronage of flowers, and Vesta, goddess of chastity who had been newly adopted into imperial cult. When Augustus became chief priest ('pontifex maximus') in 12 BCE, he created a shrine for Vesta within his house on the Palatine that was in addition to her ancient centre of worship in the Roman forum. The physical elevation of the goddess of chastity made clear her symbolic elevation as a key element of Augustan moral reform. The concluding section of Book 4 of the *Fasti* (943–54) celebrates Vesta's new shrine and acknowledges her as one of the new imperial triad of deities on the Palatine, joining Apollo and Augustus himself (951–2).[62]

But Vesta's elevation creates tension with Flora's festival, which began on 28 April and extended over several days to 3 May. The poet acknowledges the problem, but instead of juxtaposing the two occasions, as he did with Anna Perenna, he announces that he will delay an account of Flora's festival to the following month (4.947–8):

> The sacred rites of Flora continue to the start of May;
> I will turn to her then, now a grander task presses upon me.

In a reversal of his strategy with Anna Perenna, the poet privileges the imperial occasion over a fertility cult, the 'grand occasion' over elegiac pleasure. On the other hand, although Vesta ousts Flora and occupies the final position in Book 4, she is given eight lines to the almost 200 for Flora (5.183–378).

Flora has her due in the following book. Her episode takes the form of a lengthy interview with the poet in which she herself in direct speech explains her origins and cult; she thus takes personal control of her reputation. As goddess of flowers, Flora brings colour to the world (5.213–4). Of all the deities in this poem, Flora comes closest to being Ovid's Muse.

Ovid emphasizes, as with Anna Perenna, the populist nature of her festival (351–2):

> She is not from the frowning disapprovers or those who profess great things;
> she wishes her festivities to be open to the company of common people.

Like Anna Perenna, Flora is a good-time goddess whose festival enjoys drinking, dancing and song on an even grander scale, with games and theatrical productions held annually in the Circus (331–54). Although, perhaps in a concession to Augustan moral legislation, she represents herself as happily married (206), her popular games enjoyed 'greater sexual licence and more freedom in comically irreverent speech' than was permitted in everyday life (331–2). Flora's powers extend from fertility in the gardens and fields to human sexuality. Her games were particularly notorious for the prostitutes who danced in her celebration, but they too formed part of the games' broad, popular appeal (349–54).[63] These games originated in the Republican age after a successful victory by the people against the elite over land rights (279–94). Flora is a goddess on the side of the people, their rights and their pleasures. Ovid's Flora offers another possible face of the Augustan peace, not strict regulation of people's private lives but the freedom to enjoy harmless sensual amusements, as well as greater freedom of speech (332): 'at her games we can joke more freely.'

Flora's interview with the poet comes across as relaxed and genial. Her eloquence renders the poet 'silent in admiration' (275). She is perfectly accommodated to the elegiac *Fasti*, an erotic goddess whose perfume frames the episode as she breathes roses from her lips (194), and when she departs her scent lingers (376). Ovid's contemporary, the antiquarian writer Varro, saw Flora rather differently. He invokes Flora as a major, archaic agricultural deity at the start of his prose treatise *Res Rusticae* (*R.* 1.1.4–6), and in his *de Lingua Latina* he claims that she was one of the few indigenous deities to have her own priest (*L.* 7.45). Flora's story of her origins in the *Fasti* denies her archaic roots, though not her importance to Roman cult. She claims that she was a Greek nymph called Chloris who was raped by the god of the west wind, Zephyr. Unlike in the *Metamorphoses*, where nymphs are often abandoned after rape, Zephyr compensated Flora by giving her marriage, a Roman name, and Roman divinity (5.195–212). This story seems to be Ovid's invention. With her Greek origins and sexy demeanour, Flora resembles an elegiac woman (most of whom bear Greek names), yet now, through marriage and deification, elevated and accommodated to the expansive view of the elegiac genre developed in the *Fasti*. With her veneer of contemporary sophistication and marital respectability, the archaic goddess Flora is granted renewed authority and visibility in the Augustan age and in Ovid's calendar poem.

Flora is also connected in the *Fasti* not only with elegy but with Ovid's poetry in general.[64] She claims that she created the flowers of Ovid's *Metamorphoses*, the hyacinth (*Met.* 10.162–219), the narcissus (*Met.* 3.339–510) and the crocus (*Met.* 4.283–4), formerly tragic young men. Her work thus complements our poet's. At the end of his account of her festival, the Floralia, the poet offers her a prayer that invokes her explicitly as the Muse of his *Fasti* (377–8):

> That Naso's poem may flourish for ever,
>   please sprinkle my heart with your gifts.

Ovid plays here upon his name, 'Naso', which means 'nose' in Latin; he is destined therefore by physiognomy to appreciate her perfume and the poetic gifts she can bring him! By contrast, in his deferential prayer to Germanicus at the poem's start, the poet is full of hesitation about what is right and proper to say (1.3–26). Flora in Ovid's *Fasti* offers not a univocal view of Augustan identity and culture but a generous and capacious one. Unlike the elegiac mistress of the erotic elegies, here in the *Fasti* she is indeed a goddess who provides not only the material for his poetry but also the divine inspiration.

Although I have emphasized the temporal and generic tensions in the *Fasti* as well as the persistent theme of limitations upon speech, we should not look for a single political message, either of ingratiation towards the imperial house or of consistent critique. True, as we have seen, the poem's generic expansion into comic drama includes episodes of irreverent humour. For instance, Romulus, the founder of the city and a model for Augustus who cast himself as Rome's second founder, is represented throughout Ovid's *Fasti* as, on the whole, a leader of more brawn than brain.[65] But the *Fasti* is a kaleidoscope of Roman history, myth and cult that offers its readers shifting and various perspectives on Rome and its time(s). The poem can voice the imperial line and also hint at the prevalence of Orwellian doublespeak in official imperial discourse. Like other Augustan poets, Ovid participated in the construction of imperial ideology rather than simply reflecting its imprint.[66] His *Fasti* provides a critical enquiry into the public face of the new Augustan Rome and its manipulation of time. In particular, this polyvalent calendar poem uncovers the complexity of Rome's origins and promotes the memory of cults outside the imperial purview, such as those of Anna Perenna and Flora. With its unfinished state and partial revisions in exile, moreover, the *Fasti* offers a complex view of Rome itself on the cusp of change, as the balance of power shifted from the ageing Augustus to Tiberius. Importantly, therefore, the *Fasti* fosters cultural memories of Rome that are distinct from the austere ideology promoted by the imperial house. In the time of grand, marble calendars, Ovid provided his readers with his own portable, transmittable *Fasti* and personal, elegiac view of time.

VI

EXILE AND AFTER

Remove the Bacchic garlands from my hair.
  Such symbols of good fortune suit happy poets;
  a garland is not fitting for my times.

(TR. 1.7.2–4)

OVID'S EXILE IN 8 CE to the fringes of the Roman Empire for 'two crimes, a poem and an error' (*Tr.* 2.207) was a personal tragedy for the poet, yet at the same time offered new literary opportunities.[1] This final period of Ovid's career saw the prolific output of new forms of elegy – five books of *Tristia*, published between 9 and 12 CE, and four books of *Epistulae ex Ponto*, published between 12 and 17 CE; the *Ibis*, an invective written in elegiacs; the *Fasti* too was revised in exile.[2] In writing of his downfall and suffering in his exile poetry, Ovid took charge of his narrative and of his future.

The first line of Ovid's *Tristia* addresses Ovid's personified poetry book, sending it off on its journey to Rome: 'little book, I don't begrudge you, you will go without me, to the city' (*Tr.* 1.1). Centuries later, Geoffrey Chaucer alluded to this envoy in the final lines of his romantic poem *Troilus and Criseyde*: 'Go, litel bok, go, litel myn tragedye' (V.1786). Yet whereas

Chaucer places his 'sending forth of his book' at the conventional end of his work, Ovid places his envoy at the start of *Tristia* 1. This striking inversion of the ordinary placement of a literary envoy draws attention to the poet's forced absence from Rome, and to his poetry's role as surrogate for the author. The drastic dislocation of the poet's life is reflected in the suspension of the literary rules for endings; that the 'ending' now comes first is a comment on the ruin of a poet who feels close to death, with a sword poised over his throat (43–4). But the inverted opening also signals that this, yet again, is new poetry, from one of Antiquity's most creative, ingenious poets.

Ovid's exile poetry is an innovative experiment with the elegiac genre and has no precise model.[3] The *Tristia* and *Epistulae ex Ponto* established many of the conventions of exile literature to the present day. Ovid's mysterious exile and his exile poetry inspired a 'mini-genre' of modern novels that was popularized among English readers by David Malouf's *An Imaginary Life* (London, 1978), in which Ovid rediscovers his true self and the world of nature in Tomis with the help of a 'wild child'; this radical transformation of Ovid culminates with his final freedom from the need for words or poetry.[4] Jane Alison's *The Love-Artist* (New York, 2001) and Benita Jaro's *Betray the Night* (Illinois, 2009) scrutinize Ovid's life and writings from a feminist perspective, an Ovidian device that finds the poet deserving of exile for his treatment of women. Alison too explains the loss of Ovid's tragedy *Medea* by having it destroyed by her heroine Xenia, who refuses to allow her body to be used simply as text (a common trope of Ovid's erotic works). Although *The Love-Artist* takes place mostly in Rome, Ovid's contact with Xenia, whose name means 'foreigner', ultimately transforms him into a version of his exilic self, the poet of literary decline.

Among perhaps the strangest works inspired by Ovid's exile poetry is the novel by the Czech Canadian writer Josef Skvorecky, *An Inexplicable Story* (Toronto, 2002), in which scrolls, in a fragmentary state but claiming to be written by Ovid's illegitimate son by Corinna, turn up sealed in the wall of a Mayan tomb! In a delightful play on textual scholarship, researchers go to town analysing the scrolls for their authenticity. The Mayans were famous for their sophisticated measurements of time. Thus, despite the implausibility of the plot, there is a certain appropriateness in the Mayan location for news, albeit fragmentary and enigmatic, of our poet of time. Moreover, in a further transmutation of our poet, according to the scrolls Ovid has escaped Tomis and is living a fugitive's life in Austria, enjoying some success as a comic playwright under the pseudonym Pomponius Pinnatus, that is, 'Pomponius in Flight'. The Austrian location may be a tacit acknowledgement of the award-winning novel *Die letzte Welt* (1984), published in English as *The Last World*, by the Austrian Christoph Ransmayr, in which the figure of Ovid is at its most elusive.[5] Ovid's friend Cotta goes in search of the exiled author in a Tomis that is simultaneously an ancient Roman frontier port and a decaying, industrial town of the Fascist era. Although the poet is absent, the town is peopled by grotesque reifications of the characters from the *Metamorphoses*; for example, Tereus is the town butcher, a violent man who, along with his wife and sister-in-law, does turn in the end into a bird. The dissonance between the Roman and the modern worlds transfers the cultural alienation of Ovid's exile also to the temporal realm. As a subgenre, the 'Ovidian novel' demonstrates a fascination not only with the mystery of Ovid's banishment but with exile as the motivation for change in a way of life or a psychological state.

For the past century, an age of war and mass migrations, exile has become an issue of international politics.[6] Thus the Ovid of the exile poetry has also inspired interest in the representation of what it means to be the victim rather than the beneficiary of the unfettered power of empire, a human condition that extends beyond exile. Political exiles, such as the Russian poets Osip Mandelstam (1891–*c.*1938) and Joseph Brodsky (1940–96), found in Ovid's late poetry a seminal figure of dislocation and bereavement who also heroically affirmed art's therapeutic role – the comfort derived from the memory of one's earlier poetry and from the survival of creativity even when wrenched from one's country and language.[7] Ovid could not bring his friends and supporters with him into exile, but he could bring his art.

Exile emerges in Ovid's poetry as both a legal situation and a psycho-logical condition. Post-colonial studies with their focus on the hierarchical relationship between the imperial centre and the colonial periphery have also shed light on the crisis of personal identity occasioned by exile. Ovid, abruptly moved from Rome to the frontier, or the 'edge of the world' (*ultima terra, Tr.* 3.4.52), experienced profound psychological and physical dislocation in a region that he repeatedly describes as harsh in its climate and in its people (e.g. *Tr.* 3.10; *Tr.* 5.7.9–20; *Tr.* 5.10; *Pont.* 4.7.1–12). His Tomis is a barren, physical and cultural wasteland of lengthy, icy winters, of local peoples almost constantly at war, of wine frozen in their amphoras. This last, somewhat comic detail adds further emphasis to the barbarity of Tomis, for wine was not only associated with warm and gentle climates but was an ancient symbol of (agri)culture; frozen wine distils culture shock. Ovid's external representation of the harsh landscape of his exile powerfully reflects his inner misery and sense of isolation. The five books of *Tristia* were written to anonymous friends, for Ovid did not dare name his supporters; only in the later *Epistulae ex Ponto* does he address friends (and enemies) by name.[8]

Tomis in fact was populated not only by the indigenous Geats but, from as far back as the seventh century BCE, by Greek colonists. But in describing Tomis Ovid omits virtually any reference to its Hellenic culture, beyond conjuring up, in *Tr.* 3.9, a false etymology for its name from the Greek word 'to cut' (*temnein*); at Tomis, he claims, Medea, in an inhuman act of savagery, cut her younger brother's body to pieces.[9] For Ovid, Tomis in its mythic origins epitomizes barbarity and fragmentation, the psychological tearing apart of the self in exile. When he writes in the following poem (*Tr.* 3.10.13–14) that 'snow lies continuously, and once fallen, cannot be melted by either sun or rain, for the north wind hardens it and makes it eternal', his observation more accurately reflects his psychological, inner reality, his fears that not only has he lost all familiar topographical and cultural bearings but that he is trapped in the pain of exile for all time. As Stephen Hinds has argued, losing contact with his home and his culture meant a major threat to Ovid's core sense of identity, with particular anxiety focused on his alienation from his native tongue.[10] The exile poetry is permeated with concerns about prestige, marginalization and poetic quality.

Rome thus remains at the centre of Ovid's discursive world in exile. He views Tomis not as a geographer interested in different cultures and landscapes, but with peripheral vision, as a place of hostile contrast to the imperial capital.[11] As Sebastian Matzner comments of the exiled Ovid, his clinging on to Rome as the ultimate signifier of this mode of discourse pre-empts any interaction with or engaged representation of the place of exile; instead, his Tomis remains a literary construction, largely based on Greek and Latin literary traditions.[12]

Even so, as Gareth Williams points out, Ovid's primarily literary portrayal of the Black Sea region allowed him in exile to speak to his readers back in Rome in a familiar language that they could understand. Moreover, Ovid could thus reveal not only his grief and hardship but also his continuing artistic invention and capability. For instance, the familiar generic tension between elegy and epic is now actualized in real time with the poet's displacement to barbarian Tomis. His emphasis on the warlike character of the barbarians with whom he now lived, for instance, evokes martial epic and highlights the cultural divide between the elegiac poet and his alien hosts.[13] The Ovid of the exile poetry is a displaced Roman cut off from the centre who, nonetheless, retaliates with the one asset at his ready disposal, his poetry.

Ovid's engagement with the literary past involves, in particular, his own. Thus reading the exile poetry involves also rereading Ovid's earlier poetry from fresh perspectives. The frequent reference to Ovid's own earlier poetry provides a strategic means of impressing upon his readers what Rome stands to lose by the removal of its most renowned poet to the edges of the Roman world. They are also a memorializing device, a way of preserving Ovid's poetry and name in the face of Augustan censorship. Such intratextual allusions set up a chain of reception; Ovid's rereadings of his own poetry do not end with Ovid but serve as a tacit invitation to his readers to keep his poetry alive through creative interpretation and rewritings. As Don Fowler pointed out, texts owe their survival over time to their readers – and Ovid counted heavily on them in exile.[14]

Time, whether in the sense of the 'times' in which he lives, or of the passage of time, is a constant preoccupation of Ovid's poetry. But Ovid's representation of time in both its senses changes drastically in Tomis. The warning of the personified poetry book to the reader at *Tr.* 3.1.9–10 that 'you will see nothing but sadness here, for the poetry reflects its times,' leaves ambiguous whether by 'times' only Ovid's personal circumstances are meant, or the changed atmosphere in imperial Rome with Tiberius' increasing ascendancy to power over the ageing Augustus. In exile time slows down for Ovid: 'You would think that time stands still, so slowly does it move, and the year follows its course at a sluggish pace' (*Tr.* 5.10.5–6). His physical separation from Rome is matched by his temporal separation from the normal rhythms of social life (*Tr.* 5.10.11–12): 'is it that time in general runs its usual course, while the times of my life are more harsh?' Gone are the art galleries, the porticoes, the theatres, the dinner parties, the girls, the dizzying round of social events. Ovid's company is now for the most part sabre-rattling Geats, and a year can pass between the sending and response to letters (*Pont.* 3.4.59–60). As Alphonso Lingis comments, 'the time that orders the future, present, and past in which we work appears to us to be linear [...] It appears superficial when a catastrophe reveals the time of the empty endurance of the void.'[15] The destruction of 'the structure of intelligible time in human lives' means a form of premature, metaphorical death, since Ovid is cut off from frequent communication with Rome and his family and supporters there.[16] As Jo-Marie Claassen points out, unlike for Cicero when he was in exile, we have no evidence of real consolation from Ovid's former friends and family, whose names, moreover, were suppressed in the *Tristia*.[17]

Tr. 4.6 offers the poet's most sustained reflection on the monotony of time in Tomis. In elegantly paced couplets it observes that, according to natural law, time gradually makes suffering bearable and brings change; in time horses learn to endure the bridle, seeds grow and fructify, hard metals soften and human cares lessen – apart from Ovid's own, which have multiplied by the length of time in exile (38); he alone is exempt from natural law (17–18):

> Time gliding by on silent foot can weaken all things
> except for my cares.

The image of time's 'silent foot' suggests that time at Tomis is so monotonous that its passing is scarcely felt. Moreover, since Ovid frequently puns on a physical and metrical foot, the expression suggests Ovid's fears that his own poetry (of metrical feet) will fall silent in exile and be forgotten. Here too he uses the recurrent metaphor of exile as a form of death by alluding to Tibullus' personification of death which 'comes secretly with silent foot' (1.10.34).

However, another major theme of the exile poetry is the power of the Muse to transcend death by providing continuing inspiration and preserving the memory of Ovid's poetry. True, the absence of his friends' names in the *Tristia* means that in the crucial early years of exile Ovid could not bind his friends to him through the commemorative function of poetry; they did not want their close association with Ovid made public (*Tr.* 4.3.63–72). Yet the silence about the names of his addressees in the *Tristia* is also an important rhetorical strategy that creates an atmosphere of oppression and fear that reflects negatively on the late-Augustan court. As Ellen Oliensis has argued, 'Ovid has ostentatiously written these poems as if they were liable to be read by informers, if not by the origin and end of informers, Augustus himself.'[18] Thus, because his ostensible Roman audience is mute, Ovid speaks beyond them to posterity. In exile he even writes his own epitaph (*Tr.* 3.3.73–6), but follows the inscription with insistence on the surer immortality of his poetry (*Tr.* 3.3.77–8): 'but my books are greater and more lasting monuments.'

An important strategy of Ovid's exile, however, is his frequent complaint that his poetry is in decline and lacks polish and necessary revision.[19] As Gareth Williams and others have argued, the theme of poetic decline should not be taken at face value, for it serves to arouse the readers' sympathy and admiration, since Ovid can indeed write so well![20] Such complaints about inferior poetic composition also again draw attention to what Rome stands to lose in terms of cultural prestige if it does not continue to nurture its most famous contemporary poet by bringing him home.

But perhaps the most effective strategy for keeping his name and fame in the public eye at Rome is the frequent allusion in Ovid's writings from exile to his earlier works, a continuation of his previous practice whereby core texts 'talk to each other'.[21] Thus Ovid's work is kept alive in the memory of his readers, both present and future. Ovid also explicitly invites rereadings of his poetry, notably in *Tristia* 2 where he argues to Augustus that the *Ars Amatoria* does not encourage sexual misbehaviour, for love is at the core of the Greco-Roman literary tradition.[22] In *Tr.* 1.7 he even provides a six-line elegiac epigraph to be attached to the *Metamorphoses* that draws attention to the fact that the author is in exile and cannot give the work its final polish (33–40). As Stephen Hinds points out, in *Tr.* 1.7.35–40 the new preface that Ovid has written for the *Metamorphoses* keeps the author and his plight in the public eye, while it also changes the *Metamorphoses* by inviting a new pessimistic reading of the poem, one suited to the age of *Tristia*.[23]

Ovid also makes poetic capital out of the necessity that the exile poetry is written across distance and that return post is slow to arrive. Hence many of the poems look back in particular to Ovid's *Heroides*, which articulated a poetics of isolation. The mythical situations of Ovid's abandoned heroines are now realized in the real-life drama of Ovid who thus, in part, adopts a gendered, abject position, and, like his heroines, expresses a complex of emotions – conciliatory appeal, hurt, anger and fears that his letters from exile will never be read or acted upon. But Rome, not a mistress, is now the object of his frustrated desires.

In the *Tristia* and *Epistulae ex Ponto* Ovid adapts to the experience of exile many of the amatory tropes of the *Heroides* such as separation, desire, illness and difficulty in writing. For instance, the personified book addressed in *Tristia* 1.1 is stained with 'blots', which are the marks of the poet's tears (1.1.13–14). We are reminded of *Heroides* 3 and Briseis' apology for the blots that her tears make on her epistle to Achilles (3–4), signs of her grief at his abandonment but also of her fears of miscommunication, for the smudges might make her words unreadable. In *Tr.* 3.1, where the personified book itself speaks, blots too are associated with grief and fear of failure in communication. A further fear intrudes into this poem, namely that Ovid's poetry might betray its origins in barbarian territory with slips in its command of Latin and thus, it is implied, be scorned and set aside (15–18). Again Briseis is recalled, apologizing for her difficulty as a barbarian in writing Greek (*Ep.* 3.1–2) – the irony of course being that 'she' writes fluent Latin. Such links with the *Heroides* associate Ovid's new elegiac poetry of exile with elegy's origins in lament. It is thus also characterized as poetry which, like the *Heroides*, attempts to move its recipients with the writer's suffering and persuade them that the writer deserves clemency, or at least a response.

A further strategic development of Ovid's former elegy occurs with the creation of 'the new sub-genre of spousal love poetry,'[24] as the elegiac woman is adapted to the model of 'the good wife' and moved into the sphere of piety and fidelity.[25] Thus, as Ovid once instructed women how to deceive their partners, he now instructs his wife to 'fulfil the role of the good wife' (*Tr.* 4.3.72). Moreover, as he once propositioned an unnamed girl by telling her to give him 'promising material for his poetry' (*Am.* 1.3.19), so now he asks his wife to 'fill his sad [*tristem*] material' with her virtues (*Tr.* 4.3.72–3); and as he promised his unnamed girlfriend worldwide fame through his poetry (*Am.* 1.3.25–6), so too he promises his wife that she will gain great fame – but now by a difficult path (*Tr.* 4.3.74–84). Ovid's wife is never named in the exile poetry, but she seems to have had ties to the imperial household through her probable membership of the distinguished family of Paullus Fabius Maximus, Ovid's patron and a close friend of Augustus;[26] she had access to the empress Livia, who appears in the exile poetry as the primary example of the good wife, a sign of the poet's shift in moral emphasis as well as genre.[27]

The women of the *Heroides* are not his only models in exile. Ovid also represents himself as the epic hero of his exile narrative, and in this regard the Homeric hero Ulysses is his closest analogy. The comparison endows Ovid's exile with epic proportions. Beginning with *Tr.* 1.5.57–84, he claims a detailed likeness: like Ulysses, Ovid faced near death when storm-tossed at sea (on his way to Tomis; see *Tr.* 1.2), and has endured long separation from his native land and loved ones. But Ovid claims even greater suffering and heroic endurance than Ulysses, for the Homeric hero at least had Athena on his side, whereas Ovid has no divine aid (*Tr.* 1.5.76). Moreover, he is not separated from a small, insignificant island like Ithaca, but from Rome, centre of the empire and home of the gods (*Tr.* 1.5.67–70). And Ulysses reached home, unlike Ovid, unless the emperor shows clemency (*Tr.* 1.5.81–4). In the following poem, *Tr.* 1.6, his wife is favourably compared to Penelope as a way of encouraging her to remain loyal. Indeed, Penelope's fame is second to his wife's (21–2), and she would now take first place in his *Heroides* (33–6) were it not that that position is reserved for Livia (23–8).[28]

As Ulysses, Ovid associates himself also with supreme eloquence. Words are the poet's major means of survival, defence and personal glorification.

In his first poem of exile, however, Ovid associates himself with one of the most nefarious myths of Antiquity, that of Oedipus. As we have seen, in *Tr.* 1.1 Ovid personifies his poetry book, which is fortunate, unlike the poet, to be able to travel to Rome and return to Ovid's former home. But when the book is imagined to head for Ovid's bookcases, it is warned that it should avoid the three books that are 'lurking apart in a dark section of the bookcase – as everyone knows these are the very ones that teach how to love' (*Tr.* 1.1.111–12), that is, the *Ars Amatoria*. The poet suggests that if the book has 'enough voice or guts', it should insult these three with the names of Oedipus and Telegonus (*Tr.* 1.1.113–14). As Stephen Hinds points out, the insult is apt, because both Oedipus and Telegonus (son of Ulysses) killed their fathers; just so, the *Ars Amatoria* caused Ovid's exile and cultural death. Ovid here wittily develops the metaphor of the relationship between author and book as that between parent and child. But as Hinds further points out, both Oedipus and Telegonus killed their fathers unwittingly; thus, even as Ovid seems to blame his *Ars*, he also subtly exonerates his poem from the moral charges levelled against it. Ovid works the tragic myth of Oedipus with subtle craft into his personal myth of exile.[29] In addition, we should remember that Oedipus is a figure whose suffering is finally redeemed through his elevation after death in hero cult. Thus Oedipus, 'the swollen footed one', whose deformity, as Hinds argues, signifies troubled elegiacs (with their uneven metrical feet), is also, I suggest, a figure of the immortal triumph of Ovid's poetry.[30]

The exile poetry also interacts closely with Ovid's *Fasti*, which was partly revised in exile, despite Ovid's claim that exile meant a violent rupture of this work (*Tr.* 2.551–2).[31] Like the *Fasti*, the exile poetry is work written under constraint. The opening two lines of the *Tristia* establish some hallmark features that the exile poetry shares with the *Fasti* (*Tr.* 1.1.1–2):

> Little book, you will go to Rome without me, and I don't begrudge you;
>> but I am sorry that your master is not allowed to go.

The Latin word for 'book' is *liber*, which echoes the idea of 'liberty' (Latin *libertas*); the phrase 'is (not) allowed' is pervasive in the *Fasti*, beginning with the proem to Germanicus (1–26) which concludes: 'if is allowed and permitted, as poet guide a poet's reins' (*Fasti* 1.25). The opening lines of *Tr.* 1.1 thus announce the familiar themes of constraints on freedom of speech, coupled now with constraints on the poet's very movements. For whereas the poet of the *Fasti* is concerned with freedom of speech but can roam the city at will, the poet of exile is unhappily rooted in one desolate spot; he can roam freely only in his imagination.

The new gods at Rome

A distinctive feature of the exile poetry is frequent reference to the emperor and his immediate family. Indeed, the exile poetry develops a language of imperial courtship and address that was to influence later post-Augustan writers such as the epigrammatist Martial and the epic poet Statius.[32] *Tr.* 2, a self-defensive poem of 578 lines addressed to Augustus, is a case in point. Although in the opening poem of the *Tristia* Ovid claims that the *Ars Amatoria* is disgraced (*Tr.* 1.1.105–16), he refers to this poem frequently in the exile poetry, and nowhere more so than in *Tr.* 2 where he attempts to exonerate it. Here Ovid acts again as teacher, instructing the emperor on how to read literature in a more open-minded way so that he can place the *Ars* in a broad literary historical context. At lines 361–468 Ovid offers a version of literary history that validates the importance of the erotic in the Greco-Roman literary heritage. The *Ars Amatoria* therefore does not stand out as encouraging adultery but is a culmination and indeed perfection of literary trends present in all major genres.[33] Ovid thus fights the emperor on the grounds he knows best, poetry.[34]

The gods are mentioned frequently in the exile poetry, but they are usually the 'gods' of the imperial family, not the Olympian gods; the latter appear mostly as points of comparison for Augustus and immediate family members. Such divine terminology emphasizes their status as gods-in-waiting.[35] Augustus was worshipped as a god in the East during his lifetime, following Hellenistic practices; but it was not until his death that he was honoured in the West with deification, a process decreed by the Senate that also involved the institution of a cult to the deified emperor.[36] All the same, the 'divine presence' within the living emperor (Latin *numen*) could be addressed and worshipped. Ovid's late poetry thus participates in an ongoing discourse not only about deification per se but also about the language of imperial address. Just as the imperial family was engaged in a continual shaping of its public image, so too writers, most notably Ovid, sought out terminology to describe the new autocratic rulers of Rome.

In addressing the imperial family in his exile poetry, Ovid shows a particular propensity for divine analogies. This is not simply a strategy to curry favour. As we saw in Chapter 4, such comparisons between humans and gods are often unstable and can slip between glorification and accusation. As Denis Feeney aptly comments of the *Metamorphoses*, 'the gods are not [...] neutral ground of praise, nor can the terms of comparison be easily fixed or controlled.'[37] Divine analogies are central to the poet's creation of the narrative of his exile, whereby he is the victim – cruelly punished and misunderstood – of divine power and wrath. In the *Tristia* and *Epistulae ex Ponto* Ovid, ever the supreme narrator, creates a powerful personal myth that connects current political ideology with the representation of the gods in the *Metamorphoses* as powerful beings who frequently abuse their power.

In the exile poetry Augustus is often compared to Jupiter, an analogy that frames the *Metamorphoses* (1.168–76; 199–205; 15.857–60; 15.871–2);[38] in both the epic's opening and conclusion, moreover, Jupiter is characterized by anger. Augustus wished to be remembered for his clemency, as he records in his public testament of his achievements (*Res Gestae* 34.2). Indeed, at *Tr.* 2.33–42 Ovid reminds the emperor that even Jupiter knew when to exercise mercy, and Augustus as his namesake should follow suit.[39] But, conjointly with reminders that clemency befits a ruler, the wrath of Augustus runs through the exile poetry, starting with *Tristia* 1.1.[40] Here, as the earthly counterpart of Jupiter, Augustus hurls from the summit of the Palatine the thunderbolt that causes Ovid's ruin (*Tr.* 1.1.72). Indeed, the poet fears the emperor may strike again (*Tr.* 2.179–80):

> I beg you, hands off your thunderbolt, store away your savage weapons,
> alas, weapons known only too well to wretched me.

Again arguing that his suffering is greater than that of Ulysses, the poet points out that the Homeric hero was crushed by the anger of Neptune, who is second in command to Jupiter, whereas 'the anger of Jupiter' crushes Ovid (*Tr.* 1.5.77–8).

Since Ovid insists that his 'error' was not a 'crime' but a ghastly mistake, at most a 'fault' (*Tr.* 2.104), the cruelty of Augustus/Jupiter in persisting in Ovid's punishment is further emphasized.[41] 'I have been struck by the cruel fires of Jupiter' (*Tr.* 4.3.69), Ovid complains to his wife, and only poetry can save him.[42] As Jennifer Ingleheart points out of *Tristia* 2, Ovid's letter of self-defence to Augustus, there is an unresolved duality in Ovid's representation of Augustus as the poet alludes to the discrepancy between the emperor's roles as beneficent 'father of his country' and as unmerciful, hostile judge of Ovid who has committed the poet to prolonged suffering.[43]

The *Tristia* and *Epistulae ex Ponto* thus participate in the development of imperial ideology, while simultaneously revealing its rich potential for ambiguity. After Augustus' death in 14 CE, his deification is acknowledged in elevated language at *Pont.* 4.9.127–34, and also in *Pont.* 4.6, where Ovid claims he wrote an encomiastic poem celebrating the new god (17–18). Such divine imagery highlights the startling new formations of supreme, autocratic power in Rome, now legitimated by apotheosis. Yet there is a political angle to Ovid's encomiastic language of the deceased Augustus. The relative silence of the exile poetry about the new prominence of Germanicus, and the continuing privileging of Augustus over the new emperor Tiberius, seem to hint at the dynastic strains in the imperial household as well as indicate the strategic difficulties of Ovid's negotiations for recall.[44]

Livia, who plays no role in the *Metamorphoses* or in the *Ars Amatoria* beyond a provocative reference to her Portico as a good place to pick up girls (*Ars* 1.71–2), has a significant place in the *Fasti* and exile poetry.[45] In keeping with the turn in the exile poetry to 'good wives', Livia is praised as an exemplary spouse. Livia was the public face of Augustus' moral legislation on virtuous family life and marriage. As Kristina Milnor points out, women's domestic virtues were regarded by Augustus as inseparable from civic virtue.[46] Yet Livia presented the poet with a particular challenge, for she also transgressed feminine social norms. She had exceptional standing in the state as the wife of Augustus and after 4 CE, with Augustus' adoption of her son Tiberius, as the mother of Augustus' successor; she inherited a third of Augustus' considerable estate on his death.[47] She thus had considerable political and economic power. She used her wealth to engage in the time-honoured masculine system of patronage, bestowing gifts not only at home but in the provinces, where she cultivated relationships with political rulers.[48] Her public visual presence, moreover, was unprecedented. She was the first woman in the history of the West to be depicted systematically in portraits.[49] Indeed, Livia's portraiture defined the imperial female for the next 300 years, presenting an image of calm dignity, propriety and chastity, yet the very fact of her portraiture emphasized her exceptional presence in the traditionally masculine sphere of public life.

Ovid is the first Augustan poet to mention Livia by name, in the notorious reference to her Portico in the *Ars* (1.71–2).[50] She first appears in the exile poetry in *Tr.* 1.6, where, as we saw above, she displaces Ovid's wife and even Penelope herself to claim first place in a new *Heroides* as an exceptional model of the good wife (21–34).[51] Ovid perhaps invents in this poem a new term for Livia, *femina princeps* ('the female *princeps*', *Tr.* 1.6.25; *Pont.* 3.1.125), an oxymoron that indicates her unprecedented role in affairs of state.[52] Indeed, Livia not only usurps the position of Ovid's wife, she also usurps Ovid's role as 'teacher' (*Tr.* 1.6.25–6): 'the female head of state teaches you [i.e. Ovid's wife] the example of a good wife.' She marks the shift in the poet's elegiac identity by directing his poetry to new didactic ends. The married women ostensibly excluded from the readership of the *Ars Amatoria* now take centre stage in the new spousal love poetry of exile.

Yet by granting Livia first place in the 'new' *Heroides*, the poet inserts her into an elegiac discourse of dominance, servitude and gender ambiguity, as we see in *Pont.* 3.1. Here Ovid asks his wife to petition Livia as an intercessor for Augustus. He advises her to accompany her spoken pleas for his pardon with tears, for 'sometimes tears have the weight of words' (*Pont.* 3.1.158). He echoes Briseis' words from the third *Heroides*: 'but tears too have the power of words' (*Ep.* 3.4), when she interrupts her letter to Achilles to ask the Greeks to allow her to make an emotional plea to Achilles in person (127–34). The representation of Ovid's wife as a barbarian slave girl makes her a clever surrogate for her husband who is confined to barbarian territory; it also gives an erotic colour to the scene with Livia, who is thus implicitly gendered as male and as an Achilles figure.

In the exile poetry, the development of a new language of courtly address and petition can be seen as an ironic development of the language of erotic courtship that was demonstrated and taught in Ovid's earlier elegiac poetry.[53] As spouse and empress, Livia stands at the intersection of the new elegy of marital virtue and the former elegy of courtship, now politically attuned to her extraordinary and ambiguous powers. The *Heroides* in particular provide a model here not only for expressing Ovid's feelings of powerlessness and isolation in exile but also for drawing attention to the drastically unequal relationships between subjects and rulers in the imperial hierarchy in Rome. In *Pont.* 3.1 the allusion to Briseis' words depicts the relationship between empress and petitioner as one between owner and slave. As Matthew Roller has shown, Roman public discourse about the principate often used the metaphor of slavery to condemn the dynast who subjected a 'free' Roman citizen to his (or her) dominance.[54] In *Pont.* 3.1 the poet adapts the familiar elegiac metaphor of *servitium amoris* (the slavery of love) to the social context of the imperial court. Disturbingly, powerlessness and fear mark not only the exiled poet but also the Roman subject who has physical access to the court.

But while the metaphor of slavery suggests the seemingly arbitrary power of Livia to grant or reject favours, it also plays upon the gendered ambiguity of her person, here rendered elegiac. In *Pont.* 3.1 the representation of Livia is coloured by the two senses of *domina*, the owner of slaves and the cruel, elegiac mistress. Her ambiguity is enhanced by her subtle association with Achilles, who was famous not only for his great prestige as warrior and for his wrath but also for his transgression of gender norms, having played the part of a woman while in hiding from the war on the island of Scyros – a story told in Ovid's *Ars* (1.681–706), and a popular theme of imperial Roman art.[55] The eroticization of the relationship between the empress and her subjects dramatizes in familiar elegiac terms the injustice and inequality that underpin the outwardly divine splendour of the imperial house – as well as the political and cultural enigma of the new, transgressive phenomenon of 'Livia'.

In *Pont.* 3.1 Livia is also referred to as the goddess Juno (117, 145), and Ovid counsels his wife to prostrate herself at 'the immortal feet' (149–50), a pious, suppliant gesture that is also slavish. The reference to Livia as Juno is a double-edged compliment, for not only did Juno have prestige as Jupiter's wife, in Roman literature she embodied jealousy and anger. She drives the plot of Virgil's *Aeneid* with her deadly passion; in the *Metamorphoses*, on hearing of the terrible death of Actaeon she alone feels joy, so great is her hatred of the Theban family (*Met.* 3.256–9). However, at *Pont.* 3.1.119–25 the poet reassures his wife that Livia is not one of the dangerous women of myth such as Procne, Medea, the Danaids, Clytemnestra, Scylla, Circe or Medusa. Yet by saying who Livia is *not* touches on anxieties of who this exceptional woman might *be*. Myth suggests the elusiveness of Livia's categorization. His wife's immediate petition may fail, yet through the reminder of his *Heroides*, Ovid can emphasize the writer's power to shape and perpetuate reputations, including those of the new gods at Rome: 'If it is permitted to say this, gods too are made by poetry, and their great majesty needs the poet's voice' (*Pont.* 4.8.55–6).

In the exile poetry, Ovid plays with the slippage between positions of power and powerlessness and casts in vivid mythological terms the narrative of his banishment. But it is the story of Actaeon, the hunter punished for seeing the goddess Diana naked, that offered him perhaps the most compelling analogy for his own exilic condition. A striking feature of Ovid's narrative in the *Metamorphoses* (*Met.* 3.131–255) is the emphasis on Actaeon's innocence. From what we can tell of earlier tradition about this myth, Actaeon was a voyeur who planned to see Diana naked;[56] Ovid, however, seems to follow a short, alternative reference to the myth found in Callimachus' *Hymn to Athena* (5.107–18), namely that Actaeon saw Artemis at her bath unintentionally (113–14). In his commentary on Callimachus' *Hymn*, Antony Bulloch points out that in the Greek view, 'intrusion on divine privacy is no less a crime because it is unintentional: the issue is one of a mortal encountering an overwhelming immortal force, not one of morality.'[57] Ovid attempts to counteract this traditional attitude by making Actaeon's punishment very much a question of morality.

That moral slant is emphasized from the start. Unusually, the Actaeon myth in the *Metamorphoses* is prefaced by a form of prologue summarizing the myth and offering an interpretation that emphasizes Actaeon's innocence (*Met.* 3.138–42):

> Amidst so much good fortune, Cadmus, your grandson
> was the first cause for grief, with the alien horns fixed to his brow
> and you, dogs, sated with your master's blood.
> But if you care to investigate, you will not find a crime,
> just a fault of Fortune; for what is criminal about an error?

Ovid inverts the usual structure of an ethical tale by beginning with the moral rather than attaching it to the ending. Moreover, the moral itself represents a further inversion in its insistence on the innocence of the transgressor, for there is no doubt that Actaeon strays into forbidden territory sacred to the goddess of virginity. Ovid, who is often open-ended in his narratives in the *Metamorphoses*, here creates a reciprocal bond with his readers by guiding their response to the myth from its start, as a tale of a man brutally and unjustly punished for an innocent mistake. Diana's angry reaction is swift, but her punishment of Actaeon into a stag is drawn out over 70 lines and is highlighted as extraordinarily cruel and out of proportion to the original offence (186–205). Actaeon's metamorphosis involves transformation into his very opposite – from hunter to hunted, from human to animal, from prosperous prince to lowly, terrified creature of the wilds. His physical transformation is described in meticulous detail, starting with the top of the head as ears become horns, and ending with the covering of the human body in a spotted hide; the process of physical change is completed by the psychological metamorphosis, the planting of fear in Actaeon's heart (*Met.* 3.194–99). He becomes a hybrid creature who retains his human capacity to think but loses his human voice to express his thoughts; he is a man trapped in an animal body (*Met.* 3.201–3):

> 'Alas,' he was about to say, but no voice followed;
> he groaned; that was his voice; tears flowed over a face
> that he did not recognize as his own; only his mind remained as before.

The loss of the human ability to communicate leads to his gruesome death at the jaws of his own hounds.

The physical and cultural alienation of Actaeon, a man trapped in an alien body unable to communicate with the human, social world, has captured the modern imagination. The National Gallery exhibition *Metamorphosis: Titian 2012* made Actaeon's story its central focus. 'Actaeon' is one of the 24 tales selected by the British poet Ted Hughes in his *Tales from Ovid*. His version particularly expands on the horror and violence of Actaeon's death:

> These three pinned their master, as the pack
>
> Poured onto him like an avalanche.
> Every hound filled its jaws
> Till there was hardly a mouth not gagged and crammed
>
> With hair and muscle. Then began the tugging and the ripping.
> Actaeon's groan was neither human
> Nor the natural sound of a stag.[58]

Hughes skilfully manipulates sentence length to describe rapid, then slow and agonizing action. The predominant use of monosyllables and of basic English, not Latinate, diction, represents Actaeon's death as brutal and ignoble, not a death for a great prince of the Theban royal line; the bare language powerfully strips Actaeon to his bodily essentials before our eyes. Hughes focuses on the cruelty and suffering of Actaeon's death. In his painting *The Death of Actaeon*, Titian focuses instead on the power and injustice of the gods. Unlike in the *Metamorphoses*, he brings Diana in for the kill, a gigantic figure with bow and arrow aiming at the helpless, diminutive figure of a semi-metamorphosed Actaeon, already buckling under the weight of his mauling dogs. The landscape is no longer beautiful, as in Ovid's myth, but portrayed as dark and wild. Titian's painting does not portray the psychological drama or inner torment of Actaeon. But the striking physical discrepancy in size between the goddess and the hunter draws attention to the Ovidian theme of the brutal inequity between the gods and humans and their harsh forms of injustice; Actaeon, a prince of the royal line, is a mere disposable speck in the vision of the gods.

In *Tristia* 2 Ovid claims that, like Actaeon, he saw by sheer accident something forbidden (*Tr.* 2.103–8):

> Why did I see something? Why did I inculpate my eyes?
>> Why was I careless about knowing a fault?
> Accidentally Actaeon saw Diana without her clothes;
>> nonetheless he was prey to his own dogs.
> Clearly, where the gods are concerned, you have to pay for bad luck;
>> an accident is no excuse when a divinity is wronged.

This passage has been read as a key to the reasons for Ovid's exile, for it suggests that the poet saw something he should not have. Beyond that, however, is speculation and, as Jennifer Ingleheart cautions, it would be absurd to try to see every detail in the Actaeon myth as analogous to Ovid's own 'crime'.[59] Significantly, however, as at the start of the myth in the *Metamorphoses*, Ovid here emphasizes his own innocence and the accidental nature of his 'crime'. The story of Actaeon was a popular theme of Greek tragedy; in *Tristia* 2 the myth elevates Ovid's fate to a tragic level, evoking sympathy for the fate of a poet who, from great prosperity, ended his days as an outcast on the Roman frontier, trapped in an alien environment that threatened to destroy his very identity. The tragic figure of Actaeon, moreover, implicitly casts the emperor as an unjust deity who has cruelly overreacted to Ovid's accidental transgression.[60] But even as the mythological allusion evokes sympathy for the poet's plight, it is also inscribed with resistance, for Ovid's Actaeon, as he appears in both the *Metamorphoses* and the *Tristia*, differs from a conventional tragic hero in that he is not marked by a fatal flaw in his past or in his character; rather he is guilty only of a mistake.

Actaeon is a potent figure of Ovid's marginalization in exile, for, read through the *Metamorphoses'* particular version, this tragic figure embodies the poet's suffering and his fears surrounding his isolation from human – that is, from Ovid's perspective, Roman – contact and language. Through the Actaeon myth Ovid dramatizes his exile as a form of psychological metamorphosis. Actaeon encapsulates the inner terrors of exile, bringing out the fragility of human identity and of the human voice. There is irony in Actaeon's attempt to cry to his dogs, 'I am Actaeon – know who I am' (*Met.* 3.230), for since he lacks a human voice and outwardly human form, he cannot be 'known'. Actaeon is a hybrid figure who can represent the indeterminate status of Ovid in exile, a Roman citizen with full rights, except the right to live in his native land (*Tr.* 4.9.11–12), and thus without political power; a man trapped in an alien environment struggling to communicate with the Roman world; an urbane figure poised between civility and savagery, innocence and transgression.[61] As Thomas Habinek comments, in exile Ovid describes himself as placed 'in the front line between civilization and barbarism'.[62]

The figure of Actaeon is also a conduit for Ovid's fears of losing his Roman voice, the supreme command of the Latin language which is his main instrument of power in exile. That Ovid's poetry reveals his literary decline may well be a rhetorical strategy of exile, as Gareth Williams has argued.[63] Yet the fear of inferior composition must have been omnipresent for a poet who so prided himself on his art. As Richard Lanham comments, 'Ovid, until the exile at least, seems a cheerful man. Surely it came from the confidence, the instinctive psychological certainty, that only a total control of language can bestow.'[64] In exile the poet worries, for instance, that his own language is now being contaminated by the native Getic (*Tr.* 3.1.15–18). He is more explicit about his fears of linguistic hybridity at *Tr.* 3.14.45–50 (my emphasis):

> Often when I attempt to speak – I am ashamed to confess it,
> > words fail me and I have *unlearned* proper speech.
> I am surrounded by the sound of Thracian and Scythian voices
> > and I think I could write in Getic measures.
> Believe me, I am afraid that Pontic words might be mixed
> > with Latin in my writings.

'Unlearned' is a powerful, rare word for a poet who was heavily vested in 'teaching', particularly in the *Ars Amatoria* where he claimed he knew everything one needed to know about love (*Ars* 1.29): 'follow [the teachings of] the experienced poet.' 'Unlearned' suggests the tragic metamorphosis of the poet not only in speech but in poetic authority and material. But the word also points to the poet's reinvention in exile and reluctant attempt at a degree of cultural assimilation, for later he admits to having composed a kind of hybrid poem, written in the Getic language but with a purely Roman subject, the apotheosis of Augustus and the transfer of power to Tiberius (*Pont.* 4.13.17–38).

Although Rome is represented many times in the exile poetry as his beloved object of desire, sometimes the view from the margins of the empire raises the question of who are the true barbarians. Ovid's local audience for his Getic poem showed their appreciation by nodding, murmuring and rattling their quivers (*Pont.* 4.13.33–6). One of the Geats remarks that Ovid should be restored to favour by the emperor (*Pont.* 4.13.37–8), thus showing that these hard barbarians had more human compassion than the leaders in Rome and, unlike the imperial administrators, were moved to clemency by Ovid's encomiastic poetry.[65]

Over the course of the exile poetry we see some change in the expression of the poet's attitudes to his fate. At the start of the *Tristia* Ovid announces that the tragic change in his life makes him a possible addition to his *Metamorphoses* (*Tr.* 1.1.119–20). But at the start of the *Epistulae ex Ponto* Ovid laments that he cannot even seek the release of metamorphosis, unlike, for example, Niobe and the sisters of Phaethon, the Heliades, who turned respectively into stone and tree and ceased to suffer (*Pont.* 1.2.29–36).[66] In his final words from exile in *Pont.* 4.16 Ovid turns again to the mythological paradigm of Actaeon. At *Met.* 3.237 the poet describes the ghastly scene when the mass of hunting dogs swarm over Actaeon, ripping him so savagely to death that 'now there is no more place for wounds' (*Met.* 3.237); these words are reprised by the plangent final line from Ovid, addressed to hostile critics (*Pont.* 4.16.52): 'I have no place left in me now for a new wound.'[67]

Ovid's final poem, *Pont.* 4.16, is a defence against 'Envy', a personification, as Alessandro Barchiesi suggests, that stands for the envious literary critics and the moralists who have sent Ovid into exile and refused to recall him.[68] The poem begins by claiming that death is not an end to great genius, which survives beyond the grave (1–3). Then comes a roll call of past and present poets for whom this has been or will be true, ending with Ovid's hopes for his own immortal fame (4–46); the modern reader will realize by how slender a margin Ovid's own poetry survived, since the majority of the poets listed are now only names to us. The last line of *Pont.* 4.16 and his last published words from exile, 'I have no place left in me now for a new wound,' return to one of his most notable, poignant characters and his famous epic in order to make a final accusation to the political powers and poetry haters who inflicted on him a cruelly ironic metamorphosis.

A poet who brilliantly captures the tensions and paradox within Ovidian metamorphosis is the contemporary Scottish poet Robin Robertson, a contributor with his poem 'The flaying of Marsyas' to the modern collection of new poems written in response to the *Metamorphoses*, *After Ovid*.[69] His poetry shows a particular fascination with the figure of Actaeon, whose tragic life is explored in three poems across Robertson's poetic career, 'Actaeon: the early years', 'The death of Actaeon' and 'The ghost of Actaeon'.[70] Robertson, who grew up in north-eastern Scotland, transposes Ovid's *Metamorphoses* to a Scottish landscape of the mind and imagination. He is drawn not to Ovidian love but to Ovidian violence. He chooses texts with a relation to his own historical and cultural predicament, writing in standard English that at times is enlivened by striking Scots words. Reacting against the association of classical myth with high culture and the affairs of gods and kings, Robertson adapts Ovidian themes to ordinary lives undergoing extraordinary experiences. In his trilogy of poems based on the myth of Actaeon, the classical hunter is translated to a contemporary northern landscape. Playing against the 'Actaeon' of Ted Hughes' *Tales from Ovid*, Robertson explores the hero's inner consciousness not only at his final moments of transformation and death but also with reference to the early deprivations of childhood. The perennial themes of classical myth are thus renewed with raw psychological energy on Scottish soil.

Robertson's Ovidianism is encapsulated in the title of his 2006 collection, *Swithering*, that is, 'being in a state of flux'. Here, for instance, from 'The death of Actaeon', in *Swithering*, is his rendition of Actaeon's entry into Diana's fateful grove:

Edging into the open,

he saw stillness

and grace, in the space of one heartbeat;

then he saw his own death.

Robertson's poetry differs from Ovid's lush style and achieves some of its notable effects through sparse spacing and use of the monosyllable and the pause. But in this new transformation of one of Ovid's most powerful myths, Robertson conveys the universal truth at the heart of Ovid's great poem on change, namely how swiftly epiphany can turn to slaughter.

But we will not end there. The dramatic intersection of Ovid's powerful mythological fictions with his own life allowed him, though trapped in Tomis, ultimately to control the terms of discourse. Although Ovid's Diana hopes to silence Actaeon by turning him into a stag – 'now say that you saw me without my clothes on – if you can say' (*Met.* 3.192–3), she mocks, as she showers him with her avenging water – the story became one of Ovid's most powerful narratives, told and retold again and again, up to the present time by Robertson, and vividly dramatized in sculpture and painting.[71] The figure of Actaeon therefore is not simply a powerful focus for Ovid's charge that he has been unjustly punished or a riddling symbol of his political 'error'; rather it reveals the complex tensions of exile and the social, cultural and psychological metamorphosis he undergoes in Tomis. Actaeon provides a model for the expression of the inner self and, through the transmission and repetition of his story, he is also a paradigm of literary survival.

Ovid's strategy of memorializing his earlier poetry and his name repeatedly in his work was crucial to their survival. An imperial poet to the end, he relies on an empire-wide readership and its flourishing book trade to preserve his work, along with his own fierce belief in its enduring value.[72] He constantly reminds his readers of his literary greatness and of the blight cast upon Roman culture by the banishment of their most famous poet. As he says at *Tr.* 5.1.10, 'I am the author of my own narrative,' and he is also its hero. In *Tr.* 3.7 he transcends the limits of the Actaeon myth in a recasting of the epilogue to his most famous poem (*Met.* 15.871–9), where he declares his work will survive the 'wrath of Jupiter' and the erosion of time to live on for ever in the mouths of the people. Adapting these last words of his epic to the conditions of exile, he speaks nonetheless with similar pride and confidence in his worldwide fame to a female poet he calls Perilla, and to us, his readers of the future (*Tr.* 3.7.45–52):[73]

> Look at me, though I am deprived of my country, of you, and my home,
>> and all that could be taken from me has been violently seized,
> I still have nonetheless my genius as my companion and my delight;
>> Caesar has no control over that.
> Though someone finishes my life with a cruel sword,
>> my fame will survive my death,
> and as long as Mars' Rome looks out victorious from her seven hills
>> over the entire world, I shall be read.

VII

THE RECEPTION
OF OVID

AS MY RECENT WORK WITH the Wiley Blackwell *Handbook to the Reception of Ovid* showed me, arguably no Roman poet has had such extensive influence on European literature and the arts as has Ovid.[1] I shall attempt in this chapter to highlight major moments in the history of the reception of Ovid's poetry. Since, inevitably, my discussions must be partial, my main emphases will be the Middle Ages and the subsequent English literary tradition. However, the story begins with the first century CE. Although both the Middle Ages and our own times have been called *Aetas Ovidiana*, the 'Ovidian age', that designation could also apply to the century following Ovid's death, for in this period particular strategies of reading Ovid developed that were to influence his later reception.[2]

Although generally classified as an Augustan poet, Ovid's poetry exhibits many tendencies that were developed in post-Augustan writers of the first century CE, who in turn influenced writers of the Middle Ages and Renaissance. After Ovid, the genre of epic was profoundly altered. Although the imperial epics of the Neronian poet Lucan and the Flavian poets Silius Italicus, Statius and Valerius Flaccus returned to martial themes, they owe much to the stylistic, structural and thematic emphases of Ovid's *Metamorphoses*.[3] For instance, Ovid developed the role of personification in epic.[4] In the *Metamorphoses* personifications of Envy (2.760–82), Hunger (8.799–808), Sleep (11.592–632) and 'Fama' ('Rumour', 12.39–63) are given not only human form and character but also dwellings that graphically realize their nature. Hunger, a grotesque figure of starvation with swollen joints, scabrous skin and hollow belly – 'she had a space for a stomach where a stomach should be' (8.805) – inhabits a barren landscape where she scratches the earth for bare sustenance; she personifies hunger as a state of lack and want. This innovative use of personification was expanded further in Statius' *Thebaid* (published 92 CE), where personifications play a major part in the epic action.[5] This development led to the emergence of allegorical epic in the late fourth century with Prudentius' *Psychomachia*, a Christian poem of battling Virtues and Vices.[6] In English literature Chaucer's goddess 'Fame' in *The House of Fame* is a direct descendant of Ovid's 'Fama'; the culmination of this allegorical trend is Spenser's *Faerie Queene*.[7] Likewise Ovid's emphasis throughout his poetry on female experience and voice becomes an important feature of imperial epic and the medieval transmutation of epic into vernacular romance.[8] Imperial panegyric as well, which emerges as a key element of the *Metamorphoses* in its final book, becomes a standard, if controversial topos of imperial epic.[9]

The most Ovidian of the imperial epics is Statius' fragmentary *Achilleid*, which plays on themes of the instability of gender and human identity with its central plot of Achilles' unconventional education. First he was raised by the centaur Chiron, who taught him the arts of war and peace; then he hid on the island of Scyros, disguised by his mother as a young woman in order to avoid his fated death at Troy. On Scyros he learned social arts and also fell in love. The narrative opposition between love and war reflects the poem's generic tensions between elegy and epic.[10] This text became a staple of the medieval classroom.[11] Thus important features of post-Augustan epic introduced by Ovid's *Metamorphoses* re-emerge later in a variety of forms through the chain of Roman imperial reception.

Ovid's elegiac poetry also took on new life in the first century, particularly, as was mentioned in Chapter 6, in the occasional poetry of Statius (*c*.45–96 CE) and Martial (*c*.41–103 CE), who drew on Ovid's development of a language of courtly address and of a poetry of social occasion.[12] In his epigrams Martial, an astute reader of Ovid's amatory poetry, often makes its eroticism sexually explicit.[13] Martial also responds to the reinstitution of Augustan-style moral legislation in Flavian Rome and to the *Ars Amatoria* by illustrating a moral relativism that lacks, however, Ovid's authoritative didacticism.[14] A satirical reference in one of Martial's epigrams to 'all the would-be Virgils and Ovids of his day shivering in their cloaks' (3.38.9–10) emphasizes the canonical status and popularity of these two poets in the late first century. And such remained the case through the period of late Antiquity and into the medieval Christian era.[15]

Ovid was one of the most widely read authors in the Middle Ages and Renaissance.[16] He appears in multiple guises: as a moralizing figure, a teacher of courtly love, an authority on the history of the world and an example of tragic error.[17] His elegiac works as well as his *Metamorphoses* were important school texts for teaching eloquent Latin style and also crucibles for the rise of medieval Latin and vernacular lyric and romance.

We have no ancient 'Life' of Ovid as we do for Virgil. Yet, fostered by Carolingian interest in the works of Ovid, the medieval manuscript and commentary tradition for Ovid is extensive.[18] Beginning from the eleventh century, the *accessus* attached to Ovid's works and commentaries – that is, introductory, biographical sketches of the poet with interpretive comments suggesting the useful lessons to be learned from the work – provide insight into medieval reading practices.[19] They endorse the reading of Ovid by bringing out the apparently hidden moral meaning in his poetry, including the elegies. Inevitably perhaps, the exile poetry was introduced as a warning about Ovid's mistakes. The *Amores* circulated in the Middle Ages under the rubric '*sine titulo*' (without title); commentators suggested that Ovid feared to give the work a title that advertised its erotic content.[20] The *Ars Amatoria*, however, remained popular as a school text for teaching ethical conduct. The one surviving copy of the *Ars Amatoria* from tenth-century England (Book 1 only) is included in a manuscript of Christian homilies and grammatical texts whose frontispiece shows a figure of Christ with the saintly compiler at his feet.[21] The *Heroides* were core pedagogical texts which provided both a model of eloquence and a moral warning of the perils of sexual desire.[22] In some instances they were regarded as authentic historical documents; in the thirteenth and fourteenth centuries vernacular translations of the *Heroides* were inserted into historical texts, used as documentary evidence for the Trojan War and of female experience.[23] Their study in schools as performative texts also contributed to the rise of the medieval lyric tradition and the development of the first-person female voice in poetry.[24] The scholastic tradition thus fed into the flourishing of vernacular literature.

To start first with elegy, Ovid's love poetry made available a language of desire as *amor* became a cultural and courtly ideal, expressed in a range of vernacular poetry. The most ambitious expression of that ideal, perhaps, was the *Roman de la Rose*, the French thirteenth-century allegorical romance begun by Guillaume de Lorris and continued by Jean de Meun. This lengthy poem was influenced by Ovid's teachings in the *Ars* as well as by the *Metamorphoses*.[25] Desmond argues that 'Ovidian eroticism was critical to the formation of poetic subjectivities, particularly feminine subjectivities, in medieval vernaculars'.[26] This included the appearance of women authors such as the French writer Christine de Pizan (1364–*c*.1430), who engages polemically with Ovidian myth throughout her works;[27] and, in the early twelfth century Héloïse, whose letters between herself and the philosopher Peter Abelard are modelled on Ovid's *Heroides*.[28] But Ovid's poetry also set the precedent for male writing about the self. As we have seen, more than any other Roman poet Ovid carefully fashioned a literary monument of himself in his writings, particularly the exile poetry where he addresses both a contemporary audience and posterity. Thus Gur Zak has argued that Ovid's defensive self-portrait influenced Peter Abelard's account of his life and downfall, *Historia Calamitatum* ('History of his calamities', *c*.1132).[29] Like Ovid, his self-representation is directed not to an apology for his mistakes but to glorifying his abilities and achievements and claiming his innocence.

Abelard's *Historia* is an early example of the revival of the Ovidian self-portrait in the later medieval period. In fourteenth-century Italy Petrarch (1304–74) used Ovid's *Tr.* 4.10 as the departure point for his self-analytical 'Letter to posterity'.[30] But Petrarch's greatest debt to the Augustan poet was in his revitalization of Ovid's first-person elegiac poetry in his vernacular *Rime*

Sparse, a sequence of songs and sonnets about an unattainable woman, Laura. Her name, however, also takes us to Ovid's *Metamorphoses*, for it evokes Daphne, transformed into a laurel tree (*Met.* 1.452–567).[31] Petrarch's poems respond to Ovid's erotic elegy in their articulation of frustrated desire, situated, however, in a moralized rhetoric of constancy to one woman; Petrarch expels the libertine Ovid from his love poetry.[32] Catherine Keen has shown that Ovid's exile poetry, which was well known from the Carolingian period, influenced Italian poets during the period of political instability between the twelfth and the fourteenth century, among them Dante and Petrarch.[33] But as she argues, in his lyric poetry Petrarch gives a new, non-Ovidian turn to the theme of exile by embracing isolation and solitude and rejecting the city as corrupt.[34]

The *Metamorphoses* remained popular throughout the Christian Middle Ages as a great encyclopedia of ancient knowledge. Two interpretive traditions coexisted throughout the Middle Ages: the mythographic, which provided summaries of Ovid's stories, and the allegorical, beginning with Fulgentius in the sixth century.[35] The culmination of the latter tradition was the French anonymous *Ovide moralisé* ('The moralized Ovid') of the early fourteenth century, which offered a commentary on Ovid's myths that was six times the length of the Latin poem.[36] Later in the same century the French Benedictine Petrus Berchorius (Pierre Bersuire) produced in Latin his own shorter, moralized Ovid (*Ovidius Moralizatus*), which paraphrased Ovid's myths and offered multiple interpretations of them for use in sermons. For example, in the Apollo and Daphne story Apollo represents the Devil and Daphne the Christian soul that flees vice; or, allegorically, Daphne is the cross and Apollo is Christ, 'the sun of righteousness'.[37] The use of Ovid's pagan fables for Christian devotional instruction was a radical transformation not only of the *Metamorphoses* but of the image of the poet Ovid.

In fourteenth-century England the two great Ovidians were Geoffrey Chaucer (*c*.1343–1400) and John Gower (*c*.1330–1408).[38] Both were influenced by Ovid directly and as relayed through the French, Italian and Latin traditions of Jean de Meun, Guillaume Machaut, Petrarch, Boccaccio and the moralized Ovids. In the *Confessio Amantis*, a poem in the didactic and consolatory tradition of Ovid's *Remedia Amoris*, Gower uses a range of stories drawn from the *Metamorphoses* and the *Fasti* as moralizing warnings of the perils of sexual desire. Chaucer's unfinished poem *The Legend of Good Women*, on the other hand, is Chaucer's *Heroides*, in that the poem is conceived as an apology to Cupid for speaking ill of women in his *Troilus and Criseyde*; most of the women are introduced as 'martyrs' (of love). Chaucer's legend of Philomela, for example, omits the sisters' terrible revenge and ends with Philomela's rescue. With a deliberate understatement Chaucer drolly comments, 'the remenaunt is no charge for to telle' (2383). At the end of the legend of Dido Chaucer refers explicitly to the seventh *Heroides*, Dido's letter to Aeneas, when he directs the external reader to 'rede Ovyde, and in hym he shal it fynde' (1367).[39] Here and in the *House of Fame* (239–382), Chaucer's Dido demonstrates the powerful influence of Ovid's Dido on subsequent readings of Virgil's poem in the Middle Ages.[40] Chaucer also draws extensively on the *Metamorphoses*: in the *Book of the Duchess* with the tale of Ceyx and Alcyone (*Met*. 11.379–748), and in the *Legend of Good Women* with the tales of Pyramus and Thisbe (*Met*. 4.55–166) and Philomela (*Met*. 6.424–674). The Manciple's tale in the *Canterbury Tales* retells Ovid's story of Apollo and the crow (*Met*. 2.549–95).[41] In the Wife of Bath's prologue, as Desmond has shown, Chaucer turns to medieval, ethical interpretations of the *Ars Amatoria*.[42] For Chaucer, Ovid is primarily the poet of love:

> Venus clerk Ovide
> that hath ysowen wonder wide
> the grete god of Loves name (*House of Fame*, 1487–9)

Turning now to England in the sixteenth and seventeenth centuries, we see a tremendous surge of interest in Ovid among poets, dramatists and translators. The libertine Ovid and the shape-shifting Ovid return to centre stage, although the influence of the moral Ovid continues to be felt. The first major Ovidian poet of the Elizabethan age is Edmund Spenser (*c*.1552–99).[43] As Philip Hardie observes, Spenser often combines imitation of Ovid with imitation of the Ovidian tradition. Thus his most famous work, *The Faerie Queene*, bears the weight of the entire allegorical tradition. Nevertheless, the poem is 'a tour de force of metamorphic imagining'.[44] Moreover, 'Ovid inhabits the morally ambiguous zones' of the poem, as Ovidian sexuality, including its treacherous landscapes of desire, plays a central role in the poem's dialectic between chastity and eroticism.[45] As Maggie Kilgour argues, Spenser's allegorical epic owes much also to Ovid's *Fasti*, particularly in its vision of time.[46] Spenser's *The Shepheardes Calendar* draws upon the tradition of the poetic calendar, Ovid's *Fasti*. It also interacts with contemporary humanist culture in which poetic calendars, using Ovid's *Fasti* as a political, calendrical model, played a part in contemporary religious conflicts.[47] Indeed, the influence of the *Fasti* on the early modern period was pervasive. Shakespeare knew the *Fasti*, as we see from his narrative poem *The Rape of Lucrece*, which is based on Ovid's *Fasti* 2.685–852,[48] while one of the most famous paintings of the Italian Renaissance, Botticelli's *Primavera*, illustrates the seduction of Flora in *Fasti* 5.195–212, and melds Ovid's calendar poem with his epic by depicting Flora's metamorphosis into a goddess.[49]

In his plays Shakespeare departs from the learned tradition and puts Ovid on stage before a popular audience. He draws repeatedly on Ovidian themes and plots.[50] For instance, Ovid's tale of Pyramus and Thisbe inspired both the tragedy of star-crossed lovers, *Romeo and Juliet*, and the comedy of the 'rude mechanicals', complete with walk-on parts for the Wall and the Moon, in *A Midsummer Night's Dream*. The *Metamorphoses* is explicitly acknowledged as a source for tragic violence in *Titus Andronicus*. Lavinia, a noble woman who has been raped and mutilated by the loss of both tongue and hands, shows what has happened to her by using a stick in her mouth to point to the tale of Procne, Philomela and Tereus in a text of the *Metamorphoses* (*Titus* 4.1.30–60). In the late play *Cymbeline*, another vulnerable young woman sleeps with a copy of the *Metamorphoses* open to that story by her bedside (2.2.44–6). Shakespeare is the most metamorphic of playwrights. In *The Winter's Tale* a statue comes to life;[51] in *A Midsummer Night's Dream* the queen Titania falls in love with an asinine labourer; in *The Tempest* a magician rules an island realm through the power of metamorphosis. In general, Shakespeare's plays offer a panoply of disguises and constant gender play. Particular attention has focused also on Shakespeare's educational background and on the Elizabethan classroom, where Ovid was a staple Latin poet.[52] Shakespeare would have been introduced to Ovid through school Latin texts, but he also had available the first English translation of the *Metamorphoses* by Arthur Golding.

Translation of Ovid's works into English was key to the revitalization of English poetry.[53] William Caxton, printer and publisher, produced a late-Middle English translation of the *Metamorphoses* around 1480, using however a French prose source that was based on the *Ovide moralisé*.[54] Arthur Golding's *Ovid's Metamorphoses* (1567) was the first complete English translation of Ovid's Latin epic. Written in popular 'fourteener' couplets, it is a key work of early modern English literature in its influence on contemporary poets and dramatists, including Shakespeare.[55] Golding's was the definitive translation of Ovid's epic until George Sandys' translation of 1626, composed in the new colony of Virginia; Sandys published a second edition in 1632, this time with notes, commentary and illustrations. Golding 'Englishes' Ovid by the use of 'fourteener' couplets, a popular ballad metre, and by vernacular details such as the transformation of King Midas' 'mitre' into a 'nightcap'; Sandys, on the other hand, offers a Latinate version in rhyming pentameter couplets, although he adds some contemporary details from the New World. Sandys monumentalized the English *Metamorphoses* and showed that Ovid was a major part of the literary canon for contemporary English writers.[56]

Of Ovid's elegiac works, the *Heroides* were translated by George Turberville in 1567, the same year as Golding's complete translation of the *Metamorphoses*.[57] The first translation of the *Amores*, by Christopher Marlowe, was published posthumously around 1599, though it was probably known earlier in manuscript form. His translation offered a lyric persona radically different from the Petrarchan model of the constant lover, that of the libertine, an influential figure on seventeenth-century English poets from Donne to Rochester.[58] When Marlowe's *Amores* was first published, copies were burned by episcopal edict, as the work was considered scandalous, but it had 'great impact on the late-Elizabethan literary scene'.[59] While there were several sixteenth-century translations of the *Remedia Amoris*, the *Ars Amatoria* remained underground; a translation by Thomas Heywood, his

Loves Schoole, was published abroad in Amsterdam around 1625, and it was through pirated copies that his book reached England. After the English Restoration it was reprinted frequently.[60]

The complete exile poetry and the *Fasti* were not translated until the seventeenth century, possibly in response to the current political instability, when England was on the eve of civil war.[61] The *Fasti* was first translated into English as *Roman Festivalls* by a rather obscure scholar and poet, John Gower, in 1640. The translation was workmanlike but ambitious, and seems designed as an intervention in contemporary discussions of monarchical authority.[62] Three books of the *Tristia* were published by the occasional poet Thomas Churchyard in 1572, but the complete exile works were published in the period just before the civil war, when many prominent men and families were forced into exile.[63] The *Tristia* and the *Ex Ponto* by Wye Saltonstall, 'not a particularly distinguished poet', appeared in English in 1633 and 1639 respectively.[64]

Although seventeenth-century translations of the elegiac Ovid lacked distinction, Heather James has shown how deeply the poetry of Ben Jonson (*c.*1572–1637) was indebted to Ovid's elegiac poetry.[65] Not only does Ovid play a major, if controversial role in Jonson's play *Poetaster* (1601),[66] his exile poems offered Jonson a model for court poetry and for finding a language of counsel and dissent, as well as praise on moral and political themes. Ovid's grief in exile and his anxieties about bodily and mental change also spoke to Jonson's spiritual exile as a Catholic in Protestant England. As James comments, Jonson admired Ovid for his 'commitment to the liberties of verse and speech'.[67]

In *Poetaster* Jonson portrays the character Ovid as an overreacher, like Phaethon and Icarus in the *Metamorphoses*, who aim beyond their limits and suffer a tragic fall.[68] The violent overreacher is a popular figure in Renaissance drama: Shakespeare's character Macbeth is of this type, as is Christopher Marlowe's Faustus. One of the most poignant moments in *Dr Faustus* occurs when the hero, on the eve of his perpetual damnation, cries out a line from Ovid's *Amores* (1.13.40): '*lente, lente, currite, noctis equi*' (slowly, slowly run, horses of the night). Marlowe here adapts to a startlingly different context Ovid's desire for a longer time in bed with his mistress. In

'The sun rising', the metaphysical poet John Donne (1572–1631) makes a richly metaphorical, yet deeply personal poem about love from Ovid's same poem. Donne's 'The flea' brilliantly plays in Ovidian, paradoxical vein upon themes of love, sexual desire and generic inversion within the Latin tradition of the 'animal poem'.

John Milton's early Latin poetry was heavily influenced by Ovid. Ovid too permeates *Paradise Lost*, notably its treatments of Eve and Satan.[69] Thus, whether through the Latin text, through translation or through literary tradition, Ovid's poetry profoundly enriched English literature. This too was the age of the great European painters of Ovid, Titian, Poussin and Velázquez among them. In sculpture Giovanni Bernini created in the early 1620s great masterpieces of Ovidian art, his *Daphne and Apollo*, and his *Pluto and Persephone*. These brilliant works of statuary display an Ovidian paradox by their metamorphosis of Ovid's narratives into stone, while conveying the illusion of living, breathing, passionate forms.[70]

But an ambivalence about Ovid's poetry that was not merely moral but also stylistic affected the poet's reputation in the next century. True, the next major translation of the *Metamorphoses* after Sandys' appeared in 1717, a collective enterprise masterminded by Samuel Garth that assembled translations by the leading poets of the day, including John Dryden. But Dryden himself did not fully embrace Ovid's poetics. In the Preface to *Fables, Ancient and Modern* (1700), he castigated Ovid's wit as often unseasonable and unmanly, although he admired his eloquence and dramatic power.[71] In an interesting development in cultural history, however, Ovid's treacherous, mutable landscapes of desire became domesticated as early modernity adopted an Ovidian aesthetic in garden and landscape design for its great country houses.[72] As in gardens, so in poetry Ovidian 'excess' could be smoothed away according to prevailing standards of taste.

An exception, however, was Ovid's *Heroides*, whose popularity and prestige were at their height in the eighteenth century, possibly because they were thought to represent authentic female experience and sentiments; moreover, they appealed to the vastly increased number of female readers.[73] They influenced the development of the epistolary novel and spurred a tradition of verse letters written in the voices of historical or pseudo-historical characters. For example, letters between an Amerindian slave and her European lover, 'Yarico to Inkle', reflect the Ovidian epistle's concern with injustice, but directed now at slavery.[74]

The nineteenth century is generally regarded as a period when Ovid's reputation was at its lowest. The Romantic revolution made satire and irony out of fashion, as painters and poets immersed themselves in passion and nature and turned to the Greeks for aesthetic models. Unlike his contemporary Pre-Raphaelites, who were drawn to medieval and classical Greek models, John Waterhouse (1847–1917), however, was influenced by classical myth, especially Ovid, and painted several Ovidian narratives such as Echo and Narcissus, Apollo and Daphne, Thisbe, and Flora and the Zephyr (from the *Fasti*). In France the academic painter Jean-Léon Gérôme (1824–1904), contemporary of the Impressionists, painted with photographic realism various stages in the Pygmalion myth.[75] Although there is no single English author of the nineteenth century as influenced by Ovid as was, for instance, Shakespeare in the sixteenth century or Milton in the seventeenth, arguably the development of the dramatic monologue in, for instance, Browning's poetry (such as 'My last duchess'), and the abandoned women of Tennyson's poetry, such as Mariana and Oenone in the poems of that name, or 'the lady of Shalott' would be unthinkable without the precedent of Ovid's *Heroides* as mediated particularly by the development of that genre in the previous century.[76]

Ovid has proved particularly congenial to our own self-questioning age, which has capitalized on the creative, transgressive impulses inherent in metamorphosis. As we saw in Chapter 6, Ovid's frequent allusions to his immortality in his poetry have stimulated modern poets and novelists to create new afterlives for Ovid, focused on his period of exile, though also influenced by his pervasive themes of metamorphosis and human sexuality.[77] In particular Ovid's poetry underwent generic transformation in the novel, which, along with film, could be considered the 'epic' of our time.[78] Modern novelists have responded to Ovid's depiction of a world where all things are in flux, where shape-shifters of all sorts abound, where anything can be possible; a world, however, also of surveillance and injustice – a world in short like our own but vividly and magically rendered.

In the visual arts, Ovid's mythic imagination has been liberated from the 'Old Masters' and expressed in a variety of provocative forms that reflect on the pleasures and fears of our age. In the 1930s, for instance, the feminist artist 'Madame Yevonde' (aka Yevonde Middleton) challenged the tradition of 'Old Masters' with her photographs of society women posing as goddesses from classical myth and the *Metamorphoses*, including a provocative 'Europa' and the bull (*Met.* 2.836–75). In the same decade Salvador Dalí painted his enigmatic *Metamorphosis of Narcissus* (*Met.* 3.339–510). In 2002 Anish Kapoor's installation in the Tate Modern – enormous red, PVC tubing of 'Marsyas', epic in scale – gave brutal, imagistic expression to Ovid's violent myth of a satyr flayed alive by Apollo, earlier painted with graphic realism by Titian (*Met.* 6.382–400).[79] In the modern, global era Ovid's poetry has shown its resilience by its adaptability to different media, by its perennial themes of human cruelty, injustice and erotic desire, and by its endless capacity for change.

To return to poetry, in *After Ovid: New Metamorphoses*, edited by Michael Hofmann and James Lasdun (London: 1994), contemporary poets aimed to modernize Ovid's narratives in the light of current poetic practices.[80] Although Ted Hughes' *Tales from Ovid* (1997) used a variety of poetic forms for his renditions of myths from the *Metamorphoses*, he presented a consistent view of Ovid as a tormented soul, rather like Fränkel's 'poet between two worlds'.[81] Hughes finds closure, however, by abandoning Ovid's chronology and ending with the tale of Pyramus and Thisbe, true lovers joined in death.[82] Like Hughes, Mary Zimmerman, in her award-winning play *Metamorphoses*, first performed in 1996 and on Broadway by 2001, selected stories that convey the overall message of love's indomitable power; the play ends with the tale of the pious couple, Baucis and Philemon (*Met.* 8.611–724). The effect of Zimmerman's selectivity is somewhat anodyne, lacking for the most part Ovidian irony or the persistent idea of universal flux.[83]

Carol Ann Duffy's poem 'Mrs Midas' (from her anthology *The World's Wife*, 1999) offers a refreshing, modern rewriting of the *Heroides*, where women talk back to literary tradition, here to the dominance of the *Metamorphoses*. In Ovid's version of the story, Midas is a king without a wife

(*Met.* 11.85–193). Duffy's Mrs Midas, a contemporary housewife, describes in a dramatic monologue how, when she was home making supper one ordinary evening, the extraordinary happened, namely the transformation of everything her husband touched to gold. Nonetheless, though terrified, 'I served up the meal. For starters, corn on the cob. / Within seconds he was spitting out the teeth of the rich.' Later, having separated from her dangerous and selfish husband, Mrs Midas finds herself sometimes filled with regret. The poem ends, 'I miss most, / even now, his hand, his warm hands on my skin, his / touch.' Duffy appropriates Ovidian myth for a contemporary feminine voice, eschewing the original tale's aristocratic context but maintaining her own Ovidian touch: the ability to integrate the miraculous into the everyday, and with wit.

Jeremy Dimmick perhaps best sums up the complex, transformative nature of Ovid's reception as 'a rich and complex network of readings, claims, counter-appropriations, repudiations and retractions, in which Ovid's works never ceased to strive'.[84] His reference is to the Middle Ages, but it could equally be to our present.

NOTES

I. OVID IN THE THIRD MILLENNIUM AND THE FIRST

1   See Ingo Gildenhard and Andrew Zissos (eds), *Transformative Change in Western Thought: Metamorphosis from Homer to Hollywood* (London, 2013), who argue that Ovid's *Metamorphoses* is a seminal text for the history of ideas.

2   Charles Martindale, *Latin Poetry and the Judgement of Taste: An Essay in Aesthetics* (Oxford, 2005), pp. 200–1.

3   Hermann Fränkel, *Ovid: A Poet between Two Worlds* (Berkeley and Los Angeles, CA, 1945). See the brilliant rebuttal of Ovidian 'shallowness' by Stephen Hinds, 'Generalising about Ovid', *Ramus* 16 (1987), pp. 4–31.

4   Ted Hughes, *Tales from Ovid* (London, 1997). On Ovid's extensive use of tragic sources in the *Metamorphoses* see Dan Curley, *Tragedy in Ovid* (Cambridge, 2013).

5   Peter Knox, 'The poet and the second prince: Ovid in the age of Tiberius', *Memoirs of the American Academy in Rome* 49 (2004), pp. 1–20.

6   Strictly speaking, Ovid was 'relegated', not 'exiled'; according to Roman law, this meant that he kept the rights of a Roman citizen with control over his property and wealth, while being banished from Rome. See *Tr.* 4.9.11–12: 'in case you don't know, Caesar left me all my rights; my sole punishment is to lose my native land.'

7   The classic investigation into the reasons for Ovid's exile remains John C. Thibault, *The Mystery of Ovid's Exile* (Berkeley, CA, 1964).

8   See Jennifer Ingleheart, *A Commentary on Ovid, Tristia Book 2* (Oxford, 2010) on *Tr.* 2.207. That the poem was the *Ars Amatoria* seems confirmed by lines 211–12: 'having composed a disgraceful poem, I am accused of being a teacher of disgusting adultery.'

9   See Katharina Volk, *Ovid* (Oxford, 2010), pp. 122–7, for recent novels about Ovid's exile.

10 Ovid may have been influenced by the intertwining of discontinuity and continuity in the schematic structure of Book 4 of Propertius. See Gregory Hutchinson, *Propertius Elegies Book 4* (Cambridge, 2006), pp. 16–21.

11 On the chronology of Ovid's works see James C. McKeown, *Ovid: Amores*, vol. i (Liverpool, 1987), pp. 74–89.

12 On the 'preface' to the *Amores* see Francesca K. A. Martelli, *Ovid's Revisions* (Cambridge, 2013), pp. 35–8.

13 Alessandro Barchiesi and Philip Hardie, 'The Ovidian career model: Ovid, Gallus, Apuleius, Boccaccio', in Philip Hardie and Helen Moore (eds), *Classical Literary Careers and Their Reception* (Cambridge, 2010), pp. 59–88, p. 59.

14 See Seneca the Elder (*c.*54 BCE–*c.*39 CE), *Contr.* 2.8, 2.12; Quintilian (*c.*35–*c.*100 CE), *Inst.* 10.1.88.

15 On Ovid's scrupulous editorial practices see Martelli, *Ovid's Revisions*.

16 See the discussion of E. J. Kenney (ed.), *Heroides XVI–XXI* (Cambridge, 1996), pp. 20–6.

17 Quintilian, *Inst.* 8.5.6 = Ovid, *Medea* fr.1; Seneca, *Suas.* 3.7 = Ovid, *Medea* fr. 2. See Curley, *Tragedy in Ovid*, pp. 19–58.

18 For commentaries in English see Adrian S. Hollis (ed.), *Ars Amatoria Book I* (Oxford, 1977); Roy K. Gibson (ed.), *Ars Amatoria Book 3* (Cambridge, 2003).

19 Charlotte Higgins, *Latin Love Lessons: Put a Little Ovid in Your Life* (London, 2007).

20 On Augustus' moral legislation see Chapter 2.

21 See Victoria Rimell, *Ovid's Lovers: Desire, Difference and the Poetic Imagination* (Cambridge, 2006), ch. 1.

22 Cf. *Tr.* 2.549–52, where Ovid speaks enigmatically of having 'written' the full 12 months. Critics have generally taken this to mean that the second half existed in draft, not yet in publishable form; Ingleheart, *Tristia 2* on *Tr.* 2.549–50, prefers the argument that the poem was complete but that Ovid refused to release the second half, with its two prominent Caesarean months, July and August.

23 Barchiesi and Hardie, 'The Ovidian career model', p. 62.

24 On the chronology of the exile works see Ronald Syme, *History in Ovid* (Oxford, 1978), pp. 37–47. There is debate over whether the poems in Book 4 of the *Epistulae ex Ponto* were collected and published posthumously; Niklas Holzberg, *Ovid: The Poet and His Work*, tr. G. M. Goshgarian (Ithaca, NY, 2002), pp. 193–6, makes the attractive case that this final book was planned by Ovid as the culminating sequel to his exile poetry. On the *Ibis* see Gareth Williams, *The Curse of Exile: A Study of Ovid's Ibis* (Cambridge, 1996); Darcy Krasne, 'The pedant's curse: obscurity and identity in Ovid's *Ibis*', *Dictynna* 9 (2012), pp. 1–42.

25 See further Chapter 6.

26 Philip Hardie, *Ovid's Poetics of Illusion* (Cambridge, 2002), p. 15. As Hardie points out (pp. 27–9), Ovid's 'illusionistic poetics of presence' makes his work particularly amenable to post-structuralist criticism in particular.

27 Niklas Holzberg, 'Playing with his life: Ovid's autobiographical references', in Peter Knox (ed.), *Oxford Readings in Ovid* (Oxford, 2006), pp. 51–68, p. 52.

28 See Maria Wyke, 'Mistress and metaphor in Augustan elegy', *Helios* 16 (1989), pp. 25–47.

29 Hinds, 'Generalising about Ovid', pp. 4–11.

30 Ibid., pp. 6–8.

31 See Paul Allen Miller's discussion of this poem, 'What's love got to do with it?', in Karen Weisman (ed.), *The Oxford Handbook of the Elegy* (Oxford, 2010), pp. 46–66, pp. 62–4.

32 Derek Mahon, *Selected Poems* (London, 1991), p. 77.

33 Ellen Greene, *The Erotics of Domination* (Baltimore, MD, 1998), pp. 77–84.

34 See Alison Keith, 'The *domina* in Roman elegy', in Barbara Gold (ed.), *A Companion to Roman Love Elegy* (Oxford, 2012), pp. 285–302, pp. 297–9.

35 Joan Booth, 'Negotiating with the epigram in Latin love elegy', in Alison Keith (ed.),

Latin Elegy and Hellenistic Epigram: A Tale of Two Genres at Rome (Newcastle, 2011), pp. 51–65, p. 63.

36   The description of Corinna's body is based on a Greek epigram of the late Republic by Philodemus, *AP* 5.132. See Booth, 'Negotiating with the epigram'.

37   McKeown, *Amores*, vol. i, p. 21.

38   See Stephen Hinds, 'Martial's Ovid/Ovid's Martial', *Journal of Roman Studies* 97 (2007), pp. 113–54, pp. 122–3.

39   After incurring Augustus' wrath when he held political office, Gallus committed suicide; only a few lines of his work remain. He was revered by the other Latin elegists, and also by Virgil, who devotes his tenth *Eclogue* to Gallus.

40   On Latin elegy's reversal of gendered power relations see Sharon James, *Learned Girls and Male Persuasion: Gender and Reading in Roman Love Elegy* (Berkeley and Los Angeles, CA, 2003), pp. 12–13. On the distinctions between Ovid and the earlier elegists see Joan Booth, 'The *Amores*: Ovid making love', in *Blackwell Companion*, pp. 61–77.

41   As Barbara Boyd, *Ovid's Literary Loves* (Ann Arbor, MI, 1997), p. 89, comments, the *Amores* are characterized by 'multiple allusions' that allow Ovid to break free from readers' expectations and traditions.

42   Booth, 'The *Amores*', p. 76.

43   Gian Biagio Conte argues that Cupid should not be entirely appeased by Ovid's words. See 'Love without elegy', in his *Genres and Readers*, tr. Glenn W. Most (Baltimore, MD, 1994), pp. 57–8. Richard Tarrant, 'Ovid and the failure of rhetoric', in Doreen Innes, Harry Hine and Christopher Pelling (eds), *Ethics and Rhetoric: Classical Essays for Donald Russell* (Oxford, 1995), pp. 63–74, argues that generally the speeches in Ovid's poetry that are persuasive in character are in fact failures or deceptive in various ways; see for instance p. 65 on *Am.* 1.1.

44   See James C. McKeown, *Ovid: Amores*, vol. ii (Leeds, 1989), on *Am.* 1.2.41–2.

45   E. J. Kenney, 'The poetry of Ovid's exile', *Proceedings of the Cambridge Philological Society* 11 (1965), pp. 37–49, p. 46.

46   Conte, 'Love without elegy', p. 62, argues that Cupid assumes here the language of philosophical diatribe, though in skewed form.

47   On the programmatic importance of this myth see Martindale, *Latin Poetry*, pp. 203–17.

48   On Apollo's supposed presence at Actium, Augustus' victory over Mark Antony and Cleopatra in 31 BCE, see John F. Miller, *Apollo, Augustus and the Poets* (Cambridge, 2009), pp. 54–94.

49   Kenney, 'The poetry of Ovid's exile', pp. 46–7.

50   See also *Am.* 1.2.51.

51   Betty Rose Nagle, *The Poetics of Exile* (Brussels, 1980), pp. 22–32.

52   See Gareth D. Williams, *Banished Voices: Readings in Ovid's Exile Poetry* (Cambridge, 1994), esp. Chapter 2, where he argues that 'poetic decline' is a rhetorical trope. See also Chapter 6 below.

53   See Syme, *History in Ovid*, pp. 135–55.

54   See Michael Putnam, *Artifices of Eternity: Horace's Fourth Book of Odes* (Ithaca, NY, 1986), pp. 33–47.

55   Ovid probably aligns himself with Virgil here whose *Eclogues*, evidence suggests, were also performed in the theatre. Ovid says his poems were 'danced', which suggests the medium of pantomime, a popular ancient form of ballet. See Jennifer Ingleheart, 'Ovid and the pantomime', in Edith Hall and Rosie Wiles (eds), *New Directions in Ancient Pantomime*

(Oxford, 2008), pp. 198–217; Elaine Fantham, 'Foreword', in *Change Me: Stories of Sexual Transformation from Ovid*, tr. Jane Alison (Oxford, 2014), pp. xxix–xxxi.

56 See Peter E. Knox, 'Ovidian myths on Pompeian walls', in *Handbook*, pp. 36–54.

57 Martindale, *Latin Poetry*, p. 217.

II. WRITING FOR AN AGE OF GOLD: THE LOVE ELEGIST

1 Alison Sharrock, 'Gender and sexuality', in *Cambridge Companion*, pp. 95–107.

2 Alison Sharrock, 'Ovid and the politics of reading', *Materiali e discussioni per l'analisi dei testi classici* 33 (1994), pp. 97–122, p. 101.

3 See Chapter 1, note 48.

4 See Alessandro Barchiesi, *The Poet and the Prince* (Berkeley and Los Angeles, CA, 1997), pp. 214–9.

5 On the extensive visual ideology of Augustan Rome see Paul Zanker, *The Power of Images in the Age of Augustus*, tr. Alan Shapiro (Ann Arbor, MI, 1988).

6 C. Brian Rose, *Dynastic Commemoration and Imperial Portraiture in the Julio-Claudian Period* (Cambridge, 1997), pp. 15–16. Before the Ara Pacis, women and young children were extremely rare figures in public reliefs.

7 Anthony J. Boyle, *Ovid and the Monuments: A Poet's Rome* (Bendigo, Victoria, 2003), pp. 15–18.

8 On the dating of the *Ars* see Roy K. Gibson (ed.), *Ars Amatoria Book 3* (Cambridge, 2003), pp. 37–9. The first two books were published in 2 BCE, and the third around 2 CE.

9 Roy Gibson argues that the *Ars* conforms with Augustan morality by counselling moderation in male and female dress and behaviour and also literary style; see ibid., pp. 22–3. Gibson cites Cicero's *de Officiis* on decorum as a central concept for Ovid's teachings.

10 On the Augustan Golden Age, see Zanker, *Power of Images*, pp. 167–83. On the Augustan reverence for the past as the repository of moral values see Catharine Edwards, *Writing Rome* (Cambridge, 1996), pp. 27–43.

11 Boyle, *Ovid and the Monuments*, p. xi.

12 See Maria Wyke, 'Mistress and metaphor in Augustan elegy', *Helios* 16 (1989), pp. 25–47, pp. 37–41, on Roman moral discourse about women.

13 Thomas A. J. McGinn, *Prostitution, Sexuality and the Law in Ancient Rome* (Oxford, 1998) is fundamental. See also Catharine Edwards, *The Politics of Immorality in Ancient Rome* (Cambridge, 1993), pp. 34–62; Gibson, *Ars 3*, pp. 25–37.

14 Alison Keith, *Propertius: Poet of Love and Leisure* (London, 2008), pp. 148–9.

15 Paul Veyne, *Roman Erotic Elegy: Love, Poetry, and the West*, tr. David Pellauer (Chicago, IL, 1988). See the critique of Veyne in Duncan F. Kennedy, *The Arts of Love: Five Studies in the Discourse of Roman Love Elegy* (Cambridge, 1993), pp. 91–101.

16 Barbara Boyd, *Ovid's Literary Loves* (Ann Arbor, MI, 1997), pp. 9–18.

17 Apart from Corinna, the only other woman Ovid names, however, is Cypassis, Corinna's maid, whom he seduces (*Am.* 2.8).

18 See Wyke, 'Mistress and metaphor'.

19 Sharon James, *Learned Girls and Male Persuasion: Gender and Reading in Roman Love Elegy* (Berkeley and Los Angeles, CA, 2003), pp. 35–68.

20 See further on Ovid's exile in Chapter 6; also the discussion in Gibson, *Ars 3*, pp. 36–7.

21 See Chapter 7.

22   On the didactic tradition see Gibson, *Ars 3*, pp. 7–21.

23   Sharrock, 'Politics of reading', pp. 106–7, argues that after Virgil's *Georgics*, it was impossible to read didactic poetry apolitically in Rome.

24   See also *Ars* 3.57–8: the poem is for 'girls whom modesty and the laws allow'.

25   Robert Edwards, *The Flight from Desire: Augustine and Ovid to Chaucer* (New York, 2006), pp. 47–51.

26   See the discussion of these lines in Sharrock, 'Politics of reading', pp. 110–12.

27   Gibson, *Ars 3*, pp. 32–6.

28   On hunting as a primary seductive metaphor of the *Ars* see Carin M. C. Green, 'Terms of venery: *Ars Amatoria* I', *Transactions of the American Philological Association* 126 (1996), pp. 221–63.

29   Ibid., pp. 232–4.

30   See Roy K. Gibson, 'The *Ars Amatoria*', in *Blackwell Companion*, pp. 90–103, p. 92.

31   Keith, *Propertius*, pp. 148–9.

32   See further Chapter 3 on *Ep.* 14; Ellen O'Gorman, 'Love and the family: Augustus and the Ovidian legacy', *Arethusa* 30 (1997), pp. 103–23, pp. 109–111.

33   On the close connection between the temple of Palatine Apollo and the house of Augustus see John F. Miller, *Apollo, Augustus and the Poets* (Cambridge, 2009), pp. 185–91.

34   Livy 1.9–13; Dionysius of Halicarnassus 2.30; 2.45–6; Plutarch, *Life of Romulus* 14.1–19.7.

35   See J. S. C. Eidinow, 'A note on Ovid *Ars Amatoria* 1.117–9', *American Journal of Philology* 114 (1993), pp. 413–17.

36   See Victoria Rimell, *Ovid's Lovers* (Cambridge, 2006), pp. 70–2, 97–103.

37   The major mythological narratives are: the rape of the Sabine women (1.101–34); Pasiphae and the bull (1.289–326); Bacchus and Ariadne (1.525–64); Achilles and Deidamia (1.681–706); Daedalus and Icarus (2.21–96); Calypso and Ulysses (2.123–44); Mars and Venus (2.561–92); and Procris and Cephalus (3.685–746). For the argument that Ovid in the *Ars* subverts his 'persona' as teacher see John M. Fyler, '*Omnia vincit amor*: incongruity and the limitations of structure in Ovid's elegiac poetry', *Classical Journal* 66 (1971), pp. 196–203. Alison Sharrock, *Seduction and Repetition in Ovid's Ars Amatoria II* (Oxford, 1994) suggests two readers of the *Ars*, the figure addressed within the didactic discourse, and the more educated, external reader.

38   Victoria Rimell, *Ovid's Lovers: Desire, Difference and the Poetic Imagination* (Cambridge, 2006), p. 99; see her discussion of this myth, pp. 97–103.

39   Edwards, *Flight from Desire*, pp. 39–40.

40   Gibson, *Ars 3*, p. 36.

41   Gibson, 'The *Ars Amatoria*', p. 98.

42   Apart from Ovid, see Tibullus 1.7; 2.1; 2.5; Propertius 1.16.1–4; 2.1.25–34; 3.1. For an overview of the triumph theme in Roman elegy see Karl Galinsky, 'The triumph theme in the Augustan elegy', *Wiener Studien* 82 (1969), pp. 75–107; John F. Miller, 'Reading Cupid's triumph', *Classical Journal* 90 (1995), pp. 287–94.

43   Mary Beard, *The Roman Triumph* (Cambridge, MA, 2007), pp. 111–14.

44   See Miller, 'Cupid's triumph'.

45   See Wyke, 'Mistress and metaphor'.

46   Beard, *Roman Triumph*, p. 123.

47   Ibid., pp. 118, 133–9.

48   See Propertius 3.4.19–20 for a possibly more solemn reference to the link between Venus and Augustus in a poem about a political triumph.

49 On the historical background to this campaign see Adrian S. Hollis (ed.), *Ars Amatoria Book I* (Oxford, 1977), pp. 65–73.

50 Ibid., p. 72.

51 The second-/third-century historian Dio Cassius claims that there were reservations about Gaius' youth and lack of experience at the time and that Augustus was reluctant to give him the command (55.10.18).

52 See also the similar complaints at *Tr.* 4.2.47–74.

53 Matthew McGowan, *Ovid in Exile* (Boston, MA, and Leiden, 2009), pp. 160–1.

54 As Mary Beard argues, in 'Roman street theatre', in Catharine Edwards and Greg Woolf (eds), *Rome the Cosmopolis* (Cambridge, 2003), pp. 21–43, pp. 34–7, that fictional quality is also on display in Ovid's account of Gaius' projected triumph in *Ars Amatoria* 1; accurate identification does not matter in a triumph that could well be 'just another of those diplomatic stitch-ups passing as heroics that characterized most Augustan encounters with the Parthians and their neighbours' (p. 36); the real interest is in showing off to a girl.

55 Galinsky, 'The triumph theme', pp. 102–7; Beard, 'Roman street theatre', pp. 34–7.

56 See also *Pont.* 2.1.37–8. This particular triumph by Germanicus was postponed because of the disaster in Germany in 9 CE when three legions were lost.

57 See also *Tr.* 4.2.41–2.

58 Alessandro Barchiesi and Philip Hardie, 'The Ovidian career model: Ovid, Gallus, Apuleius, Boccaccio', in Philip Hardie and Helen Moore (eds), *Classical Literary Careers and Their Reception* (Cambridge, 2010), pp. 59–88, p. 67.

III. WOMEN AS AUTHORS: LETTER WRITING AND THE *HEROIDES*

1 In *Am.* 2.18.21–34 Ovid refers to several of the single *Heroides* and to the replies that his friend Sabinus has written to some of them. As James C. McKeown, *Ovid: Amores*, vol. iii (Leeds, 1998), pp. 386–7, points out, this suggests that the single *Heroides* had been recently published as a set, probably shortly before 10–7 BCE.

2 The tradition of the deceptive or secret letter goes back as far as Homer (*Il.* 6.152–70). See Patricia Rosenmeyer, *Ancient Epistolary Fictions: The Letter in Greek Literature* (Cambridge, 2001), pp. 39–44; Janet G. Altman, *Epistolarity: Approaches to a Form* (Columbus, OH, 1982), pp. 59–62.

3 Joseph Farrell, 'Reading and writing the *Heroides*', *Harvard Studies in Classical Philology* 98 (1998), pp. 307–38, pp. 311–4.

4 Philip Hardie, *Ovid's Poetics of Illusion* (Cambridge, 2002). See also Duncan Kennedy, 'Epistolarity: the *Heroides*', in *Cambridge Companion*, pp. 217–32, pp. 220–1.

5 Peter Dronke, *Women Writers of the Middle Ages* (Cambridge, 1984), p. 105.

6 On negative twentieth-century criticism of the *Heroides* see Howard Jacobson, *Ovid's Heroides* (Princeton, NJ, 1974), pp. 3–11; Kennedy, 'Epistolarity', pp. 219–20. Feminist critics led the way to a fresh appreciation. See Sara Lindheim, *Mail and Female: Epistolary Narrative and Desire in Ovid's Heroides: Transgressions of Genre and Gender* (Madison, WI, 2003); Efrossini Spentzou, *Readers and Writers in Ovid's Heroides* (Oxford, 2003); Laurel Fulkerson, *The Ovidian Heroine as Author: Reading, Writing, and Community*

in the Heroides (Cambridge, 2005); Laurel Fulkerson, 'The *Heroides*: Female Elegy?', in *Blackwell Companion*, pp. 78–89.

7　Kennedy, 'Epistolarity', p. 220. Foundational for study of the epistolary genre is Altman, *Epistolarity*. Her focus is the epistolary novel, but much of her study applies also to the form of the *Heroides*.

8　On the question of the authenticity of the *Epistle of Sappho* see Peter Knox (ed.), *Ovid's Heroides, Select Epistles* (Cambridge, 1995), pp. 11–14. The question arises in part because this *Epistle* does not come down to us in the same manuscript tradition as the rest of the single epistles; moreover, when Ovid mentions the *Heroides* in *Am.* 2.18.21–6, he does not mention all the poems that we now possess.

9　On the question of the originality of the *Heroides* as a genre see Jacobson, *Ovid's Heroides*, pp. 319–48.

10　On the dating of Propertius 4 and the relationship of 4.3 with the *Heroides* see Gregory Hutchinson, *Propertius Elegies Book 4* (Cambridge, 2006), pp. 2–3; 100–1.

11　Kennedy, 'Epistolarity', pp. 222–4.

12　Farrell, 'Reading and writing', pp. 310–11; Altman, *Epistolarity*, p. 14.

13　See the discussion of Spentzou, *Readers and Writers*, pp. 25–8. As an introduction to the topic of gender in Ovid and the ancient world see Marilyn B. Skinner, *Sexuality in Greek and Roman Culture* (Oxford, 2005); also Alison Sharrock, 'Gender and sexuality', in *Cambridge Companion*, pp. 95–107.

14　Kennedy, 'Epistolarity', pp. 227–30.

15　See Manfred Kraus, 'Rehearsing the other sex: impersonation of women in ancient classroom *ethopoeia*', in J. A. F. Delgado, F. Pordomingo and A. Stramaglia (eds), *Escuela y literatura en Grecia antigua* (Cassino, 2007), pp. 455–68.

16　Seneca the Elder, *Contr.* 2.8, 12.

17　Spentzou, *Readers and Writers*, pp. 24–8; also Fulkerson, *The Ovidian Heroine*, who argues that the heroines are acute readers of one another's texts.

18　Altman, *Epistolarity*, p. 43; see also pp. 134–42.

19　Sharon James, *Learned Girls and Male Persuasion: Gender and Reading in Roman Love Elegy* (Berkeley and Los Angeles, CA, 2003), p. 26.

20　See Genevieve Lively, 'Birthday letters from Pontus: Ted Hughes and the white noise of classical elegy', in Roger Rees (ed.), *Ted Hughes and the Classics* (Oxford, 2009), pp. 216–32.

21　See Jacobson, *Ovid's Heroides*, pp. 404–6.

22　Duncan Kennedy, 'The epistolary mode and the first of Ovid's *Heroides*', *Classical Quarterly* 34 (1984), pp. 413–22.

23　See above, note 2.

24　Patricia Rosenmeyer, 'Ovid's *Heroides* and *Tristia*: voices from exile', *Ramus* 26 (1997), pp. 29–56, pp. 33–4. For other examples of the materiality of letter writing see also *Ep.* 11.1–6; 15.1–8.

25　See Kennedy, 'Epistolarity'.

26　As Farrell, 'Reading and writing', notes, p. 335, tears also draw attention to the editorial intervention that has removed them; the mention of blots in fact emphasizes the textualization of grief.

27　Altman, *Epistolarity*, p. 88, notes that the letter is unique among first-person literary forms in its aptitude for portraying the experience of reading.

28　Marilynn Desmond, *Reading Dido: Gender, Textuality, and the Medieval Aeneid* (Minneapolis, MN, 1994), p. 41, points out that *Ep.* 7 is permeated with the language of *Aeneid* 4.

29   Kennedy, 'The epistolary mode', pp. 415–6.
30   Desmond, *Reading Dido*, pp. 45–6. For an astute analysis of *Ep.* 7 and its relationship with the *Aeneid*, see ibid., pp. 23–44.
31   Ibid., pp. 38–42.
32   See Alison Keith, *Engendering Rome* (Cambridge, 2000), p. 112.
33   Desmond, *Reading Dido*, p. 43.
34   Since Ovid's Dido is not the political leader of *Aeneid* 4, she does not curse Aeneas and his future race, as she does at *Aeneid* 4.607–29.
35   For the text see Jane L. Lightfoot (ed.), *Parthenius of Nicaea* (Oxford, 1999), pp. 312–15. On other sources see Jacobson, *Ovid's Heroides*, pp. 176–9.
36   Matthew Reynolds, *The Poetry of Translation* (Oxford, 2011), pp. 96–7.
37   On the metaphor of death as marriage see Keith, *Engendering Rome*, pp. 105–7.
38   Ellen O'Gorman, 'Love and the family: Augustus and the Ovidian legacy', *Arethusa* 30 (1997), pp. 103–23, pp. 109–114.
39   Ibid., p. 113.
40   See Jacobson, *Ovid's Heroides*, p. 345.
41   See the detailed discussion of this episode in Farrell, 'Reading and writing', pp. 318–22.
42   On the confusion of familial and social categories in this myth see Leonard Barkan, *The Gods Made Flesh* (New Haven, CT, 1986), pp. 59–63. Ellen Oliensis, *Freud's Rome* (Cambridge, 2009), pp. 78–81, points out the incestuous subtext in the myth.
43   Thus Karl Galinsky, *Ovid's Metamorphoses: An Introduction to the Basic Aspects* (Berkeley and Los Angeles, CA, 1975), pp. 129–32.
44   Elaine Fantham, *Ovid's Metamorphoses* (Oxford, 2004), p. 66, notes that Philomela is the first woman to commit murder in the *Metamorphoses*. See Patricia Joplin's influential article, 'The voice of the shuttle is ours', *Stanford Literature Review* 1 (1984), pp. 25–53, which calls for rewriting the myth in a way that foregrounds the positive, creative value of Philomela's weaving.
45   Andrew Feldherr, *Playing Gods* (Princeton, NJ, 2010), p. 217, with full discussion at pp. 199–239.
46   See John Scheid and Jesper Svenbro, *The Craft of Zeus: Myths of Weaving and Fabrics*, tr. Carol Volk (Cambridge, MA, 1996); Gianpiero Rosati, 'Form in motion: weaving the text in the *Metamorphoses*', in Philip Hardie, Alessandro Barchiesi and Stephen Hinds (eds), *Ovidian Transformations: Essays on the Metamorphoses and Its Reception*, Cambridge Philological Society supplement 23 (Cambridge, 1999), pp. 240–53.
47   Oliensis, *Freud's Rome*, p. 82.
48   Rosenmeyer, *Ancient Epistolary Fictions*, pp. 39–44. On letters and secrecy see also Altman, *Epistolarity*, pp. 59–62.
49   Some critics have suspected that the word 'poem' is a later corruption. But there are good reasons for connecting this letter with the poetic letters of the *Heroides*.
50   Kathryn L. McKinley, *Reading the Ovidian Heroine* (Leiden, 2011), p. xix.

IV. WRITING FOR AN AGE OF IRON: THE *METAMORPHOSES*

1   On the concept of universal history, see Stephen Wheeler, *Narrative Dynamics in Ovid's Metamorphoses* (Tübingen, 2000), pp. 107–10.

2   W. Ralph Johnson, 'The problem of the counter-classical sensibility and its critics', *California Studies in Classical Antiquity* 3 (1970), pp. 123–51, pp. 141–5.

3   From the Hellenistic third century BCE we hear of Boeus' lost work on the metamorphoses of birds, *Ornithogonia*; Nicander's poem *Altered Bodies* (*Heteroeumena*); Eratosthenes' *Catasterisms*, a prose work on the mythologies of the stars. On the literary, aetiological aspect of the *Metamorphoses* see Alison Keith, *The Play of Fictions* (Ann Arbor, MI, 1992); K. Sara Myers, *Ovid's Causes* (Ann Arbor, MI, 1994).

4   See Paul Forbes-Irving, *Metamorphosis in Greek Myths* (Oxford, 1990), pp. 19–37.

5   Stephen Wheeler, *A Discourse of Wonders* (Philadelphia, PA, 1999), pp. 162–3, estimates that more than a third of the *Metamorphoses* is narrated by characters other than Ovid.

6   Ibid., pp. 118–25.

7   See Alessandro Barchiesi, 'Endgames: Ovid's *Metamorphoses* 15 and *Fasti* 6', in Deborah H. Roberts, Francis M. Dunn and Don Fowler (eds), *Classical Closure: Reading the End in Greek and Latin Literature* (Princeton, NJ, 1997), pp. 181–208, pp. 182–3.

8   Erik Gray, 'The races of poetry', *Essays in Criticism* 65 (2014), pp. 75–99, pp. 79, 90–2. He cites Peter Brooks, *Reading for the Plot: Design and Intention in Narrative* (New York, 1984).

9   Gray, 'The races of poetry', p. 90.

10 See John F. Miller, *Apollo, Augustus and the Poets* (Cambridge, 2009), pp. 342–9.

11 Robert Edwards, *The Flight from Desire: Augustine and Ovid to Chaucer* (New York, 2006), pp. 56–7.

12 See Alison Keith on the challenge the *Metamorphoses* poses to epic masculine norms, 'Versions of epic masculinity in Ovid's *Metamorphoses*', in Philip Hardie, Alessandro Barchiesi and Stephen Hinds (eds), *Ovidian Transformations: Essays on the Metamorphoses and Its Reception*, Cambridge Philological Society supplement 23 (Cambridge, 1999), pp. 214–39.

13 See Carole E. Newlands, 'Ovid', in John Miles Foley (ed.), *A Companion to Ancient Epic* (Malden, 2005), pp. 476–91, pp. 481–2.

14 Stephen Hinds, *Allusion and Intertext* (Cambridge, 1998), pp. 104–22.

15 The wall is humorously given a walk-on part in the 'rude mechanicals'' play of Pyramus and Thisbe in Shakespeare's *A Midsummer Night's Dream*.

16 Philip Hardie, *Ovid's Poetics of Illusion* (Cambridge, 2002), p. 145; see also pp. 164–5.

17 Ibid., p. 165.

18 Ibid., p. 166.

19 Ibid., pp. 152–65.

20 See Stephen Hinds, 'Landscape with figures: aesthetics of place in the *Metamorphoses* and its tradition', in *Cambridge Companion*, pp. 122–49.

21 See Paul Barolsky, *Ovid and the Metamorphoses of Modern Art from Botticelli to Picasso* (New Haven, CT, 2014), pp. 18–19.

22 See also the tale of Iphis (9.666–797), discussed below.

23 Cf. *Met.* 7.11–71 (Medea); *Met.* 8.44–80 (Scylla); *Met.* 9.474–516 (Byblis); *Met.* 9.726–63 (Iphis).

24 On the popularity of the Pygmalion myth in film see Paula James, *Ovid's Myth of Pygmalion on Screen: In Pursuit of the Perfect Woman* (London, 2011).

25 Brooks Otis, *Ovid as an Epic Poet* (Cambridge, 1970), pp. 231–77. See also Hardie, *Poetics of Illusion*, pp. 258–82.

26 On the self-interest of the gods, see Steven J. Green, 'Collapsing authority and "Arachnean" gods in Ovid's Baucis and Philemon', *Ramus* 32 (2003), pp. 39–56.

27 See Alessandro Barchiesi, 'Voices and narrative "instances" in the *Metamorphoses*', in Alessandro Barchiesi, *Speaking Volumes* (London, 2001), pp. 49–55; also Gianpiero Rosati, 'Narrative techniques and narrative structures in the *Metamorphoses*', in *Brill's Companion*, pp. 271–304.

28 See Alan H. F. Griffin, 'Baucis and Philemon in Ovid's *Metamorphoses*', *Greece and Rome* 38 (1991), pp. 62–74.

29 See Amy Richlin, 'Reading Ovid's rapes', in Amy Richlin (ed.), *Pornography and Representation in Greece and Rome* (Oxford, 1992), pp. 158–79.

30 Female sexual aggression in the *Metamorphoses* is generally marked as deviant; for instance, the incestuous desires of Byblis and Myrrha (9.450–665; 10.298–502), and the treachery of Medea (7.11–71) and Scylla (8.44–80), who both betray father and country for misjudged love.

31 Gray, 'The races of poetry', pp. 90–2.

32 On the poet's delicate handling of alternating perspectives, the aggressor's and the victim's, see W. Ralph Johnson, 'The rapes of Callisto', *Classical Journal* 92 (1996), pp. 9–24. See also the discussion of Bernini's sculpture 'Apollo and Daphne' in Barolsky, *Ovid and the Metamorphoses of Modern Art*, pp. 37–45.

33 Some critics claim that Alpheus in fact has sex with Arethusa through a metaphorical 'mingling of their waters'. But the text only says that Alpheus turned back to the form of a river '*in order* to mingle his waters with hers' (*Met.* 5.636–8); at that point Diana intervenes further and sends Arethusa plunging underground, conveying her to her own island of Ortygia, in the centre of Sicilian Syracuse (5.639–41).

34 See Keith, *The Play of Fictions*, pp. 81–93.

35 Patricia J. Johnson, 'Constructions of Venus in Ovid's *Metamorphoses* V', *Arethusa* 29 (1996), pp. 125–49.

36 Charles Martindale, *Latin Poetry and the Judgement of Taste: An Essay in Aesthetics* (Oxford, 2005), p. 209.

37 Ibid., pp. 213–17; Miller, *Apollo*, pp. 348–9.

38 See Barolsky, *Ovid and the Metamorphoses of Modern Art*, pp. 33–4.

39 Emma Gee, *Ovid, Aratus and Augustus: Astronomy in Ovid's Fasti* (Cambridge, 2000), p. 176, explains that the Bears, being the most northerly of all constellations, never set for an observer in the northern hemisphere but merely chase one another in a circle around the celestial pole, almost directly overhead.

40 See Andrew Feldherr, 'Metamorphosis and sacrifice in Ovid's Theban narrative', *Materiali e discussioni per l'analisi dei testi classici* 38 (1997), pp. 25–55, p. 51.

41 Mary Lefkowitz, 'Seduction and rape in Greek myth', in Angeliki E. Laiou (ed.), *Consent and Coercion to Sex and Marriage in Ancient and Medieval Societies* (Washington DC, 1993), pp. 17–37.

42 Another rare example of upward metamorphosis is Io (*Met.* 1.583–747).

43 On Caesar's comet see Suetonius, *Julius Caesar* 88; Pliny, *Nat.* 2.94; Stefan Weinstock, *Divus Iulius* (Oxford, 1971), pp. 370–84.

44 Denis Feeney, *The Gods in Epic* (Princeton, NJ, 1991), pp. 210–12.

45 That the controversy over deification remained a live controversy well beyond the Augustan principate is shown by its satirical treatment in Seneca's *Apocolocyntosis*. See Christopher L. Whitton, 'Seneca, *Apocolocyntosis*', in Emma Buckley and Martin T. Dinter (eds), *A Companion to the Neronian Age* (Chichester, 2013), pp. 151–69, pp. 157–61.

46 See Johnson, 'The problem of the counter-classical sensibility', pp. 145–6.

47   See Carole E. Newlands, *Playing with Time: Ovid and the Fasti* (Ithaca, NY, 1995), pp. 43–4.
48   Feeney, *Gods in Epic*, p. 220.
49   Ali Smith, *Girl Meets Boy* (Edinburgh, 2007), p. 160.
50   See Forbes-Irving, *Metamorphosis*, pp. 152–5.
51   On this myth see Chapter 3.
52   On this theme in the *Metamorphoses* see Patricia J. Johnson, *Ovid before Exile: Art and Punishment in the Metamorphoses* (Madison, WI, 2008); Eleanor W. Leach, 'Ekphrasis and the theme of artistic failure in Ovid's *Metamorphoses*', *Ramus* 3 (1974), pp. 102–42; Joseph B. Solodow, *The World of Ovid's Metamorphoses* (Chapel Hill, NC, 1988), pp. 203–31.
53   On the contrasting styles of the tapestry see Feeney, *Gods in Epic*, pp. 190–4; Leach, 'Ekphrasis'.
54   See Wheeler, *Narrative Dynamics*, pp. 162–3. On the role of Pythagoras in the *Metamorphoses*, see Myers, *Ovid's Causes*, pp. 133–66.
55   Leonard Barkan, *The Gods Made Flesh* (New Haven, CT, 1986), pp. 82–5.

V. THE *FASTI*: POEM OF ROMAN TIME

1   See Elaine Fantham, 'Ovid, Germanicus and the composition of the *Fasti*', *Papers of the Liverpool Latin Seminar* 5 (1985), pp. 243–81.
2   Mary Beard, 'A complex of times: no more sheep on Romulus' birthday', *Proceedings of the Cambridge Philological Society* 33 (1987), pp. 1–15.
3   See Denis Feeney, 'Patterning of time in the *Metamorphoses*', in Philip Hardie, Alessandro Barchiesi and Stephen Hinds (eds), *Ovidian Transformations: Essays on the Metamorphoses and Its Reception*, Cambridge Philological Society supplement 23 (Cambridge, 1999), pp. 13–30, pp. 28–9. On the close generic interaction between the two poems see Stephen Hinds, *The Metamorphosis of Persephone: Ovid and the Self-conscious Muse* (Cambridge, 1987).
4   Jörg Rüpke, *Roman Religion*, tr. and ed. Richard Gordon (Cambridge, 2007), pp. 249–50.
5   Denis Feeney, *Caesar's Calendar* (Berkeley and Los Angeles, CA, 2007), pp. 184–9.
6   Andrew Wallace-Hadrill, 'Mutatio morum', in Thomas Habinek and Alessandro Schiesaro (eds), *The Roman Cultural Revolution* (Cambridge, 1997), pp. 16–18; also 'Time for Augustus: Ovid, Augustus and the *Fasti*', in Michael Whitby, Philip Hardie and Mary Whitby (eds), *Homo Viator: Classical Essays for John Bramble* (Bristol, 1987), pp. 221–31.
7   There is no certain evidence for prestigious marble calendars beyond the early principate. See Jörg Rüpke, *The Roman Calendar from Numa to Constantine*, tr. David M. B. Richardson (Chichester, 2011), pp. 140–5.
8   See Wallace-Hadrill. 'Time for Augustus', pp. 223–4; Rüpke, *Roman Religion*, pp. 251–2.
9   On Augustus' sundial see Pliny, *Nat.* 36.72–3; Wallace-Hadrill, 'Time for Augustus', pp. 224–5. Whether the shadow of the gnomon intersected the Ara Pacis on Augustus' birthday remains controversial.
10 Beard, 'A complex of times'.
11 Particularly in the early books, however, with their overlapping mythological genealogies, the progressive linear scheme is not strictly adhered to. See Frederick Ahl, *Metaformations* (Ithaca, NY, 1985), pp. 285–93.

12 See Alessandro Barchiesi, 'Endgames: Ovid's *Metamorphoses* 15 and *Fasti* 6', in Deborah H. Roberts, Francis M. Dunn and Don Fowler (eds), *Classical Closure: Reading the End in Greek and Latin Literature* (Princeton, NJ, 1997), pp. 181–208; Francesca K. A. Martelli, *Ovid's Revisions* (Cambridge, 2013), pp. 142–4.

13 On Propertius' relationship with Callimachus' *Aetia* and Greek elegy, see Gregory Hutchinson, *Propertius Elegies Book 4* (Cambridge, 2006), pp. 7–16.

14 See Emma Gee, *Ovid, Aratus and Augustus: Astronomy in Ovid's Fasti* (Cambridge, 2000). Molly Pasco-Pranger, *Founding the Year: Ovid's Fasti and the Poetics of the Roman Calendar* (Leiden, 2006), pp. 7–8, points out that Eratosthenes' *Catasterisms*, a Hellenistic prose collection of star myths, was important for content.

15 See Adrian S. Hollis (ed.), *Ars Amatoria Book I* (Oxford, 1977) on *Ars* 1.399–436.

16 For example the account of the burning of foxes at the festival to Ceres in Carseoli, a rural town in Ovid's home territory of Paelignia (*Fasti* 4.685–712).

17 See Paul Murgatroyd, *Mythical and Legendary Narrative in Ovid's Fasti* (Leiden, 2005), pp. 63–95.

18 Rüpke, *Roman Religion*, pp. 59–60. On Varro and the dependence of the *Fasti* on the Roman antiquarian tradition see Pasco-Pranger, *Founding the Year*, pp. 34–50.

19 On the Ovidian narrator of the *Fasti* see my 'Ovid's narrator in the *Fasti*', *Arethusa* 25 (1992), pp. 33–54; on Ovid's use of multiple narrators, see my *Playing with Time: Ovid and the Fasti* (Ithaca, NY, 1995), pp. 51–86. On Ovid's debt to Callimachus' narrative strategies in the *Aetia* see John F. Miller, 'Callimachus and the Augustan aetiological elegy', *Aufstieg und Niedergang der römischen Welt* 2.30.1 (1982), pp. 371–417.

20 Alessandro Barchiesi, *The Poet and the Prince* (Berkeley and Los Angeles, CA, 1997), p. 19.

21 On Janus' association with peace in the *Fasti*, see Philip Hardie, 'The Janus episode in Ovid's *Fasti*', *Materiali e discussioni per l'analisi dei testi classici* 26 (1991), pp. 47–64.

22 See Stephen Hinds, '*Arma* in Ovid's *Fasti*, part 1: genre and mannerism', *Arethusa* 25 (1992), pp. 81–112, pp. 87–90.

23 Ibid.; also '*Arma* in Ovid's *Fasti*, part 2: genre, Romulean Rome and Augustan ideology', *Arethusa* 25 (1992), pp. 113–53; Alison Keith, *Engendering Rome* (Cambridge, 2000), pp. 103–7.

24 Stefan Weinstock, *Divus Iulius* (Oxford, 1971), pp. 131–2.

25 See Paul Zanker, *The Power of Images in the Age of Augustus* (Ann Arbor, MI, 1988), pp. 210–15.

26 Denis Feeney, '*Si licet et fas est*: Ovid's *Fasti* and the problem of free speech under the principate', in Anton Powell (ed.), *Poetry and Propaganda in the Age of Augustus* (Bristol, 1992), pp. 1–25.

27 The *Fasti* seems to have been rededicated to Germanicus after Augustus' death as part of Ovid's late revisions in exile, for when Augustus was still living, Ovid claims that the *Fasti* was written in his honour (*Tr.* 2.551). See Fantham, 'Ovid, Germanicus'.

28 See Geraldine Herbert-Brown, *Ovid and the Fasti: A Historical Study* (Oxford, 1994), pp. 173–85.

29 Feeney, '*Si licet et fas est*'.

30 *Tr.* 2.549: 'I wrote six books of *Fasti* and the same number again.'

31 See Carole E. Newlands, 'Connecting the disconnected: reading Ovid's *Fasti*', in Helen Morales and Alison Sharrock (eds), *Intratextuality* (Oxford, 2000), pp. 171–202.

32 Barchiesi, *Poet and the Prince*, pp. 74–6.

33 Several ancient sources, including Ovid's *Fasti*, explained this festival as originating with the flight of the 'king of sacred rites' (the high priest) from the popular assembly in Rome after performing sacrifice there (Ovid *Fasti* 5.727–8; Plutarch *Quaestiones Romanae* 63).

34 See Martelli, *Ovid's Revisions*, pp. 142–4.

35 On this myth see the final section of Chapter 3.

36 On the differences between Ovid and Livy in the representation of ancient Rome see Murgatroyd, *Mythical and Legendary Narrative*, pp. 171–80; on the story of Lucretia see ibid., pp. 191–200.

37 A complicated allusion perhaps to the tradition that Julius Caesar fell with similar modesty when assassinated at the hands of, among others, another Brutus, who in 44 BCE tried in vain to stop the resumption of one-man rule. See Matthew Robinson, *A Commentary on Ovid's Fasti, Book 2* (Oxford, 2011) on *Fasti* 2.833.

38 See Robinson, *A Commentary*, pp. 462–3.

39 Ibid., pp. 370–2; Joy Littlewood, *A Commentary on Ovid's Fasti, Book 6* (Oxford, 2006), pp. xxxi–xxxiv.

40 As in the *Metamorphoses*, so in the *Fasti* Augustus is closely compared to Jupiter; see for instance *Fasti* 2.131–2.

41 See the definition of 'comic rape' in Thomas Frazel, 'Priapus' two rapes in Ovid's *Fasti*', *Arethusa* 36 (2003), pp. 61–97, p. 66. The term both describes the humorous reaction of the characters in the narrative and suggests the influence of comic drama on the plot.

42 See however the influential article of Amy Richlin, 'Reading Ovid's rapes', in Amy Richlin (ed.), *Pornography and Representation in Greece and Rome* (Oxford, 1992), pp. 158–79, which does not distinguish between the rape narratives of the *Fasti* and *Metamorphoses*.

43 See the discussion of these narratives in Murgatroyd, *Mythical and Legendary Narrative*, pp. 63–95.

44 T. Peter Wiseman, *Roman Drama and History* (Exeter, 1998), pp. 23–4.

45 See the discussion of the Vesta and Priapus myth in Frazel, 'Priapus' two rapes', especially pp. 76–84.

46 On the playful elements, however, in this apotheosis see Chapter 4; Newlands, *Playing with Time*, pp. 43–4.

47 Wiseman, *Roman Drama*, pp. 68–9, suggests that prostitutes took part in the festival since couples camp out under togas for shelter, and only elite males and prostitutes wore the toga.

48 See Carole E. Newlands, 'Transgressive acts: Ovid's treatment of the Ides of March', *Classical Philology* 91 (1996), pp. 320–38.

49 On Anna Perenna in the *Fasti* see Wiseman, *Roman Drama*, pp. 64–74.

50 See Beard, 'A complex of times', pp. 6–11.

51 Ovid also briefly offers four other possibilities at 3.657–9: she is a moon goddess, the goddess Themis, the goddess Io, or a nymph who gave the infant Jupiter his first food.

52 See Macrobius 1.12.6; Martial 4.64.16–17.

53 Servius on *Aeneid* 4.682, citing Varro as an authority, though Varro says that Anna killed herself on the Carthaginian pyre.

54 Ahl, *Metaformations*, p. 311.

55 See Keith, *Engendering Rome*, pp. 102–11, on the important Roman political theme of the woman sacrificed for the good of the state.

56 See Ahl, *Metaformations*, pp. 309–15. He comments on the irony that 'they even appear to share the bed of Numicius together after death' (p. 312).

57   See Weinstock, *Divus Iulius*, pp. 5–7.

58   Wiseman, *Roman Drama*, pp. 72–4.

59   Julius Caesar also traced his ancestry back to Mars; see Weinstock, *Divus Iulius*, pp. 129–30, pp. 183–4.

60   Marina Piranomonte, 'Anna Perenna a dieci anni della scoperta', *MHNH* 9 (2009), pp. 251–64; T. Peter Wiseman, 'The cult site of Anna Perenna: documentation, visualization, imagination', in Lothar Haselberger and John Humphrey (eds), *Imaging Ancient Rome*, *Journal of Roman Archaeology* supplement 61 (Portsmouth, RI), pp. 51–61.

61   Stephen J. Heyworth, 'Roman topography and Latin diction', *Papers of the British School at Rome* 79 (2011), pp. 43–69.

62   See also *Met.* 15.864–5, which names her as 'Caesar's Vesta', installed among the imperial household gods with Palatine Apollo; Herbert-Brown, *Ovid and the Fasti*, p. 71; Barchiesi, *Poet and the Prince*, pp. 137–40.

63   On the wantonness of Flora's games see Valerius Maximus, 2.10.8; Martial (1 preface, 18–21) writes that the stern censor Cato walked out of Flora's games in disgust (raising the question of why he was there in the first place).

64   See Newlands, *Playing with Time*, pp. 109–10.

65   See Hinds, '*Arma* in Ovid's *Fasti*', parts 1 and 2.

66   John F. Miller, *Apollo, Augustus and the Poets* (Cambridge, 2009), pp. 5–6.

VI. EXILE AND AFTER

1   On the circumstances surrounding Ovid's exile, see Chapter 1.

2   On the chronology of the exile works see Ronald Syme, *History in Ovid* (Oxford, 1978), pp. 37–47.

3   Thus E. J. Kenney, 'The poetry of Ovid's exile', *Proceedings of the Cambridge Philological Society* 11 (1965), pp. 37–49, who challenged the prevailing scholarly view that the exile poetry reflected Ovid's literary decline. See also Jo-Marie Claassen, *Displaced Persons: The Literature of Exile from Cicero to Boethius* (London, 1999), p. 32.

4   See Philip Hardie, *Ovid's Poetics of Illusion* (Cambridge, 2002), pp. 326–31; Rainer Godel, 'Ovid's "biography": novels of Ovid's exile', in *Handbook*, pp. 454–68, pp. 459–62. In general on the 'Ovidian novel' see Theodore Ziolkowski, *Ovid and the Moderns* (Ithaca, NY, 2005); Katharina Volk, *Ovid* (Oxford, 2010), pp. 122–7.

5   Hardie, *Poetics of Illusion*, pp. 331–7; Godel, 'Ovid's "biography"', pp. 462–6.

6   See Godel, 'Ovid's "biography"', p. 454.

7   On Mandelstam and Brodsky and the importance of exile in the Russian literary imagination from the eighteenth century on see Andrew Kahn, 'Ovid and Russia's poets of exile', in *Handbook*, pp. 401–15.

8   See Ellen Oliensis, 'Return to sender', *Ramus* 26 (1995), pp. 172–93.

9   In a brief apology to the people of Tomis in one of his last poems, *Pont.* 4.14, Ovid calls them 'kindly' because of their Greek origin (47–8) – though he refuses to concede that their climate is anything but terrible.

10   Stephen Hinds, 'Black-Sea Latin, Du Bellay, and the barbarian turn', in Jennifer Ingleheart (ed.), *Two Thousand Years of Solitude: Exile after Ovid* (Oxford, 2011), pp. 59–83. See also Gareth D. Williams, *Banished Voices: Readings in Ovid's Exile Poetry* (Cambridge, 1994), p. 50.

11 Thus Thomas N. Habinek, *The Politics of Latin Literature: Writing, Identity, and Empire in Ancient Rome* (Princeton, NJ, 1998), pp. 151–69.

12 Sebastian Matzner, 'Tomis writes back', in *Two Thousand Years of Solitude*, pp. 307–21, p. 320.

13 Williams, *Banished Voices*, pp. 1–49.

14 Don Fowler, *Roman Constructions* (Oxford, 2000), pp. 193–217; see also the discussion of Fowler in Francesca K. A. Martelli, *Ovid's Revisions* (Cambridge, 2013), pp. 155–7.

15 Alphonso Lingis, *Dangerous Emotions* (Berkeley and Los Angeles, CA, 2000), p. 122.

16 On death as a metaphor for Ovid's fate in exile from Rome see Betty Rose Nagle, *The Poetics of Exile* (Brussels, 1980), pp. 22–32; Claassen, *Displaced Persons*, pp. 239–40. Nagle argues for both a 'civic' and a 'poetic' death; Claassen and others stress the innovative nature of the exile poetry.

17 Claassen, *Displaced Persons*, pp. 31–2.

18 Oliensis, 'Return to sender', p. 177.

19 Possibly the most bitter complaint occurs at *Pont.* 4.2.23–38, which confesses to inertia and lack of inspiration – for who is Ovid's immediate audience except the barbarous local tribes? But note Ovid's inspiring paean to his poetic gifts in one of his last poems, *Pont.* 4.8.31–88.

20 Williams, *Banished Voices*, pp. 50–99.

21 Alessandro Barchiesi and Philip Hardie, 'The Ovidian career model: Ovid, Gallus, Apuleius, Boccaccio', in Philip Hardie and Helen Moore (eds), *Classical Literary Careers and Their Reception* (Cambridge, 2010), pp. 59–88, p. 59.

22 See Martelli, *Ovid's Revisions*, pp. 171–4.

23 Stephen Hinds, 'Booking the return trip: Ovid and *Tristia* 1', *Proceedings of the Cambridge Philological Society* 31 (1985), pp. 13–32, pp. 24–6.

24 The term is that of Stephen Hinds, 'First among women: Ovid, *Tristia* 1.6 and the traditions of "exemplary" catalogue', in Susanna M. Braund and Roland Mayer (eds), *Amor: Roma. Love and Latin Literature*, Cambridge Philological Society supplement 22 (Cambridge, 1999), pp. 123–42, p. 124.

25 Ellen O'Gorman, 'Love and the family: Augustus and the Ovidian legacy', *Arethusa* 30 (1997), pp. 103–23, esp. pp. 115–16.

26 See Syme, *History in Ovid*, pp. 135–55.

27 When both Fabius and Augustus died in 14 CE, Ovid's wife presumably lost her influence; Ovid addresses no poems to her after that date. See Martin Helzle, 'Mr and Mrs Ovid', *Greece and Rome* 36 (1989), pp. 183–93.

28 See also *Tr.* 5.14.1–14, where Ovid claims that the *Tristia* are a lasting monument to his wife.

29 Hinds, 'Booking the return trip', pp. 17–20.

30 Ibid., pp. 17–18.

31 On revision of the *Fasti* in exile see Elaine Fantham. 'Ovid, Germanicus and the composition of the Fasti', *Papers of the Liverpool Latin Seminar* 5 (1985), pp. 243–81.

32 See Gianpiero Rosati, 'Elegy after the elegists: from opposition to assent', *Papers of the Langford Latin Seminar* 12 (2005), pp. 133–50. See also Chapter 7.

33 Jennifer Ingleheart, *A Commentary on Ovid, Tristia Book 2* (Oxford, 2010), pp. 21–4.

34 S. Georgia Nugent, '*Tristia* 2: Ovid and Augustus', in Kurt A. Raaflaub and Mark Toher (eds), *Between Republic and Empire* (Berkeley and Los Angeles, CA, 1990), pp. 239–57.

35 Kenneth Scott, 'Emperor worship in Ovid', *Transactions and Proceedings of the American Philological Association* 61 (1930), pp. 43–69.

36 On the process of deification in Rome see Stefan Weinstock, *Divus Iulius* (Oxford, 1971), esp. pp. 386–7.

37 Denis Feeney, *The Gods in Epic* (Princeton, NJ, 1991), p. 220.

38 Ibid., pp. 221–2.

39 Note however the Ovidian touch (*Tr.* 2.33–4) that Jupiter exercises clemency because he would quickly run out of thunderbolts if he hurled one every time a human being did something wrong.

40 On the analogy between Jupiter and Augustus in the exile poetry see Scott, 'Emperor worship', pp. 52–8; on the frequency of the word 'anger' in the exile poetry see Syme, *History in Ovid*, pp. 223–4.

41 A similar sentiment is expressed at *Pont.* 1.6.25–6: 'whatever it is, it should be called a fault, not a crime; or is every fault against the great gods a crime?'

42 Ovid calls Jupiter's thunderbolt 'cruel' also at *Tr.* 1.9.21 and 3.4.6.

43 Ingleheart, *Tristia 2*, p. 14.

44 See Peter E. Knox, 'The poet and the second prince: Ovid in the age of Tiberius', *Memoirs of the American Academy in Rome* 49 (2004), pp. 1–20.

45 On Livia's role in the *Fasti* see Geraldine Herbert-Brown, *Ovid and the Fasti: A Historical Study* (Oxford, 1994), pp. 130–72.

46 Kristina Milnor, *Gender, Domesticity, and the Age of Augustus: Inventing Private Life* (Oxford, 2005), p. 43.

47 Suetonius, *Div. Aug.* 101.2; Tacitus, *Ann.* 1.8.1.

48 Nicholas Purcell, 'Livia and the womanhood of Rome', *Cambridge Classical Journal* 32 (1986), pp. 78–105, p. 87; Anthony Barrett, *Livia: First Lady of Imperial Rome* (New Haven, CT, 2002), pp. 195–202.

49 Elizabeth Bartman, *Portraits of Livia* (Cambridge, 1999), p. xxi.

50 Of the Augustan poets before Ovid, only Horace refers to Livia, but indirectly and not by name; cf. *Carm.* 3.14.5: 'a woman rejoicing in her matchless husband'.

51 See Hinds, 'First among women'.

52 The term *femina princeps* occurs in Roman poetry elsewhere only in the *Consolatio ad Liviam* (303–4 and 351–6), an anonymous poem of uncertain date. See Thomas E. Jenkins, 'Livia the *princeps*: gender and ideology in the *Consolatio ad Liviam*', *Helios* 36 (2009), pp. 1–25.

53 Mario Labate 'Elegia triste e elegia lieta: un caso di riconversione letteraria', *Materiali e discussioni per l'analisi dei testi classici* 19 (1987), pp. 91–129.

54 Matthew Roller, *Constructing Autocracy* (Princeton, NJ, 2001), pp. 213–87.

55 See Jennifer Trimble, 'Greek myth, gender, and social structure in a Roman house: two paintings of Achilles at Pompeii', in Elaine Gazda (ed.), *The Ancient Art of Emulation* (Ann Arbor, MI, 2002), pp. 225–48.

56 Our sources for this earlier version are fragmentary, but, along with evidence from mythological painting, they suggest Actaeon's transgressive intent. See Paul Forbes-Irving, *Metamorphosis in Greek Myths* (Oxford, 1990), pp. 80–90.

57 Anthony W. Bulloch (ed.), *Callimachus: The Fifth Hymn* (Cambridge, 1985), p. 160 (on line 52).

58 Ted Hughes, 'Actaeon', in *Tales from Ovid* (London, 1997), p. 111.

59 See Ingleheart, *Tristia 2* on *Tr.* 2.103–4, and 105–8. On *Tr.* 2.106 ('he became the prey of

his own dogs') she discusses two possible (but 'not desirable') metaphorical interpretations of this line, first that it refers to Ovid's destruction by his own poetry; at *Tr.* 2.1–14 he complains that his own work has brought about his downfall. In support of the second interpretation that 'dogs' means faithless friends Ingleheart cites *Tr.* 4.10.101: 'what can I say about the betrayal of friends and harmful slaves?' On Ovid's faithless friends and enemies in exile see *Tr.* 1.8; *Tr.* 3.11; *Tr.* 4.7; *Tr.* 4.9; *Tr.* 5.8; *Tr.* 5.13; *Pont.* 4.3; *Pont.* 4.16.

60   Ingleheart, *Tristia 2* on *Tr.* 2.105–8.

61   On the powerful ambivalence of the myth of Actaeon for later playwrights such as Christopher Marlowe and William Shakespeare, see François Laroque, 'Ovidian v(o)ices in Marlowe and Shakespeare: the Actaeon variations', in A. B. Taylor (ed.), *Shakespeare's Ovid: The Metamorphoses in the Plays and Poems* (Cambridge, 2000), pp. 165–80.

62   Habinek, *Politics of Latin Literature*, p. 159.

63   See note 20 to this chapter.

64   Richard Lanham, *The Motives of Eloquence* (New Haven, CT, 1976), p. 64.

65   Jo-Marie Claassen, 'Carmen and poetics: poetry as enemy and friend', Collection Latomus 5 (Brussels, 1989), pp. 252–66, p. 266.

66   Luigi Galasso (ed.), *Epistulae ex Ponto* (Chichester, 2009), pp. 204–5.

67   Thus Ingleheart, *Tristia 2* on *Tr.* 2.103–10. Habinek, *Politics of Latin Literature*, p. 166, argues that Ovid represents himself here as a gladiator dying in the arena; but the arena is a highly public space where the gladiator interacted with the crowd, and Ovid, like Actaeon, dies far from contact with his own public.

68   Alessandro Barchiesi, *The Poet and the Prince* (Berkeley and Los Angeles, CA, 1997), pp. 40–2. 'Envy' as a threat to Ovid's poetic career appears at key programmatic moments also at the end of the first book of the *Amores* (1.15.1), and at the end of the fourth book of *Tristia* (4.10.123).

69   *After Ovid: New Metamorphoses*, edited by Michael Hofmann and James Lasdun (London, 1994).

70   'The death of Actaeon' and 'Actaeon: the early years' in *Swithering* (London, 2006); 'The ghost of Actaeon' in *Hill of Doors* (London, 2013).

71   See Peter E. Knox, 'Ovidian myths on Pompeian walls', in *Handbook*, pp. 36–54.

72   See Fowler, *Roman Constructions*, p. 196: 'his works will continue to exist through constant recopying and reinterpretation by readers.'

73   Jennifer Ingleheart, 'Ovid's *Scripta Puella*: Perilla as poetic and political fiction in *Tr.* 3.7', *Classical Quarterly* 62 (2012), pp. 227–41, persuasively dismisses the biographical speculations around Perilla by arguing that she is not a real person but is modelled on the fictive mistresses of Roman elegy, adapted to reflect Ovid's modified poetic programme in exile.

VII. THE RECEPTION OF OVID

1   The *Handbook* discusses drama, film, music and the visual arts as well as literature across Europe from the first century to the present. Charles Martindale, *Ovid Renewed: Ovidian Influences on Literature and Art from the Middle Ages to the Twentieth Century* (Cambridge, 1988) also includes the visual arts; see now also Paul Barolsky, *Ovid and the Metamorphoses of Modern Art from Botticelli to Picasso* (New Haven, CT, 2014). Sarah A. Brown, *The Metamorphosis of Ovid: From Chaucer to Ted Hughes* (London, 1999) focuses

on Ovid's influence of Ovid on canonical English authors; Jennifer Ingleheart (ed.), *Two Thousand Years of Solitude: Exile after Ovid* (Oxford, 2011) surveys the complex reception of Ovid's exile poetry to the present day. The *Cambridge Companion*, *Brill's Companion* and the *Blackwell Companion* also contain excellent essays on the reception of Ovid.

2   The term *aetas Ovidiana* was coined by Ludwig Traube (1911) with reference to the twelfth and thirteenth centuries; see Charles McNelis, 'Ovidian strategies in early imperial literature', in *Blackwell Companion*, pp. 397–410, p. 397.

3   See Stephen Wheeler, 'Lucan's reception of Ovid's *Metamorphoses*', in Garth Tissol and Stephen Wheeler (eds), *The Reception of Ovid in Antiquity*, *Arethusa* 35.3 (2002), pp. 361–80.

4   Denis Feeney, *The Gods in Epic* (Princeton, NJ, 1991), pp. 241–9. Virgil, *Aen.* 4.173–86, provides the example of *Fama* ('Rumour').

5   Ibid., pp. 376–91.

6   See S. Georgia Nugent, *Allegory and Poetics: The Structure and Imagery of Prudentius' Psychomachia* (Frankfurt and New York, 1985); Martha Malamud, *A Poetics of Transformation: Prudentius and Classical Mythology* (Ithaca, NY, 1989); Paula James, 'Prudentius' *Psychomachia*: the Christian arena and the politics of display', in Richard Miles (ed.), *Constructing Identities in Late Antiquity* (London, 1999), pp. 70–94.

7   The classic treatment is C. S Lewis, *The Allegory of Love* (Oxford, 1936).

8   See Lee Patterson, *Chaucer and the Subject of History* (Madison, WI, 1991), pp. 104–14.

9   Panegyric can lay itself open to the charge of ambiguity or even subversion. See Stephen Hinds, 'Generalising about Ovid', *Ramus* 16 (1987), pp. 4–31, pp. 23–9.

10 On the Ovidianism of the *Achilleid* see Stephen Hinds, *Allusion and Intertext* (Cambridge, 1998), pp. 123–9; 135–44; McNelis, 'Ovidian strategies', pp. 406–9.

11 Paul Clogan, *The Medieval Achilleid of Statius* (Leiden, 1968); Carole E. Newlands, *Statius, Poet between Rome and Naples* (London, 2012), pp. 98–101.

12 See Gianpiero Rosati, 'Ovid in Flavian occasional poetry', in *Handbook*, pp. 55–69.

13 Stephen Hinds, 'Martial's Ovid/Ovid's Martial', *Journal of Roman Studies* 97 (2007), pp. 113–54, pp. 114–29.

14 McNelis, 'Ovidian strategies', pp. 398–404.

15 On the importance of Ovid's work for late antique poetics, see Ian Fielding, 'A poet between two worlds: Ovid in late Antiquity', in *Handbook*, pp. 100–13; the articles by Michael Roberts and Garth Tissol in Garth Tissol and Stephen Wheeler (eds), *The Reception of Ovid in Antiquity*, *Arethusa* 35.3 (2002).

16 Alison Keith and Steven Rupp (eds), *Metamorphosis: The Changing Face of Ovid in Medieval and Early Modern Europe* (Toronto, 2007) and James G. Clark, Frank T. Coulson and Kathryn L. McKinley (eds), *Ovid in the Middle Ages* (Cambridge, 2011) address Ovid's medieval reception, the latter volume focusing on various medieval European cultures, including Byzantine, French, Italian, Spanish, as well as English. See also Jeremy Dimmick, 'Ovid in the Middle Ages: authority and poetry', in *Cambridge Companion*, pp. 264–87; Ralph Hexter, 'Ovid in the Middle Ages', in *Brill's Companion*, pp. 413–42; the special edition of *Mediaevalia* 13 (1989) edited by Marilynn Desmond.

17 Ralph Hexter, 'Ovid's body', in James I. Porter (ed.), *Constructions of the Classical body* (Ann Arbor, MI, 1999), pp. 327–54.

18 Major work on Ovidian commentaries has been done by Frank Coulson. See, for instance, Frank T. Coulson and Bruno Roy, *Incipitarium Ovidianum: A Finding Guide for Texts Related to Ovid* (Turnhout, 2000).

19 See Fausto Ghisalberti, 'Medieval biographies of Ovid', *Journal of the Warburg and Courtauld Institutes* 9 (1946), pp. 10–59; R. B. G. Huygens (ed.), *Accessus ad Auctores*, Collection Latomus 15 (Brussels, 1954).

20 Ghisalberti, 'Medieval biographies', pp. 10–14; M. L. Stapleton, *Harmful Eloquence: Ovid's Amores from Antiquity to Shakespeare* (Ann Arbor, MI, 1996), pp. 39–49.

21 See *Saint Dunstan's Classbook from Glastonbury*, ed. R. W. Hunt (Amsterdam, 1961).

22 Ralph Hexter, *Ovid and Medieval Schooling* (Munich, 1986).

23 Marilynn Desmond, 'Venus' clerk: Ovid's amatory poetry in the Middle Ages', in *Handbook*, pp. 161–73, p. 169.

24 Peter Dronke, *Women Writers of the Middle Ages* (Cambridge, 1984); John F. Plummer (ed.), *Vox Feminae: Studies in Medieval Woman's Song* (Kalamazoo, MI, 1981).

25 Desmond, 'Venus' clerk', pp. 166–8; Dimmick, 'Ovid in the Middle Ages', pp. 271–3; John Fyler, 'The medieval Ovid', in *Blackwell Companion*, pp. 411–22, pp. 414–5.

26 Desmond, 'Venus' clerk', p. 170.

27 See Renate Blumenfeld-Kosinski, *Reading Myth: Classical Mythology and Its Interpretations in Medieval French Literature* (Palo Alto, CA, 1997), pp. 171–212; Marilynn Desmond and Pamela Sheingorn, *Myth, Montage, and Visuality in Late Medieval Manuscript Culture* (Ann Arbor, MI, 2003), discuss the extensive mythical iconography accompanying Christine's work.

28 Desmond, 'Venus' clerk', pp. 163–4.

29 See Gur Zak, 'Modes of self-writing from Antiquity to the later Middle Ages', in Ralph J. Hexter and David Townsend (eds), *The Oxford Handbook of Medieval Latin Literature* (Oxford, 2012), pp. 485–505.

30 Ibid., pp. 497–9.

31 See Philip Hardie, *Ovid's Poetics of Illusion* (Cambridge, 2002), pp. 71–81; Gordon Braden, 'The *Amores* from Petrarch to Goethe', in *Handbook*, pp. 262–76, pp. 265–7.

32 Stapleton, *Harmful Eloquence*, pp. 115–19.

33 Catherine Keen, 'Ovid's exile and medieval Italian literature', in *Handbook*, pp. 144–60. On the importance of the exile poetry in the Carolingian period see Hexter, *Medieval Schooling*, pp. 89–97; Dimmick, 'Ovid in the Middle Ages', pp. 284–5.

34 Keen, 'Ovid's exile', pp. 154–8.

35 Gregory Hays, 'The mythographic tradition after Ovid', in *Handbook*, pp. 129–43.

36 See Ana Pairet, 'Recasting the *Metamorphoses* in fourteenth-century France: the challenge of the *Ovide Moralisé*', in James G. Clark, Frank T. Coulson and Kathryn L. McKinley (eds), *Ovid in the Middle Ages* (Cambridge, 2011), pp. 83–107.

37 See Ann Moss, *Latin Commentaries on Ovid from the Renaissance* (Summertown, TN, 1998), pp. 86–90; Jamie C. Fumo, 'The medieval allegorical tradition', in *Handbook*, pp. 114–28, pp. 119–25.

38 See Andrew Galloway, 'Ovid in Chaucer and Gower', in *Handbook*, pp. 187–201; Katherine L. McKinley, 'Gower and Chaucer: readings of Ovid in late medieval England', in James G. Clark, Frank T. Coulson and Kathryn L. McKinley (eds), *Ovid in the Middle Ages* (Cambridge, 2011), pp. 197–230; John M. Fyler, *Chaucer and Ovid* (New Haven, CT, 1979), and 'The medieval Ovid', pp. 411–22.

39 Chaucer makes a similar allusion at the end of the legend of Hypsipyle and Medea.

40 Marilynn Desmond, *Reading Dido: Gender, Textuality, and the Medieval Aeneid* (Minneapolis, MN, 1994), pp. 33–55; 128–62.

41 Fyler, 'The medieval Ovid', pp. 416–22.

42   Marilynn Desmond, *Ovid's Art and the Wife of Bath: The Ethics of Erotic Violence* (Ithaca, NY, 2006).

43   Syrithe Pugh, *Spenser and Ovid* (Aldershot, 2005); Philip Hardie, 'Spenser and Ovid', in *Handbook*, pp. 291–305.

44   Ibid., pp. 292–3.

45   See Heather James, 'Ovid in Renaissance English literature', in *Blackwell Companion*, pp. 423–41.

46   Maggie Kilgour, 'The poetics of time: the *Fasti* in the Renaissance', in *Handbook*, pp. 217–31, pp. 224–5.

47   John F. Miller, 'Calendrical poetry', in Roland Greene et al. (eds), *The Princeton Encyclopedia of Poetry and Poetics* (4th edn, Princeton, NJ, 2012), p. 175.

48   Gordon Braden, 'Ovid and Shakespeare', in *Blackwell Companion*, pp. 442–54, p. 443.

49   See Paul Barolsky, 'Botticelli's *Primavera* and the poetic imagination', *Arion* 8.2 (2000), pp. 5–35; 'Ovid's *Metamorphoses* and the history of baroque art', in *Handbook*, pp. 202–16, p. 203. Chaucer also knew the myth of Flora; e.g. *Book of the Duchess* 397–409; *The Legend of Good Women* also draws on the *Fasti* in 'the legend of Lucrece'.

50   Jonathan Bate, *Shakespeare and Ovid* (Oxford, 1994) remains foundational. See also Leonard Barkan, *The Gods Made Flesh* (New Haven, CT, 1986), pp. 243–88; Lynn Enterline, *The Rhetoric of the Body from Ovid to Shakespeare* (Cambridge, 2000); A. B. Taylor (ed.), *Shakespeare's Ovid: The Metamorphoses in the Plays and Poems* (Cambridge, 2000); Braden, 'Ovid and Shakespeare', discusses Charles Martindale's critique of Bate, pp. 450–4.

51   Hardie, *Poetics of Illusion*, pp. 193–206.

52   For example Thomas W. Baldwin, *William Shakspere's Small Latin and Lesse Greeke* (Urbana, IL, 1944); Lynn Enterline, *Shakespeare's Schoolroom: Rhetoric, Discipline, Emotion* (Philadelphia, PA, 2012); Sean Keilen, 'Shakespeare and Ovid', in *Handbook*, pp. 232–45.

53   Invaluable for the translation of Ovid is the work of Stuart Gillespie, especially 'Translations from Greek and Latin classics, part 1: 1550–1700: a revised bibliography', *Translation and Literature* 18.1 (2009), pp. 1–42, pp. 26–9; and 'Translations from Greek and Latin classics, part 2: 1701–1800: a revised bibliography', *Translation and Literature* 18.2 (2009), pp. 181–224, pp. 208–10; also Robert Cummings and Stuart Gillespie (eds), 'A bibliography of Ovidian translations and imitations in English', *Translation and Literature* 13 (2004), pp. 207–18; Gordon Braden, Robert M. Cummings and Stuart Gillespie (eds), *The Oxford History of Literary Translation in English*, vol. ii: *1550–1600* (Oxford, 2010).

54   See Kathleen L. Scott, *The Caxton Master and His Patrons* (Cambridge, 1976); *The Middle English Text of Caxton's Ovid, Book 1*, ed. Diana Rumrich (Heidelberg, 2011).

55   Madeleine Forey (ed.), in *Ovid's Metamorphoses*, tr. Arthur Golding (Penguin, 2002), offers a full text with introduction and notes.

56   Raphael Lyne, *Ovid's Changing Worlds: English Metamorphoses 1567–1632* (Oxford, 2001), chapters 1 and 4; Dan Hooley, 'Ovid translated: early modern versions of the *Metamorphoses*', in *Handbook*, pp. 339–54. See also Liz Oakley-Brown, *Ovid and the Cultural Politics of Translation in Early Modern England* (Aldershot, 2006).

57   The *Heroides* were translated also by Wye Saltonstall in 1636, and John Sherburne in 1639.

58   James, 'Ovid in Renaissance English literature', p. 431.

59   Braden, 'Ovid and Shakespeare', pp. 443–6.

60 Gillespie, 'Translations from Greek and Latin classics, part 1', p. 27.
61 On the political role of translation in this period see David Norbrook, *Writing the English Republic: Poetry, Rhetoric and Politics 1627–1660* (Cambridge, 1999).
62 Carole E. Newlands, 'Englishing Ovid's *Fasti*', *Hermathena* 177/8 (2004–5), pp. 251–65.
63 See Liz Oakley-Brown, 'Elizabethan exile after Ovid: Thomas Churchyard's *Tristia* (1572)', in Jennifer Ingleheart (ed.), *Two Thousand Years of Solitude: Exile after Ovid* (Oxford, 2011), pp. 103–17.
64 See Sarah A. Brown, 'Wye Saltonstall', *Oxford Dictionary of National Biography*.
65 Heather James, 'Ben Jonson's light reading', in *Handbook*, pp. 246–61.
66 Hardie, *Poetics of Illusion*, pp. 97–105; James, 'Ovid in Renaissance English literature', p. 424.
67 James, 'Ben Jonson's light reading', p. 258.
68 James, 'Ovid in Renaissance English literature', p. 424.
69 Mandy Green, *Milton's Ovidian Eve* (Farnham, 2009); Maggie Kilgour, *Milton and the Metamorphosis of Ovid* (Oxford, 2012).
70 Barolsky, 'Ovid's *Metamorphoses*', pp. 37–45; 73–98.
71 Garth Tissol, *The Face of Nature* (Princeton, NJ, 1997), pp. 11–14.
72 Stephen Hinds, 'Landscape with figures: aesthetics of place in the *Metamorphoses* and its tradition', in *Cambridge Companion*, pp. 122–49.
73 James M. Horowitz, 'Ovid in Restoration and eighteenth-century England', in *Handbook*, pp. 355–70, pp. 362–7.
74 Ibid., pp. 363–4.
75 Hardie, *Poetics of Illusion*, pp. 206–26.
76 As suggested to me by Erik Gray, in correspondence.
77 See Theodore Ziolkowski, *Ovid and the Moderns* (Ithaca, NY, 2005).
78 Apuleius' novel of the second century CE, *Metamorphoses*, concerning the adventures of a man transformed into a donkey, anticipates this development by almost two millennia. See Stephen Harrison, 'Ovid in Apuleius' *Metamorphoses*', in *Handbook*, pp. 86–99; Barkan, *The Gods Made Flesh*, pp. 233–4.
79 See Jill Casid, 'Alter-Ovid: contemporary art on the hyphen', in *Handbook*, pp. 416–35.
80 On twenty-first-century developments see Sarah A. Brown, 'Contemporary poetry: after *After Ovid*', in *Handbook*, pp. 436–53.
81 Hermann Fränkel, *Ovid: A Poet between Two Worlds* (Berkeley and Los Angeles, CA, 1945).
82 For *After Ovid* and *Tales from Ovid*, see Ziolkowski, *Ovid and the Moderns*, pp. 198–203.
83 Ibid., pp. 195–8.
84 Dimmick, 'Ovid in the Middle Ages', p. 286.

SELECT BIBLIOGRAPHY

GENERAL WORKS

Barchiesi, Alessandro, *The Poet and the Prince* (Berkeley and Los Angeles, CA, 1997).
Boyd, Barbara (ed.), *Brill's Companion to Ovid* (Leiden, 2002).
Boyle, Anthony J., *Ovid and the Monuments: A Poet's Rome* (Bendigo, Victoria, 2003).
Feeney, Denis, *The Gods in Epic* (Princeton, NJ, 1991).
Hardie, Philip, *Ovid's Poetics of Illusion* (Cambridge, 2002).
—— (ed.), *The Cambridge Companion to Ovid* (Cambridge, 2002).
Holzberg, Niklas, *Ovid: The Poet and His Work*, tr. G. M. Goshgarian (Ithaca, NY, 2002).
Keith, Alison, *Engendering Rome* (Cambridge, 2000).
Knox, Peter (ed.), *Oxford Readings in Ovid* (Oxford, 2006).
—— (ed.), *A Companion to Ovid*, Blackwell Companions to the Ancient World (Oxford and Malden, MA, 2009).
Martelli, Francesca K. A., *Ovid's Revisions: the Editor as Author* (Cambridge, 2013).
Syme, Ronald, *History in Ovid* (Oxford, 1978).

ELEGY: *AMORES* AND *ARS AMATORIA*

Boyd, Barbara, *Ovid's Literary Loves* (Ann Arbor, MI, 1997).
Gibson, Roy, Steven Green and Alison Sharrock (eds), *The Art of Love: Bimillennial Essays on Ovid's Ars Amatoria and Remedia Amoris* (Oxford, 2006).
James, Sharon, *Learned Girls and Male Persuasion: Gender and Reading in Roman Love Elegy* (Berkeley and Los Angeles, CA, 2003).
Miller, John F., *Apollo, Augustus and the Poets* (Cambridge, 2009).
O'Gorman, Ellen, 'Love and the family: Augustus and the Ovidian Legacy', *Arethusa* 30 (1997), pp. 103–23.
Rimell, Victoria, *Ovid's Lovers: Desire, Difference and the Poetic Imagination* (Cambridge, 2006).
Sharrock, Alison, 'Ovid and the politics of reading', *Materiali e discussioni per l'analisi dei testi classici* 33 (1994), pp. 97–122.
Wyke, Maria, 'Mistress and metaphor in Augustan elegy', *Helios* 16 (1989), pp. 25–47.

EXILE POETRY: *TRISTIA* AND *EPISTULAE EX PONTO*

Claassen, Jo-Marie, *Displaced Persons: The Literature of Exile from Cicero to Boethius* (London, 1999).

Hinds, Stephen, 'Booking the return trip: Ovid and Tristia 1', *Proceedings of the Cambridge Philological Society* 31 (1985), pp. 13–32.

—— 'Black-Sea Latin, Du Bellay, and the barbarian turn', in Jennifer Ingleheart (ed.), *Two Thousand Years of Solitude: Exile after Ovid* (Oxford, 2011), pp. 59–83.

Kenney, E. J., 'The poetry of Ovid's exile', *Proceedings of the Cambridge Philological Society* 191 (1965), pp. 37–49.

McGowan, Matthew, *Ovid in Exile* (Boston, MA, and Leiden, 2009).

Oliensis, Ellen, 'Return to sender', *Ramus* 26 (1995), pp. 172–93.

Williams, Gareth D., *Banished Voices: Readings in Ovid's Exile Poetry* (Cambridge, 1994).

FASTI

Beard, Mary, 'A complex of times: no more sheep on Romulus' birthday', *Proceedings of the Cambridge Philological Society* 33 (1987), pp. 1–15.

Fantham, Elaine, 'Ovid, Germanicus and the composition of the *Fasti*', *Papers of the Liverpool Latin Seminar* 5 (1985), pp. 243–81.

Feeney, Denis, '*Si licet et fas est*: Ovid's *Fasti* and the problem of free speech under the principate', in Anton Powell (ed.), *Poetry and Propaganda in the Age of Augustus* (Bristol, 1992), pp. 1–25.

—— *Caesar's Calendar* (Berkeley and Los Angeles, CA, 2007).

Gee, Emma, *Ovid, Aratus and Augustus: Astronomy in Ovid's Fasti* (Cambridge, 2000).

Herbert-Brown, Geraldine, *Ovid and the Fasti: A Historical Study* (Oxford, 1994).

Hinds, Stephen, '*Arma* in Ovid's *Fasti*, part 1: genre and mannerism', *Arethusa* 25 (1992), pp. 81–112; '*Arma* in Ovid's *Fasti*, part 2: genre, Romulean Rome and Augustan ideology', *Arethusa* 25 (1992), pp. 113–53.

Miller, John F., *Ovid's Elegiac Festivals* (Frankfurt, 1991).

Murgatroyd, Paul, *Mythical and Legendary Narrative in Ovid's Fasti* (Leiden, 2005).

Newlands, Carole E., *Playing with Time: Ovid and the Fasti* (Ithaca, NY, 1995).

Pasco-Pranger, Molly, *Founding the Year: Ovid's Fasti and the Poetics of the Roman Calendar* (Leiden, 2006).

Wallace-Hadrill, Andrew, 'Time for Augustus: Ovid, Augustus and the *Fasti*', in M. Whitby, P. Hardie and M. Whitby (eds), *Homo Viator* (Bristol, 1987), pp. 221–31.

Wiseman, T. Peter, *Roman Drama and History* (Exeter, 1998).

HEROIDES

Fulkerson, Laurel, *The Ovidian Heroine as Author: Reading, Writing, and Community in the Heroides* (Cambridge, 2005).

Jacobson, Howard, *Ovid's Heroides* (Princeton, NJ, 1974).

Kennedy, Duncan, 'The epistolary mode and the first of Ovid's *Heroides*', *Classical Quarterly* 34 (1984), pp. 413–22.

Kenney, E. J. (ed.), *Heroides XVI–XXI* (Cambridge, 1996).

Knox, Peter (ed.), *Ovid's Heroides, Select Epistles* (Cambridge, 1995).

Lindheim, Sara, *Mail and Female: Epistolary Narrative and Desire in Ovid's Heroides: Transgressions of Genre and Gender* (Madison, WI, 2003).

Rosenmeyer, Patricia, 'Ovid's *Heroides* and *Tristia*: voices from exile', *Ramus* 26 (1997), pp. 29–56.

Spentzou, Efrossini, *Readers and Writers in Ovid's Heroides* (Oxford, 2003).

METAMORPHOSES

Barkan, Leonard, *The Gods Made Flesh* (New Haven, CT, 1986).

Fantham, Elaine, *Ovid's Metamorphoses* (Oxford, 2004).

Feldherr, Andrew, *Playing Gods* (Princeton, NJ, 2010).

Forbes-Irving, Paul, *Metamorphosis in Greek Myths* (Oxford, 1990).

Hardie, Philip, Alessandro Barchiesi and Stephen Hinds (eds), *Ovidian Transformations: Essays on the Metamorphoses and Its Reception*, Cambridge Philological Society supplement 23 (Cambridge, 1999).

Johnson, Patricia J., *Ovid before Exile: Art and Punishment in the Metamorphoses* (Madison, WI, 2008).

Keith, Alison, *The Play of Fictions* (Ann Arbor, MI, 1992).

Myers, K. Sara, *Ovid's Causes* (Ann Arbor, MI, 1994).

Rosati, Gianpiero, 'Form in motion: weaving the text in the *Metamorphoses*', in Hardie, Barchiesi and Hinds (eds), *Ovidian Transformations*, pp. 240–53.

Solodow, Joseph B., *The World of Ovid's Metamorphoses* (Chapel Hill, NC, 1988).

Tissol, Garth, *The Face of Nature* (Princeton, NJ, 1997).

Wheeler, Stephen, *A Discourse of Wonders* (Philadelphia, PA, 1999).

RECEPTION

Barolsky, Paul, *Ovid and the Metamorphoses of Modern Art from Botticelli to Picasso* (New Haven, CT, 2014).

Bate, Jonathan, *Shakespeare and Ovid* (Oxford, 1993).

Brown, Sarah A., *The Metamorphosis of Ovid: From Chaucer to Ted Hughes* (London, 1999).

Clark, James G., Frank T. Coulson and Kathryn L. McKinley (eds), *Ovid in the Middle Ages* (Cambridge, 2011).

Desmond, Marilynn, *Reading Dido: Gender, Textuality, and the Medieval Aeneid* (Minneapolis, MN, 1994).

Enterline, Lynn, *The Rhetoric of the Body from Ovid to Shakespeare* (Cambridge, 2000).

Ingleheart, Jennifer (ed.), *Two Thousand Years of Solitude: Exile after Ovid* (Oxford, 2011).

James, Paula, *Ovid's Myth of Pygmalion on Screen: In Pursuit of the Perfect Woman* (London, 2011).

Keith, Alison, and Steven Rupp (eds), *Metamorphosis: The Changing Face of Ovid in Medieval and Early Modern Europe* (Toronto, 2007).

Kilgour, Maggie, *Milton and the Metamorphosis of Ovid* (Oxford, 2012).

Martindale, Charles, *Ovid Renewed: Ovidian Influences on Literature and Art from the Middle Ages to the Twentieth Century* (Cambridge, 1988).

Miller, John F., and Carole E. Newlands, *A Handbook to the Reception of Ovid* (Oxford, 2014).

Taylor, A. B. (ed.), *Shakespeare's Ovid: The Metamorphoses in the Plays and Poems* (Cambridge, 2000).

Ziolkowski, Theodore, *Ovid and the Moderns* (Ithaca, NY, 2005).

SELECT MODERN TRANSLATIONS

Amores, tr. Guy Lee (London, 1968).

The Tristia of Ovid, tr. David R. Slavitt (Cleveland, OH, 1986).

Ovid, *Sorrows of an Exile*, tr. A. D. Melville (Oxford, 1992).

—— *Metamorphoses*, tr. Allen Mandelbaum (New York, 1993).

After Ovid: New Metamorphoses, ed. Michael Hofmann and James Lasdun (London, 1994).

The Metamorphoses of Ovid, tr. David R. Slavitt (Baltimore, MD, 1994).

Ovid: The Poems of Exile, tr. Peter Green (London, 1994).

Ovid's Fasti: Roman Holidays, tr. Betty Rose Nagle (Bloomington, IN, 1995).

Ovid, *Fasti*, tr. Antony J. Boyle and Roger Woodward (London, 2000).

Ovid, *Fasti*, tr. Anne Wiseman and Peter Wiseman (Oxford, 2011).

Ovid's Heroines, tr. Clare Pollard (Tarset, Northumberland, 2013).

Change Me: Stories of Sexual Transformation from Ovid, tr. Jane Alison (Oxford, 2014).

Ovid, *The Offense of Love: Ars Amatoria, Remedia Amoris, and Tristia 2*, tr. Julia Dyson Hejduk (Madison, WI, 2014).

INDEX